# Probable Cause

T0168232

# Probable Cause:
# Crime Fiction in America

## LeRoy Lad Panek

Bowling Green State University Popular Press
Bowling Green, Ohio 43403

Copyright© 1990 by Bowling Green State University Popular Press

Library of Congress Catalogue Card No.: 89-081987

ISBN:  087972-485-4 cb
       087972-486-2 pb

**Cover design by Gary Dumm**

For Susan

# Contents

# Preface

It didn't start out this way. I started out to write a book about the hard-boiled detective story. Innocently, I thought that I had better take a look back at some nineteenth century fiction to get a bit of a handle on the background of hard-boiled fiction. Once I got started with this, I realized that there is not a lot of common knowledge about the history of crime and police forces in America either. So I scrapped the book about the hard-boiled detective story and began to put together some basic facts and observations about the first one hundred years of crime literature and crime history in this country. I intended this book to be a primer or an introductory survey, and that is what it turned out to be. It is not, therefore, an exhaustive history of American crime fiction or American crime or American police forces; those books remain to be written. It is, I hope, a place for readers to begin when they want to know more about American crime fiction and American crime.

The following chapters take the one hundred years roughly between 1840 and 1940 and break them up into chunks: 1840-1890, 1890-1917 and 1917 to 1940. There are two chapters for each period. The first treats historical developments related to crime and the police, as well as developments in American publishing, and then makes some generalizations about the detective or crime fiction of the period. The second treats significant books of crime fiction written during the period and makes some summary observations about them. Throughout I assume that a connection, not always a direct one, exists between the history of crime literature and historical developments of crime, police forces and the publishing industry in America.

Writing about the background was not always simple. Nobody has written comprehensively about the history of crime, violence and police forces in the United States. And it's easy to tell why. Views of crime often depend on the public's perception of it, and there was scarcely a time from 1840 to 1940 when Americans did not think that they were experiencing a crime-wave of immense proportions. Also, books about crime and criminals tend to be sensational—they usually have a macabre picture of an electric chair or a hanging on their covers—and they focus only on extraordinary and bizarre crimes. Every public library has a small section of them, but they were not much help here. Factoring in the history of American police forces makes it even more difficult. Every major city in the United States has its own police department with its own unique history, but that history has only been written for a few of them. Furthermore, when the police do their job properly they are invisible, but when they do not it is news, so perceptions about the history of our police are almost invariably skewed.

Dealing with books was a bit easier. In the chapters on texts I have tried to discuss significant or representative books from each period. For the periods after 1890, though, I have had to do a good bit of picking and choosing for just what books are significant or representative. As sort of a rule I have operated under the sometimes true assumption that writers' first books are their most significant. On top of the either/or of significant and representative, however, I have tried with the later periods to consider availability: I selected, for instance, Daly's *Murder from the East* rather than one of his earlier novels because it has been reprinted not too long ago. But because even the most eager critic or fan simply cannot find many of the books I discuss (in some cases, like Futrelle's, modern editions do not contain all of the stories in the original editions) I have summarized books' contents before I discuss their significance. I hope that this is helpful. Although I have developed some pretty firm notions about the literary form and function of detective fiction, I have largely passed over them here. I have done this because I wanted to avoid a lot of niggling, because I wanted to do more than write a history of the detective story in this country, and because a number of books that influence both literary and public perceptions about crime and detectives are clearly not detective stories.

I introduce the following pages to you in the hope that they will present some initial considerations about crime and crime fiction in this country, that they will be a small step toward both fuller discussion and fuller understanding of this area of our past. Too much of our early popular literature lies in tatters, known only to collectors; too much of it has disappeared and remains only as titles in publishers' lists. To those who have spread the word—J. Randolph Cox, E.F. Bleiler, Sam Moskowitz, Ron Goulart and others—all of us interested in literature, popular and otherwise, owe a debt of thanks.

Finally, I would like to thank the librarians at Western Maryland College, most especially Cheri Smith, for their help. My thanks, too, to Keith Richwine for occasional dips into his profound knowledge of American literature and culture. Also I thank my colleagues for their patience with me every time my obsessions transform me into the lounge bore.

# Chapter 1
# Contexts
# 1840-1890

It all started with Poe and then, with a boost from Dickens and Collins and Gaboriau, it started again with Doyle. So goes the standard history of the detective story in the nineteenth century. But this line of succession ignores a great deal, and it especially ignores what went on in America during the period. Even when writers do consider the significance of Poe and the dime novel, they neglect to ask enough questions. Why did Poe start writing detective stories when he was living in Philadelphia in the early 1840s? Why did popular American literature latch on to the character of the detective in the decade after the Civil War? Why were detective characters so popular in sensational fiction of the last quarter of the nineteenth century? The answers to these and many other questions may lie with the police.

For a long time few people even thought about the history of police forces in America: look in any history book and try to find any mention of the development of law enforcement in the United States. Ask even knowledgeable people to name two or even one important police officer or detective. You will draw a blank. We are supposed to know about things like the Gadsden Purchase, and maybe we should, but we're not supposed to know about the police. Recently a few scholars have done some work on the history of police forces in America: among them are David Johnson with his *Policing the Urban Underworld* and Larry Hartsfield with his *The American Response to Professional Crime*. We can learn a great deal about our history and, by extension, our literature, from examining the growth and development of America's police forces. Likewise, taking another look at the history of publishing can refresh our knowledge of crime literature, which, in turn, yields insights about our history. Books like Michael Dennings' *Mechanic Accents* have begun to take a new look at the place and significance of cheap popular literature. Much of that literature deals with crime. Looking into the history of American crime and crime-fighters, as well as the books written about these subjects, yields some new questions and perhaps some new answers about the birth and growth of the detective story in this country and maybe even abroad.

The growth of cities and the increase in wealth are two of the governing facts of much nineteenth century history. They had much to do with the successes of Western culture, and they had, perhaps, as much to do with its failures. Cities grew like weeds. In 1800 the population of New York and Philadelphia was scarcely 100,000; by 1890 not only did the population

1

of New York and Philadelphia reach 1,000,000, but so did Chicago's. Along with this urban population growth, cities irrevocably changed in character. Prosperous people, prosperous beyond the dreams of their ancestors, no longer lived above their shops. Cities developed clearly defined districts, Wall streets, shopping districts, industrial areas, posh precincts, ghettos for blacks, Italians, and every other immigrant group. The same thing happened all over the industrialized world. And as cities changed so did people's relationships with one another. One of the most drastic results of these changes was a marked increase in crime. Early in the nineteenth century it became obvious that available means of providing domestic security to people in big cities simply didn't work. The new lineaments of the cities, the recent explosion of wealth, and the new social ills, unemployment, horrendous over-crowding, racial and ethnic tensions, combined with all of the old motives for crime to make London, New York, Philadelphia and other large cities unsafe places to live. Additionally, elected politicians and newspapers periodically looked at their cities and found that crime was worse than ever before. At the turn of the nineteenth century, however, British and American cities relied on institutions inherited, essentially, from Elizabethan times, the watch and constabulary, to deter and detect crime. They did a conspicuously bad job of it.

From the middle ages members of the watch patrolled, at first city walls, and then specific parishes or precincts at night, on the lookout for obnoxious behavior and also on the lookout for fires. Constables, originally petty or parish constables, were appointed by courts or by justices of the peace or, in London, by the ratepayers of each ward to act as conservators of the peace. They had wider powers of arrest than the watch and sometimes acted as detectives. Whether watchmen or constables ever provided much in the way of domestic security is not altogether clear: Shakespeare, at least, does not suggest that Elizabethans held either group in much esteem. It is clear that neither body provided much security once cities began to burgeon in the nineteenth century. As early as the sixteenth century, citizens from the middle class and up routinely shirked their duty to help maintain a secure community and fobbed off "policing" on paid, usually badly paid, watchmen and constables. Who, after all, wants to leave a comfy chair and cozy fire to tramp around the streets at night? Who wants to deal with drunks and hoodlums when someone else can be hired to do it? In early nineteenth century America it was especially difficult to move people to perform these civic duties in large cities. Just as upper—and middle—class men deserted volunteer fire companies in Philadelphia and New York, usually because they had "better things to do," they failed to support the institutions of the watch and the constabulary. So they simply did not work. Antique answers to protecting life and property failed in Britain to do either; they failed even more profoundly in the United States. Something else had to be done.

In Britain, Sir Robert Peel established modern policing with the founding of the Metropolitan Police in 1829, followed by the creation of a detective division in 1842. The organization of the Metropolitan Police, and later the detective division, responded not only to the need to police an increasingly complex and crime-ridden city, the police and detective movement also had to deal with a democratic society's fears, fears that an established police force would become the tool of political repression, become a standing army, and fears that plain clothes police would become spies who would pry into one's private affairs. Not only did Peel and early police commissioners have to try to counter these fears, they also occasionally had to contend with public exposure of police inefficiency, like the Fenian bombings, and police corruption, witnessed by the corruption trials of the 1870s. For much of the nineteenth century, from Godwin to Lytton, to Dickens, and even to Collins, the police officer and the detective are equivocal figures in British literature, often sinister and sometimes repugnant. It is, then, the triumph of British police officials and officers as well as writers who concerned themselves with crime and police work that by the end of the nineteenth century the detective became a standard hero in British popular fiction.

Now if Robert Peel thought that he had problems establishing a modern police force in London, he should have cast some thought to the problems of establishing police forces in the United States: no entrenched class system, few hard-and-fast notions of social decorum, an enshrined prejudice against standing armies, a large itinerant population, a citizenry familiar with frontier justice, massive and persistent ethnic and racial problems, a half dozen large cities and a political system with legislative authority scattered among federal, state and local jurisdictions. Those establishing police forces in the United States faced the same problems that Peel did, in spades, and they also faced homegrown problems unique to this country.

Nevertheless Americans quickly recognized the significance of the establishment of a professional police force in Britain. As early as 1830 a group of Philadelphians proposed the establishment of protective police in that city, and in 1831 Philadelphia philanthropist Stephen Girard left a sum in his will for the creation of a police force in his adopted city. It was not until the next decades, however, that most large cities in the United States began to establish police departments: New York in 1845, Philadelphia in 1854 and Chicago in 1854. These early police departments happened only after long and protracted civic and journalistic arguments about crime, about taxes and about the corruption of the old system of constables. Indeed some spectacular instances of constables' corruption in New York and Philadelphia spread over the newspapers and caused some of the most effective movement toward the creation of the new police forces. In each case, these new organizations were to be preventive police; their conspicuous presence on the streets (hence their badges and eventually uniforms) was intended to deter crime. But the resources allocated to the new police forces scarcely reached adequate levels. In Chicago, for example, nine men comprised the total strength of the original day police. Early American police forces scarcely terrified malefactors with their presence. To make even small sections of the cities safe they frequently adopted what can be politely called aggressive methods: Chief George Walling introduced "strong arm squads" in New York composed of policemen who descended on locations pestered by criminals and drove the criminals away with their nightsticks. Obviously, nineteenth century American police forces never attained the professional status established for the police in Britain. Political bosses viewed police jobs as simply additions to the spoils system: in 1857 the New York State Legislature fired all of New York City's policemen, considering the city "too corrupt to govern itself" and, with the help of the Seventh Regiment State Guard, replaced them with new policemen and an Albany-appointed chief. The same kind of state take-over of city police departments happened elsewhere with some regularity. In addition to all of this, American cities quickly discovered that a police force conceived as a preventative organization cannot cope with what happens when crime is not prevented.

Although some constables acted as *de facto* detectives during the transitional years, soon after establishing police forces American municipalities began to create detective forces within their police departments. The first was in Boston in 1846, followed by New York (1857), Philadelphia (1859) and Chicago (1861). Establishing detective police, however, creates a good bit of difficulty if one grants that the police have to do not only with protecting life and property but also with upholding the law. For most of the nineteenth century individual and institutional victims of robbery or burglary commonly offered rewards for the return of all or part of the stolen goods. They offered either no reward or a substantially lower amount for the apprehension of the criminal. John Reilly in his article "Beneficient Roguery" tells of one of the most spectacular beneficiaries of the reward system, Boston detective George Heath, who on one case earned a reward of $8,000, eight times his official salary. Following the financial incentives, detectives with some frequency pursued the stolen property versus the man, and there were even a number of notorious cases of detectives who routinely served as middlemen between crooks and their victims. They would make a bargain for the return of stolen property and split the reward with the thieves. The mid-century history of official detective forces in America reflects a cycle of disgust by civic officials for cops on the take (Boston and Chicago both temporarily eliminated their detective divisions in 1864) followed by recognition that modern city police departments cannot do without detectives.

From the hurley-burley of the creation of regular police forces in American cities arose private detectives. In 1845 Gil Hays, a constable put out of work by the creation of the new police in New York, became the first American private detective, and ex-chief Cyrus Bradley set up as a private detective in 1857 after he lost his policing job in Chicago. Private detective agencies sprang up in American cities even before some of them had modern police forces: private detectives offered their services in St. Louis in 1846, Baltimore in 1847, and Philadelphia in 1848. Pinkerton opened his shop in Chicago in 1851. This flurry of private enterprise partly reflects the difficulties municipalities faced in devising organizations to deal with crimes before, during and after their commission. In many cases the new private detectives were men, like Hays, who had acquired thief-catching skills as constables but who had no place in the new "preventive" police. It partly reflects the reality of money in the middle of the nineteenth century—the rich could buy their own security. Pinkerton established his agency and his reputation working for the railroads, and nobody in mid-century America was richer than the railroads. The growth of private detectives also reflects the lack of professionalism in regular police forces: in Chicago the Pinkerton Agency offered to take over municipal policing at two-thirds of what the city paid its police and to guarantee "that citizens would actually be protected." It also reflects the growth of crime in American cities. Nevertheless, by the middle of the nineteenth century Americans had taken some steps to combat crime. Between 1830 and 1860, widespread public discussion and debate led to the creation of modern police forces in most major American cities. For the next decade these organizations, as well as the new private detective agencies, grew, sometimes painfully, and adapted themselves to the realities of policing American cities and protecting life and, to a far greater extent, property. And they did this just in time, for in the 1870s the country witnessed not only a dramatic increase in crime, but also a substantial change in the nature of crime.

Coming to terms with crime statistics is not terribly easy. No national crime records exist for periods before 1933. Likewise, crime statistics still cover only reported crimes and it is likely that a substantial number of crimes were never reported. Nevertheless it seems fairly certain that after the Civil War the crime rate in American cities rose dramatically. David Johnson, in *Policing the Urban Underworld*, has compiled figures for Philadelphia in the middle of the nineteenth century from the *Public Ledger*. In 1840, for instance, Johnson lists 122 crimes against property and 68 crimes against persons reported in Philadelphia. For the next twenty-five years there are small increases in the crime rate: by 1865 Johnson's sample shows 164 crimes against property and 55 crimes against persons. There was not really much change. In 1870, however, things got bad. Johnson counts 272 reported crimes against property and 104 crimes against persons: a drastic increase. The atmosphere in the rest of the United States seems to indicate the same thing. Although public anxiety about crime persists in most times, the late 1860s and the 1870s seem to be particularly hysterical times. Inventors and entrepreneurs quickly responded to the public mood, with devices like Linus Yale's "burglar proof" lock in 1862 (which was not especially burglar proof until James Sergeant invented the time lock in 1873) and with various electronic burglar alarm systems which became popular in the 1870s. Henry Ward Beecher had an electronic burglar alarm in his home in the late 1860s, and, in a piece in *The New York Ledger*, complains about the nuisance of false alarms. There were, however, contemporary alternatives to locks and alarms. In 1871 Colt introduced a new revolver called the "House Pistol" and advertised that it was "particularly adapted for house defense against burglars, or for the pocket." Colt and other arms manufacturers also sold a weapon called the "pocket pistol," obviously designed for use when people had to leave their homes. People in the late sixties and early seventies were skittish about crime, and sought means to protect their lives and their belongings.

Not only did the post Civil War period see more crime but that crime was also different; it was more often violent. This is not to say that the early nineteenth lacked violence. There was a great deal of mob violence, often involving firearms: street gang fights, race riots, the infamous draft riots, rivalry among volunteer fire departments, and differences among political factions—all involved clubs, knives and sometimes firearms. For profit criminal activity in the early part of the century, however, seems to have been relatively non-violent. Before the establishment of national currency it was relatively easy to make a lot of literally dishonest bucks by counterfeiting the bills of state banks. Likewise, before the Civil War, safecracking was either simple (in that most safes came from the factory mounted on wheels) or it was a skilled trade because criminals had to open safes either by cunning—studying locks and keys so as to open even the newest strong box—or by simple physics—using wedges and levers to force open the safe. Prominent bank robbers prior to the war viewed themselves, and were viewed, as gentlemen criminals who were loath to stoop to violence. By the late 1860s many perceived that crime in America had grown dangerously and repugnantly violent. Indeed the term "hoodlum" entered American English in the 1860s, derived from a San Francisco gang. In May, 1866, the most popular family story paper *The New York Ledger* ran an editorial on "Infatuated Monsters" which lamented that "within the last twelve months, at least a dozen wholesale murders have been perpetrated in different parts of the country, and, in the majority of these cases, the perpetrators have not taken even the ordinary precautions against detection which a pickpocket would adopt to baffle the police. This seeming recklessness of consequences is a terrible and alarming feature of modern ruffianism." Charles Brace, in his 1872 study *The Dangerous Classes of New York*, reflects on this by comparing homegrown crime to European crime:

...If the vice and pauperism of New York are not so steeped in the blood of the populace [as it is in Europe] they are more dangerous...They rob a bank when English thieves pick pockets; they murder where European proletaires cudgel or fight with fists; in a riot they begin what seems about to be the sacking of a city, where English rioters merely batter policemen or smash lamps...

Bringing the matter closer to home, in 1873 *Harpers* contemplated the effects of a New York gas strike and the loss of street lights:

Even with the streets lighted, assaults and robberies are frequent, in total darkness crime would hold high carnival...Every dwelling house would have to be converted into a fortress.

*Wood's Illustrated Handbook* advised visitors to New York in 1872 to visit dance halls only if they were armed or accompanied by a policeman. The Civil War not only accustomed thousands of men to violence, it trained them in the use of firearms and made firearms readily available for domestic use. In 1843 Colt arms went out of business largely because of its failure to procure government contracts, but the reestablished company flourished after the Civil War in part because it catered to the demand for personal pistols, not only in the West but in cities as well. For urban use Colt manufactured the House Pistol, the Pocket Pistol and their version of the derringer. After 1865, Remington produced 50,000 vest pocket pistols. Smith and Wesson manufactured a pistol they called "the Ladies' Friend," and muff pistols, cane guns and alarm guns attachable to doors and windows appeared. Postwar firearms were relatively inexpensive (West's Pocket Revolvers, advertised in *The Fireside Companion* of 1869, sold for $1.50), and they were far easier to use because of the invention of the modern cartridge in 1860. In spite of this, the police of the time carried no firearms: Philadelphia and Boston armed their forces in the 1880s, but the New York police waited until the 1890s to give policemen official permission to carry firearms. And it was not just firearms that made crime more violent. In 1848, David Johnson tells us, gunpowder was first used to open a safe, but gunpowder was messy and tricky stuff. Alfred Nobel made things neater and easier in 1866 when he invented dynamite; a decade after its invention, criminals were "cooking" the nitro glycerin out of dynamite and blowing safes open with it.

People could, and did, arm themselves to protect themselves and their property against this new sea of crime, but increasingly society sought organized means to curb crime besides keeping a house pistol in the nightstand. Newspapers editorialized about the need for better education as a means of reducing the "criminal class." Most significantly, organizations designed to create wholesome citizens by suppressing vice arose in the 1870s: in 1878 the Society for the Prevention of Crime began in New York, but it had no real impact until the 1890s. More significantly, in 1872 the New York Y.M.C.A. created a committee for the suppression of vice, and in the following year this became The New York Society for the Suppression of Vice. This organization, and others like it, gained the support of many prominent Americans (J.P. Morgan supported the New York society, and the roster in Boston sounds like a who's who in New England) because it offered the utopian prospect of suppressing vice and crime and because it promised to bring the morals and social control of rural America to the chaos of the metropolis. The vice societies, and Anthony Comstock (the presiding genius of the vice suppression movement), chiefly targeted erotic pictures and books, abortionists and birth control for suppression. They also, however, went after literature about crime; indeed Comstock had an absolute mania about crime stories in story papers, devoting a full chapter in his *Traps for the Young* (1883) to haranguing against story papers and listing examples of youths who committed crimes because they had been steeped in the crime fiction of story papers. Comstock moved the

Massachusetts legislature to pass a law that prohibited the sale to minors of books or magazines containing "criminal news, police reports, or accounts of criminal deeds, or pictures and stories of lust and crime." In his crusade to extinguish criminality by abolishing it from the printed page, after *The National Police Gazette,* Comstock held the family story paper *The Fireside Companion* as his chief nemesis. In 1872, early in his smut-fighting career, Comstock caused the arrest of the editor of the paper, and *The Fireside Companion* may have been the paper he summarized as an example of perniciousness of crime in literature in *Traps for the Young.* In the long run, the societies for the suppression of vice had some impact upon American literature. They, however, had very little success in suppressing vice or eradicating crime.

If suppressing vice was either not possible or not the answer to doing away with crime and criminals, during the last half of the nineteenth century others, police officers, private detectives and journalists, began to reflect on what it all meant. They thought about the meaning of new cities, new police forces and new kinds of crime and criminals. Perhaps the first of these professional studies was *A chronological history of the Boston watch and police, from 1631 to 1865; together with the Recollections of a Boston Police Officer, or Boston by daylight and gaslight* published by the author, Edward H. Savage, in 1865. By the end of the century other metropolitan forces had their own histories: Howard O. Sprogle chronicled *The History of the Philadelphia Police* in 1887, and DeFrancis Folsom did the same in 1888 with his *Our Police: History of the Baltimore Force.*

The same period also saw works intended to either facilitate police work or to analyze crime and the police officer's experience in America. Philip Farley in 1876 published *Criminals of America: or, tales of the lives of thieves. Enabling everyone to be his own detective. With portraits, making a complete rogues' gallery.* Ten years later, Thomas F. Byrnes, a New York detective of legendary proportions, did much the same thing as Farley by publishing a rogues' gallery in his *Professional Criminals of America.* In the days before fingerprints or even Bertillion measurements the photographs in these books did one elementary but important thing; they identified known criminals. Analyzing the conditions that led to crime began during this period with Charles Brace's *The Dangerous Classes of New York* and Edward Crapsey's *The Nether Side of New York; or, the vice, crime and poverty of the great metropolis* (1872). A somewhat less sociological view comes in *Our Rival, the Rascal, A faithful Portrayal of the Conflict between the Criminals of this Age and the Defenders of Society—The Police,* written in 1897 by two Boston police officials, Benjamin P. Eldridge and William B. Watts.

On a personal level, in the last quarter of the century professional detectives recorded their recollections of their careers and calling. These began with George S. McWatters, a detective in New York from 1858 to 1870, and his *Knots Untied; or Ways and By-Ways in the Hidden Life of an American Detective* in 1873. This was followed in 1875 by John H. Warren, Jr.'s *Thirty Years Battle with crime, or, the crying shame of New York, seen under the broad glare of an old detective's lantern.* Another New York police official, George W. Walling, added *Recollections of a New York Chief of Police: an official record of thirty-eight years as patrolman, detective, captain, inspector and chief of the New York Police* in 1887. Covering the same period, although published in the twentieth century, were Alfred H. Lewis' *Confessions of a Detective* (1906) and Thomas Furlong's *Fifty Years a Detective*(1912). Many of these police biographies not only described the nature of the policeman's job but also added lamentations about crime, police work and urban society in general. McWatters, for instance, sees his profession in two lights:

...aside from the fact that the detective, in his calling, is often degraded to a sort of watchman or ordinary policeman, to help the big thieves, the merchants, etc., protect themselves from the small thieves, who are not able to keep places of business, and to perform sundry other undignified work, his calling is a blessed one...

Parallel to these police memoirs, we find works which either use fiction to embellish facts or which turn fact into fiction. Probably the most influential of these were Allen Pinkerton's seventeen books (beginning with *The Expressman and the Detective* and including *Criminal Reminiscences and Detective Sketches*). The books, ghost written under Pinkerton's name, which served in part as advertisements, chronicle the successes of Pinkerton agents and because of their narrative embellishments move from the realm of personal memoirs into what some would call "novelizations." Thomas Byrnes, one-time head of the New York City detective division, moved police autobiography literally into the world of fiction. Byrnes helped turn fact into fiction by, in effect, becoming the main character in a series of novels written by Nathaniel Hawthorne's son Julian: these included *The Great Bank Robbery* (1887), *An American Pennman* (1887), *Another's Crime* (1888), *Section 558; or The Fatal Letter* (1888), and *A Tragic Mystery* (1888).

At about the same time that policemen and detectives began to describe their trade in print, American popular literature was undergoing a significant change. From the 1830s the family story paper was the staple of American popular literature. Essentially a newspaper in format, the eight-page family story paper supplied light fiction to huge audiences: 200,000 and even 300,000 yearly subscribers were typical for the most popular publications. Over the years one paper succeeded another in terms of popularity. First *Brother Jonathan* and then *The Flag of Our Union* and *The New York Ledger* succeeded in the race for the crown of being the paper with the largest circulation in the country or, so the papers claimed, the world. This popularity accrued in part because, especially at mid-century, story papers spent huge sums on what was sometimes clever and original advertising. Mostly, though, their popularity came from the fact that story papers served up an amazing amount of fiction at a low price.

Family story papers ran editorials, correspondence, advice columns, news pieces as well as some short fiction, but the heart of the story paper was serial fiction, and each issue continued a lot of it: *The Fireside Companion*, for instance, typically ran episodes of eight serials in each weekly issue. Considering that family story papers began in the 1830s and lasted almost until the twentieth century, they collectively published a whopping, almost inconceivably whopping, amount of fiction. Not that much of it was original or very good. In fact, a substantial amount of early family story fiction was simply pirated from England, there being no international copyright protection in America until 1891. No matter how industriously the papers pirated English fiction, sometimes even going abroad ships before they docked so as to rush their new load of booty to the printer, piracy alone could not fill all of the empty columns. In the 1840s, therefore, editors began to search for and nurture American writers, going to the extreme of actually paying them well—in the forties and fifties, in fact, popular writers made more than many establishment literary figures.

Much of the original fiction nurtured by story paper editors was scarcely original. The staple serial developed along lines typical of popular British fiction, that is, it was a romance with some kind of exotic setting, episodes of threat to a helpless heroine from lawless brigands or pirates or the like, fates worse than death, separations of families and lovers, scenes oozing with sentiment, and the distribution of just desserts followed by a grand reunion at the close. "Lady" authors like Mrs. Southworth and Ann S. Stephens were among the most popular contributors to family story papers. Western or, more precisely, frontier stories were an original contribution, as was the serial genre known as "miseries and mysteries." These were as close as early story paper serials came to the detective.

Misery and Mystery stories began in France with Eugene Sue's *Mysteries of Paris* of 1842. Sue's work was quickly imitated and soon fictional explorations of the "mysteries and miseries" of most European cities appeared in print, contrasting the degradation of lower-class life with the sybaritic entertainments of the rich and famous. In America cheap pamphlet or serial fiction exposed the "mysteries and miseries" of New York, Baltimore, Boston, San Francisco and, among other smaller towns, Lowell and Fitchburg Massachusetts. Ned Buntline, a story paper giant, weighed in with *The Mysteries and Miseries of New York* in 1848, but the king of mysteries and miseries was George Lippard. Lippard, one of Poe's Philadelphia acquaintances, achieved celebrity with his *The Quaker City, or the Monks of Monk Hall: A Romance of Philadelphia Life, Mystery and Crime* (1844) and went on to start his own story paper, *The Quaker City*, to serve as a vehicle for more of his mysteries and miseries. This "new" kind of fiction used the same old titillation romance motifs but replaced exotic settings with the sensational background of the corrupt city. We can taste some of the flavor of the genre in this story paper ad for Justin Jones' *Hasserac the Thief-Taker* in *Star Spangled Banner*:

In the first number of the new volume will be commenced a Great Local Novelette, Illustrative of *Life in Boston*; in which none but Conspicuous Living Characters!! Will be introduced. In it the "Mysteries and Miseries" of the great metropolis will be faithfully portrayed; scenes among the rich and the Poor, the High and the Low, the Strong and the Weak, will be truly and graphically given. Hasserac the Thief Taker!!

Is one of the most prominent characters.

The dens of *Thieves, Counterfeiters, Gamblers,* and the *Splendid Palaces of the Cyprians!*

Will be opened to view. In short the Vice and Villainy of this immoral city will be revealed, and those who are deepest dyed in Crime and Cruelty will be exposed.

After thirty years of purveying English sensational fiction in its original form or in American imitations, after twenty years of mysteries and miseries, and after twenty years of frontier or western stories, the family story papers underwent a period of change. Mary Noel, in *Villains Galore...The Heyday of the Popular Story Weekly*, tells us that the eighteen seventies were "the time of the great story paper flood." More and more publishers went into the story paper business, perhaps because they saw the immense profits Robert Bonner made with *The New York Ledger*. Not only were there more story papers than ever before in the late 1860s and 1870s, but their fiction began to change too. The story papers now faced real competition from Irwin Beadle and other dime novel publishers who began to scoop up large numbers of readers, often with fiction that originally appeared in story papers. Story papers had to compete; sometimes they did this by becoming super sensational (in the seventies Norman Munro tried a story paper that announced that it would feature "all the divorce suits and spiciest kind of reading"), by aggressive promotions (such as offering premiums, often paper bound books) to subscribers, by accepting advertising (which earlier story papers staunchly refused to do) and by introducing new kinds of heroes—if not new kinds of fiction. On December 23, 1868, Ned Buntline in *The New York Weekly* introduced Buffalo Bill. Story papers, dime novels, plays and Cody's Wild West Show made Buffalo Bill one of these new heroes. In 1877 Edward L. Wheeler introduced another new hero, the outlaw, in *Beadle's Half Dime Library* with *Deadwood Dick, the Prince of the Road; or, The Black Rider of the Black Hills.*

Along with these new kinds of heroes, family paper publishers and the new dime novel publishers adopted a new attitude toward the production of fiction. When family story papers began in the forties, editors saw readers' allegiance to well paid and publicized authors as the way to sell lots of papers. By the eighties the old, well-paid authors had died off and publishers replaced them with a corps of writers whom they paid meager wages. In 1846 Longfellow met Joseph Ingram and noted, perhaps with some envy, that Ingram pulled down $3,000 a year by writing story paper serials. In 1892 Joseph Bok, editor of the *Ladies Home Journal*, described what were perhaps typical conditions for the second generation of popular writers for "the cheaper sensational weeklies":

Of course we all know that all kinds of factories exist in New York, but until last week I never knew that the great metropolis boasted of such a thing as a real and fully equipped literary factory...It employs over thirty people, mostly girls and women. For the most part these girls are intelligent. It is their duty to read all the daily and weekly periodicals in the land...Any unusual story of city life—mostly the misdoings of city people—is marked by these girls and turned over to one of three managers. These managers, who are men, select the best of the marked articles, and turn over such as are available to one of a corps of five women, who digest the happening given to them and transform it to a skeleton or outline for a story. This shell, if it may be so called, is then returned to the chief manager, who turns to a large address book and adapts the skeleton to some one of the hundred or more writers entered on his book.

Beginning in the seventies, cheap fiction became a manufactured commodity, and publishers realized that in many cases the hero was more important than the writer. Readers did not particularly care who wrote about Buffalo Bill or Deadwood Dick as long as the story featured that hero. Indeed in 1889, after protracted litigation, the Supreme Court in the County of New York ruled that George Munro of *The Fireside Companion* owned the rights to "Old Sleuth" and prohibited others from using the name.

All of this, the histories of police and crime as well as the history of the family story paper, has, I think, significant implications for the development of the detective story.

That American discussion and debate about establishing modern police forces began in Philadelphia is particularly important. The prominent stages in this discussion were: in 1830 Recorder Joseph M'Ilvaine proposed establishing a police force in the city; in 1831 Stephen Girard's will left a sum of money to "provide more effectually than...now...for the security of the persons and property of the inhabitants of said city by a competent police force"; in 1833 M'Ilvaine, John Swift and Joseph Watson issued a report suggesting the creation of an "efficient preventive police;" in February 1840 a Philadelphia grand jury reflected upon the corruption of the old system by finding that constables often "go bail for felons arrested by themselves; in some cases compounding felonies with thieves, and dividing the stolen property between themselves, thieves and the plundered"; and in 1840 John Swift, who contributed to the 1833 report, became mayor of Philadelphia and immediately moved sixteen men from the watch to become de facto day police.

In 1838 Poe moved from New York to Philadelphia to be editor of *Gentleman's Magazine* and then *Graham's Magazine*. Among his friends there were Henry Beck Hirst, an attorney who sparked Poe's interest in the law, and George Lippard. In the spring of 1842, when Poe wrote "The Murders in the Rue Morgue," Lippard wrote a fiction column called "City Police" for the story paper *The Spirit of the Times*, the offices of which were across the street from *Graham's* offices. Lippard also editorialized in the same paper about the misappropriation of Girard's legacy, and he later used an 1843 Philadelphia murder case as the grain of sand that eventually produced the mysteries and miseries of *The Quaker City*. Now I take it as virtually certain that Poe knew about Stephen Girard: Girard at his death was worth almost $7,000,000 and was one of the wealthiest men in America. Even without legal friends, Poe must have known about Girard's will, along with its provision for a Philadelphia police force, because it was the subject of public and protracted litigation by his relatives, to whom he bequeathed a mere $140,000. Poe may have even known something of Girard the man, a native Frenchman devoted to French rationalism (his finest ships were the *Montesquieu, Rousseau* and *Voltaire*), whose wife became mentally ill and died in a Pennsylvania Hospital, and who, in spite of his conspicuous exertions for the public good, led, according to the *Dictionary of American Biography*, a "lonely and self-centered life."

Just as Poe must have heard about Girard and his public spirited concern about municipal police, he must have been aware of the agitation in the city for a modern police force. Newspapers in Philadelphia and New York frequently ran news stories and editorials about police corruption, and we know that Poe read newspapers and particularly that he read about crime in them; *The Mystery of Marie Roget* provides proof enough of this. And how about Poe's friend George Lippard? Not only was Lippard's father elected constable in Philadelphia's South Ward, he had an active interest in the police courts and crime. Lippard also had a passing interest (along with Poe) in opium, and, in the early forties, he lived a somewhat irregular or Bohemian existence, occupying for a time, at least legend would have it, a huge abandoned mansion near Franklin Square.

Now much has been made of the French sources of Poe's detective tales: *Zadig* and Vidocq's *Memoirs*. They are real enough. But his Philadelphia sources are just as, perhaps more, important. I think that it is likely that, even though Poe's fiction displays little in the way of social or political concern, Poe's knowledge of American cities' efforts to establish modern police forces, his knowledge of the inefficiency and corruption of the old system of the watch and especially the constabulary had something to do with his use of crime, police and detectives in his "detective tales" of the 1840s. It also strikes me that it is conceivable that the background of Stephen Girard, the lonely philanthropist, and George Lippard, the eccentric court reporter who wandered the streets of his Quaker City (and whom Poe called a "genius"), may have something to do with Dupin, the focus of detection in "Murders in the Rue Morgue," "The Mystery of Marie Roget" and "The Purloined Letter."

After 1844 and "The Purloined Letter," Americans lost Dupin and did not get him back until the last decade of the century when the rational-romantic detective hero reappeared in the form of Sherlock Holmes. Nobody in this country took up on Poe's creation. His friend Lippard ignored the detached amateur detective and made the heroes in his mysteries and miseries books agents selected by Providence to avenge the wrongs of the downtrodden. During the middle of the nineteenth century American popular fiction neglected the character of the detective and police officer. The Civil War had something to do with the break in the development of detective fiction: the country and its popular press had other things to do than develop a new popular hero. The detective character also lay fallow after Poe because the figure of the police officer and the detective were too equivocal. During the thirty years from the 1840s to the 1870s, American cities experimented with establishing modern police and detective forces. Their record was, at best, a mixed one, what with foot-dragging municipal authority, local political conflicts and periodic dysfunctions of police officers leading to the on-again, off-again detective divisions in several cities. This in spite of the fact that during the same period crime increased significantly, became more violent and became more of a threat to middle-class citizens. In mid-century fiction detectives are largely significant by their absence, but, when they do appear, they tend to be much like the detectives in mid-Victorian fiction in Britain, characters who are dangerous, morally questionable or just socially embarrassing.

By the late 1860s and early 1870s, however, story papers began to cast about for new ways to attract readers. They began accepting advertising, they began to run stories with new kinds of Western heroes in them, and they began to experiment with others: the plucky boy (eventually to become Alger's hero), the African adventurer, the knight (for example, *The Black Squire; or, St. George's Cross. A Story of Cressy* appeared in 1871), the physician and the detective. Trials of this new kind of hero, the detective, began as early as the mid-1860s. John B. Williams' *Leaves from the Note-Book of a New York Detective* (1864-5) contains 15 short stories about James Brampton, a New York private detective. Entering the world of the story paper, *Beadle's Monthly* ran what is perhaps the first American detective novel, Seeley Register's (Mrs. Metta Victoria Fuller Victor) *The Dead Letter*. *The Saturday Journal* of June 10, 1871, ran *The Detective's Ward; or, The Fortunes of a Bowery Girl* by "Agile Penne" (Albert W. Aiken). George Munro's *The Fireside Companion*, however, seems to have played the most significant role in this initial attempt to establish the detective as a popular hero.

Munro, who began his career as a clerk at Beadle's dime novel house, displayed a long-term interest in the development of British detective fiction: he ran Collins' *The Woman in White* (originally published in 1860) as a serial in *The Fireside Companion*, offered *East Lynne* (originally published in 1861) as a premium for new subscribers to his story paper, and on January 31, 1870 ran a piece ("Quick Work. From the Diary of Hardshaw [sic], the Detective") featuring Hawkshaw, the detective in Tom Taylor's 1863 *The Ticket of Leave Man*.

Almost inevitably, American detective fiction began to appear in *The Fireside Companion*. Although some earlier pieces lay claim, "I had not been in the detective service long when a singular case came to my notice" from "My First Case" by Frank Dumont (June 27, 1868) seems to announce the first native detective piece in *The Fireside Companion*. Munro went on to publish a number of short detective sketches before moving to the serial detective novel, with *The Bowery Detective* by Kenward Philip (beginning April 4, 1870). But detective serials did not suddenly take over the paper, and there was not another one until *The Broken Dagger; or, The Mysteries of Brooklyn* (starting February 6, 1871). In 1871, though, things moved a bit, for on April 28 Munro followed up with *The Boy Detective; or, The Chief of the Counterfeiters*. There seems to have been a conscious move to feature detectives in *The Fireside Companion* in 1872: on May 6 began the fifteen part series *Perils and Escapes of a Detective*, and on June 10, *Old Sleuth the Detective; or, the Bay Ridge Mystery* hit the streets. 1872 was the year that Anthony Comstock caused the arrest of the editor of *The Fireside Companion*. This may have influenced their turn to detective stories in an attempt to show people who effectively deal with serious crime as opposed to nit-pickers like Comstock who went around arresting clerks in stationery stores for selling naughty books.

At any rate, thereafter, *The Fireside Companion* commonly ran two detective pieces at the same time. Although Harlan Page Halsey actually wrote *Old Sleuth*, the advertised author was Tony Pastor. This also seems to indicate a new emphasis on the detective story, for Pastor, one of the fathers of vaudeville, was not only a well-known theatrical entrepreneur but also an extremely popular song and dance man. Indeed, Munro probably had some investment in the use of Tony Pastor's name, because it quickly shows up on a number of serials: Pastor's name appears on *The Fastest Boy in New York*; and *The Irish Detective; or, On His Track*; and *Down in a Coal Mine* by the fall of 1873. But it wasn't Pastor's name that made Old Sleuth popular, it was the detective hero. Old Sleuth made the detective into a marketable hero and Munro marketed him. In a little more than a decade Munro claimed to have spent $200,000 (a figure in line with the expenses of other grandiose family story paper promotions of the time) advertising his detective. It did pay off: *The Fireside Companion* barely eaked by in 1870 and 1871, but had nearly a quarter of a million subscribers a decade later. Rather than being Beadle's dime novels (which ran mostly westerns during the 1870s), the story papers made the detective story come to life in America. Its beginnings, however, were neither smooth nor miraculous.

Before the arrival of Old Sleuth as a continuing character, the detective story struggled to establish itself in the family story paper. Detectives, first of all, did not appear as urban types; in the earliest short sketches, like "Job Percy's Plot" (June 6, 1868), "My First Case" or "A Detective's Sketch" (August 3, 1869) the crimes and detection occur in small towns. Because of this, even with American settings, the cases sound European: American detective fiction did not acquire its own character until it came to terms with geography, that is, in essentially American fiction the detective's problems are not so much logic and proof as they are tracking and finding the criminal in the city.

Most of the detective sketches in *The Fireside Companion* appeared on page four, the place reserved for editorials and brief news stories ("Remarkable Case of Poisoning in Boston," for instance graces page four on October 21, 1868). Linked to sensational news items, these sketches, therefore, are one-shot affairs. Secondly, the early pieces do very little to establish the detective as a character. Later detective fiction establishes the hero by delineating two sets of characters: those people in the normal society of the fiction and the detective who reacts with but who remains aloof from and does not join the community of the story. In some early fiction the detective is an alien and potentially frightening form: in "Job Percy's Plot" the unnamed detective is only identified as "a dark man with a heavy beard." Most early pieces, however, portray the detective as a neutral observer or as a reporter—a depersonalized agent of justice who finds "clews" (the clues in "My First Case" are printed in italics) and establishes justice.

These early detectives possess little character because of the entrenched sentimental bias of story paper fiction. In spite of the fact that the detective has superior perception, that he quickly sees physical and human details that others cannot, for readers the early detectives simply act as recorders of sentimental, and frequently pathetic, passages of human experience— the dying consumptive in "My First Case," or the child murdered by his grandfather in "A Detective Story" (February 7, 1870). Some of them, like "The Detective. A Story of New Orleans" (June 29, 2869) or the crime tales in the series "Medical College Sketches" (beginning April 18, 1868), are yarns told to sentimentally gratify an audience within the sketch. Additionally, the majority of the crimes in the early sketches turn upon inheritances, the motive most amenable to sentimental fiction because inheritances invariably mean missing heirs and other romance motifs. Of course the same bias weighed down early serial fiction about detectives, and, although their names may appear on the titles ( *The Bowery Detective*, etc.), these fictions focus upon a sentimental mystery and its impact on other characters. The first Old Sleuth serial shows one way to make the detective the principal actor in a sentimental romance: Old Sleuth in disguise is the detective and out of disguise is the romantic lead. Ultimately, however, the detective was free to fully develop into the hero of long fiction only when he appeared in a series, when the crimes became more urban, moving away from sentimental domestic tangles, and when writers understood that readers wanted to know about the hero as a detective and not as a participant in tear-jerking melodrama.

To some extent all of these ingredients appeared in the early 1880s when publishers found a new vehicle, the "library." The library was, essentially, a new way of marketing cheap fiction that combined the low price of the dime novel with the postal distribution of the story paper. Weekly, or semi-weekly, readers received in what we would call a magazine form a complete novel (albeit a short one), and the serial disappeared until it was revived by the pulp magazine in the next century. The libraries tended to offer westerns at first, but detective libraries sprang up quickly. Norman Munro, who had been trying to poach his brother George's detectives for almost a decade, created a detective story "library" with his *Old Cap Collier Library,* which ran from April, 1883 until September 1899. Frank Tousey's *New York Detective Library* ran from June 1883 until April 1898. In 1885 brother George Munro's company entered the detective library competition with his *Old Sleuth Library.* Others followed.

The detective libraries were in touch with European developments in detective fiction. The *Old Cap Collier Library,* for instance, early on sent its readers *The Greatest Detective in France;* or, *Piping the Mystery of Orcival* by Emile Gaboriau and then followed with three other novels by the same author. There are several items in the Cap Collier series advertised as being by Frenchmen (numbers 25 and 44 are supposedly "by a Celebrated French Detective and number 34 is *Vibert, the Detective;* or *Piping the Crime of the Rue de la Paix* by Adolphe Belot). The *New York Detective Library* occasionally brought in a whiff of things British by identifying the author of six numbers as "A Scotland Yard Detective." In the main, however, the stories in the libraries are American stories. Here the autobiographical and analytical works of American policemen and detectives had real impact. By the 1880s a number of these factual police works had appeared and had achieved some measure of popularity. Detective library titles, in fact, focus on professional attributes (sometimes odd professional attributes) of the detective: taken at random, numbers 95 and 96 in the *New York Detective Library* are *Billy Bender, the Ventriloquist Detective* and *Old Dan Grip;* or, *the Oldest Detective on the Force.* More significantly, the libraries looked to the police when they took to creating authors' names. The two most frequent contributors to the *New York Detective Library* were Police Captain Howard, with over 85 attributions, and A New York Detective, with a similar number. The same publication also featured a U.S. Detective, Police Captain Williams, Police Sergeant Mallory, Ex-Chief of Police Mansing and a Philadelphia Detective.

The *Old Cap Collier Library* did the same thing, only here a greater variety of police officials supposedly authored items: Sergeants Rollins, Stuart Milne and Steers; Detectives Collins (of Denver), Sharp and Edenhope; Detective Sergeant Erdby; Inspectors Woglom and Jones; Captains Grace, Dawson, Dalgreen and McAnder: not to mention One of the Force, One of the Squad, a Retired Officer and others. Clearly the detective libraries tried to pass fiction off as biography. Just as Pinkerton's name appeared on stories relating real detective work, the authors' names in the detective libraries suggest autobiography or biography, and some of the titles did as well. The *New York Detective Library* offered titles such as: *Stories of World-Renowned Detectives,* by a New York Journalist; *Thrilling Adventures of a London Detective,* Written by Himself; or, *Biography of a Great Detective,* by Himself. Norman Munro, in fact, based the *Old Cap Collier Library* on the illusion that the detective himself narrated his allegedly real cases.

Real cases, that is what the libraries pretended to describe. Some of the early titles recall, and were no doubt meant to recall, the Mysteries and Miseries of the last generation of story papers, suggesting exposes of the dark side of urban America. The *Old Sleuth Library* published titles such as *Night Scenes in New York: In Darkness and by Gaslight*, and *The New York Detective; or, Startling Phases of City Life* and, to be quite obvious, *The Mysteries and Miseries of New York*. Tousey's library, the *Young Sleuth Library*, offered readers *Young Sleuth's Night Trail; or, The Slums of New York* and *Young Sleuth in the "Lava Beds" of New York; or, the Tenderloin District by Night*. By the nineties the libraries seem to shift from dwelling on the seamy side of urban life to providing a variety of urban vistas for their readers: Young Sleuth, therefore, detects in New York, Chicago, Boston, Baltimore, San Francisco, Denver, Cincinnati and a list of other cities. In addition to a grounding in the atmosphere of Mysteries and Miseries and local color, the detective libraries recall Bok's description of "fiction factories" in New York that turned sensational news items into even more sensational fiction. Following Poe and then Lippard, Irwin Cobb based the first Cap Collier number, *Old Cap Collier, Chief of Detectives; or, Piping the New Haven Mystery* (1883), on an actual murder that occurred in 1881. Almost as soon as they happened the Molly Maguire trails and the march of Coxey's army were both converted into detective stories.

Additionally, stories in the detective libraries began to move away from the sentimental domestic mystery that powered early detective serials. Although the libraries continued to provide what are really romances with detective additions—suggested, for instance, by titles like *Under a Cloud; or, A Detective's Work for a Poor Boy* (New York Detective Library #189)— they began to treat crimes against property, the principal theme of many non-fiction police memoirs of the time: *New York Detective Library's* titles such as *The Forged Checks* and *The Vault Detective* and *$200,000 in Bounds* and *Shoving the Queer* and *Silent the Harbor Detective; or, Tracking a Band of Thieves*, as well as Cap Collier Library's subtitles such as *Piping a Series of Bank Frauds* and *A Great Safe Robbery* and *The Counterfeiters of Death Gultch* and *Tracking the Thugs* and *Tracking the Nitro-Glycerine League* allude to the kinds of crime that preoccupied police writers. They shift from heroines with dreadful secrets and villains of melodrama to contemporary crimes and criminals. Not only did the focus on these new varieties of crime coalesce with other publics' awareness of them, crimes against poverty also provided writers with plots that allowed them to show detectives as detectives, as opposed to awkward participants in the sentimental drama of the story paper serial.

By the turn of the century, the story paper and the detective library began their slide into oblivion. The passage of the international copyright agreement did them no good: free foreign copy went out the window. Postal rates did not help either: strict enforcement of postal regulations in 1901 increased mailing costs for "libraries" from one to eight cents a pound. Publishers could have surmounted both of these problems; for instance, they had to simply drop the term "library" from their banners to once again be considered magazines. By the late 1890s, however, magazine publishing changed. Middle-class journals were now available for a dime a copy, and aggressive magazines like *McClure's* and *Collier's* took up much of the market. In part, though, they were victims of their own success: in January, 1893 *Harper's Weekly* ran "The Cardboard Box" and others took over the genre that they had pioneered.

Today we know very little about the earliest forms of the American detective story: there are but two contemporary collections of "dime novels," some mostly bibliographical data in collectors' journals and little in the way of meaningful analysis and criticism. And yet there ought to be. The American detective story is, in fact, a unique manifestation of the genre. Just as the detective story in Britain and France grew out of specific backgrounds, the history of police and crime as well as American popular fiction have shaped our detective stories. That American detective fiction gravitates to unmasking corruption and hypocrisy in high persons and places goes back to the mysteries and miseries of the 1840s. That American detective fiction uses more realistic crime than the artificial problems of British fiction goes back to the story papers and libraries of the 1870s and 1880s. That there is a tension between public and private detectives is not simply a literary convention but a response to the way things were in nineteenth-century America. In the 1890s the detective grew out of cheap fiction and, partly because of Sherlock Holmes, became the subject of fiction in more respectable venues and, thereby, became the victim of his own success. Nevertheless, in any number of essential ways the backgrounds of the nineteenth century are inextricably tied to the detective story in America. And we ought to know more about this.

# Chapter 2
# Texts
# 1866-1890

Let us get one thing straight from the start. Having spent some time and thought on a book can deaden one's critical faculties. The rediscovery of old books especially inclines writers to confuse age with quality. I don't want to do that here. In the following chapter I intend to discuss significant detective works written during the 1870s and 1880s. As literature, they are significant only because they are early. Altogether they are noxious books, incompetent in style, characterization, setting and plot. Their popularity derived from the fact that their authors did something first, not from the fact that they did something well. Nevertheless, they show the evolution of the figure of the detective in popular fiction, they show writers struggling with the problem of how to reconcile the detective and what he does with the demands of contemporary fiction, and they show writers trying to figure out exactly what a detective plot ought to be. The following works are not without a peculiar kind of charm...but I said that I wasn't going to do that.

*The Dead Letter (1866)* by Seeley Register (Metta Victoria Fuller Victor)
On a dark and stormy night the Argyll family awaits the arrival of Henry Moreland. Moreland, by all accounts a spotless youth of position and fortune, is bethrothed to Eleanor Argyll. The family includes Mr. Argyll, a prosperous lawyer, his daughters Eleanor and Mary, his nephew, James Argyll, and Richard Redfield, the narrator, an energetic young man with connections to the family, who is reading law with Mr. Argyll. News arrives that Moreland has been murdered, stabbed in the back while he walked from the station to the Argyll house. The family goes into shock. No clues point to a specific culprit, although it does come out that someone has stolen the $2,000 dowry from Mr. Argyll's desk. Moreland's parents arrive from New York City and take their son's body back with them, and James and Redfield go to the city to hire a detective.

They come up with Mr. Burton, an individual who is not a city detective but a private individual who, as a result of past wrongs done to him, has become an unofficial detective. But not much comes to light: the stolen money seems untraceable and there is no apparent suspect. For one hundred or so pages Burton and Redfield hunt for Lessy Sullivan, a seamstress who has acted suspiciously. When they finally find her hiding in the Morelands' vacant summer home we find that she had a hopeless passion for Moreland, but she isn't very much help.

All this time James Argyll has been making insinuations that Redfield caused Moreland to be murdered because of his passion for Eleanor. This hardens the family against Redfield, and he is, in effect, booted out. Wronged and emotionally desolated, Redfield gives up the law and winds up in Washington working as a clerk in the dead letter office. Here he finds an undelivered letter which seems to be from the murderer to the person who hired him. Redfield takes the letter to Burton who figures out that it was written by one George Thorley, a discredited pharmacist who has connections to Lessy Sullivan. Burton and Redfield take ship for California, where, news has it, Thorley has fled. While on board, Burton receives evidence that the criminal is in Mexico. He, therefore, leaves the ship at Acapulco, and finds Thorley, who has worked his way into the confidence of the Mexican grandee. Burton induces Thorley to write out a confession, and then the detective's party scoots back to New York, hoping to get there before Mary Argyll and James are married. Burton gathers the family in the parlor, presents his case and James confesses that he hired Thorley to murder Moreland so that he could marry one of the daughters (it doesn't matter which) and gain the family fortune. Mr. Argyll declines to have James arrested but warns him to leave the country or else. Mary Argyll and Redfield are married, Eleanor does good works and Burton is poisoned by his enemies.

*The Dead Letter* in many ways typifies the Victorian novel. First of all, it is full of sympathetic nature: dark and stormy nights accompany the bad things in the novel while love connects with the beautiful and soothing in nature. It also contains a full measure of woman worship: we're supposed to regard Eleanor and Lessy's eternal devotion to Moreland as awesome and admirable, we're supposed to see Redfield's exertions in behalf of the family as chivalrous, and we're supposed to see Redfield's exaggerated respect for his mother as healthy. Indeed, Victor portrays Redfield as the model of Victorian gentility, actually Christian gentility, but Victorians like to show it without saying the word. Redfield acts cleanly and charitably and thinks the same way: he does not upbraid the Argylls for their mistreatment of him, does not defend himself and, indeed, does not mention his suspicions for fear that he will wrong another. Honoring Eleanor for her devotion, but—more importantly—vowing to bring Moreland's killer to justice, simply demonstrate principle turned into action: another typical Victorian theme. So does Victor's treatment of James. We know from the very beginning that James is a bad one because he slouches and sneers and makes cynical comments. Then we find out that he is lazy and, on top of that, a secret gambler. The narrator tells us that James is also a sweet talker, but I don't think that readers are or ever were convinced of this. Only Victor's faith in the Victorianism of her readers keeps Redfield from looking like a sap for not pouncing on James at once. For readers who aren't Victorians, though, Redfield is a dope: he tells us about how James goes all queer around

Moreland's corpse and around items associated with the murder, but he can't put two and two together.

That is why we have Mr. Burton, the detective. In Mr. Burton, Victor conglomerates not Victorian notions of the detective but Romantic ones. Like Gaboriau's Tirauclair, Burton began life as an energetic and prosperous merchant. Then rich and powerful merchants resorted to arson to collect insurance money and accidentally also destroyed Burton's uninsured goods. He gathered evidence to convict them, but the courts set them free. Vowing to protect the weak and oppressed from the rich and powerful, vowing to work for justice, Burton became a consultant to and private agent for the police. At the end he lets Thorley and James go free out of regard for the feelings of rich folks. This simply states in action what the novel has preached all along: that a guilty conscience is its own worst punishment.

As a detective Burton uses some pretty standard detective techniques: gathering material evidence (the pieces of the murder weapon), knowledge of the underworld (the dead letter is a contrary one—it means the opposite of what it says), tracking ("He was like an Indian on the trail of his enemy— the bent grass, the broken twig...to him were 'proofs strong as Holy Writ' '') and profiting from the information gained by a far-flung network of "agents." He further insists that he is a master of a new police science:

'I do not know his name and I have never met him. All the acquaintance I have with him is through the medium of chirography. It is sufficient for me: I can not mistake,' then observing my puzzled and incredulous look, he smiled as he added, 'By the way, Richard, you are not aware of my accomplishment of reading men and women from a specimen of their handwriting. It is one of my greatest aids in the profession to which I have devoted myself. The results I obtain sometimes astonish my friends. But, I assure you, there is nothing marvelous is them. Patient study and unwearied observation, with naturally quick perceptions, are the only witchcraft I use.'

Now I suppose that we can accept that Victor took chirography as a science (even while most in the nineteenth century saw it only as a means of guessing character) but it is a bit harder to accept clairvoyance.

Burton puts his young daughter, Lenore, into trances: in one she sees where Lessy Sullivan has hidden and in another she glimpses Thorley. Neither of these spiritual sightings gets Burton and Redfield nearer to the solution of the case, and Victor uses them primarily to show her readers that Burton does not detect by material alone. After James' confession, Burton says:

I owe, still, a good many explanations both to you, Mr. Argyll, and to Mr. Redfield. I cannot lay before you the thousand subtle threads by which I trace the course of a pursuit like this, and which makes me successful as a detective; but I can account for some things which at times have puzzled both of you. In the first place, there is about me a power not possessed by all—call it instinct, magnetism, clairvoyance, or remarkable nervous and mental perception. Whatever it is, it enables me, often, to feel the presence of criminals, as well as of very good persons, poets, artists, or marked temperaments of any kind.

We have here a detective who uses logic and material evidence simply to confirm what he knows by mystical means. Throughout the novel, in fact, both Redfield and Burton point out that the progress of the investigation is actually the manifestation of Providence. Burton is its agent. His dedication to justice and the oppressed, his employment of transcendental or mystical or intuitive intelligence and his death at the hands of his enemies at the close of the novel mark Victor's detective as a descendant (albeit a homogenized and pasteurized one) of Poe or maybe Lytton. Mr. Burton is, essentially, a Romantic hero who acts as a detective because Redfield is, also essentially, a Victorian hero.

*The Dead Letter*, typical of the early detective novel, joins a number of plot conventions. It has a gothic section when Redfield and eventually Burton hunt the ghost that haunts the Morelands' summer villa, discovering that the ghost is actually Lessy Sullivan and her niece. A small episode in New York City, when Burton takes Redfield to the posh gambling establishment, tastes of the mysteries and miseries tradition, showing the exquisite but degenerate habitats of vice. The novel contains a good bit of travelling. First the plot moves repeatedly from Blankville to New York, alternating in typical Victorian style from the beautiful and healthy countryside to the crowded and corrupt city: Thorley, in fact, comes from the city to the country to murder young Moreland. Then the plot takes us to California and Mexico, more for exposure to exotic people and places, in the romantic vein, than for local color. *The Dead Letter* does not intend to follow the trail of evidence to convict the murderer. Indeed readers know who the villain is from the very start. Her creation of the villain, in fact, causes Victor some trouble. On one hand, readers see James as the epitome of weakness. He is slothful, debauched and he turns to jelly at the least mention of the murder. Having a super-human detective, however, requires more of a villain than this, and so in mid-novel Victor transforms James into a super villain: as Burton says, "James Argyll is a *singular* man— a singular man! A person ought to be a panther in cunning and strength to cope with him." Nevertheless, detective work in *The Dead Letter* is really the occasion for sensational or sentimental set pieces— *tableaux vivant* Victor calls them. She intends the grief of Eleanor, the passion of Lessy, and a number of other moments to be seen and felt. Along the same lines, Burton works the denouement, the gathering of the family in the parlor, not so much as a detective trick to uncover the guilty party—as Gryce does in *The Leavenworth Case*—but for the *tableau* of James saying "Yes—I did it, Eleanor."

When Metta Fuller was 20 she published, with her sister, *Poems of Sentiment and Imagination*. She married Orville Victor, an important editor at Beadle and Adams' dime novel publishing house, and became herself a competent utility writer doing cookbooks as well as serial romances. Her novel *The Dead Letter* of 1866 demonstrates that Victor was well up to the standards of the craft in her day, but it also demonstrates that fifteen years after her book of poetry she was still writing of sentiment and imagination, only this time in prose.

### Old Sleuth (1872) by "Tony Pastor"

*Old Sleuth, the Detective; or, the Bay Ridge Mystery* was published in *The Fireside Companion* in 19 installments from June 10 to October 14, 1872. The narrative begins with a young clerk, Elmsley Merritt, leaving a card game on Staten Island having lost all because of his addiction to gambling. When he goes to his boat to return to Manhattan he finds a corpse in the water, a corpse wearing jewelry and carrying money and negotiable notes. While rifling the dead man's clothes, a Staten Island ne'er-do-well, named Hank Skinner, interrupts Merritt and claims part of the booty. After they have rowed out into the channel they begin to fight about the shares and Merritt gets the best of it and ostensibly drowns Skinner. Merritt then goes on to use the plunder to establish what becomes a fortune.

Fifteen years later, concerned about robberies at his bank, Merritt hires Sleuth. Sleuth, "a tall, elderly, handsomely dressed, business-like looking man," discovers that the banker's son, Elmsley Merritt, Jr., has been robbing his father, follows him to a gambling den and buys a curious chain from him which proves that he's been into his dad's vault. But the chain proves more than that, for Merritt Senior got it from the Bay Ridge corpse. Merritt Junior, when he is not dissipating, is forcing his attentions on Minnie Lamont, a popular singer. We witness Harry Loveland rescuing Minnie from Junior's obnoxious attentions. Here are the wheels within wheels. Minnie, who worked in the Merritt household before beginning her life on the stage, is, in fact, the daughter of Charles Henry Decker, the man found drowned at Bay Ridge. This Merritt senior discovers when he finds Minnie's notes about her past that she has written out for Loveland, and so he beings to persecute her, having her abducted and then having her arrested for the theft of a chain, a chain which is the partner to the one Sleuth now has and which connects us back to the Bay Ridge corpse. Sleuth becomes Minnie's defender and drives off the abductors and helps to prove her innocent in court.

Finally a woman in Merritt's pay, Mrs. Obitz, kidnaps Minnie while they are on an outing on Staten Island. Here Minnie also stumbles onto her father's grave and meets Hank Skinner, who escaped drowning but has amnesia. Sleuth arrives at the scene of the kidnapping and "with the sagacity of an Indian, tracked each clue," but he's diverted by discovering Skinner and trying to help him regain his memory. Sleuth then confronts Merritt, catching him as he's about to leave for Europe, and gets him to assign one third of his fortune to Minnie. But Minnie, at this point, is still in the hands of the kidnappers. Mrs. Obitz, it turns out, is not all that bad, and she's humanized by Minnie's company, so she and Minnie escape from Charley Wiseman, the nastiest of Merritt's hirelings. After several twists, all of the bad guys, Merritt and Wiseman, along with Minnie and Mrs. Obitz, end up on a ship where Wiseman almost convinces the captain that he is a detective and Minnie is a criminal, when Sleuth appears and sets everything right. At the end Mrs. Obitz and Minnie, safe and possessed of her rightful share of Merritt's boodle, sit around wondering where Loveland has been all of this time when Sleuth whips off his whig and, *voila*, he's Loveland. The serial ends with the suggestion that it has recounted an actual history and that the readers can find the originals for the characters by scanning New York society.

No doubt because it is a serial, there is not much characterization in *Old Sleuth*. First of all, we know little of Sleuth because he plays two roles, an old man wise in the ways of crime and a young gentleman anxious to achieve the love of the heroine. The two-personality hero was a popular dime novel technique, used at least as early as *Seth Jones; or, the Captives of the Frontier* (1860) to allow one character to possess simultaneously the uncivil competence necessary to deal with a hostile environment and the genteel manners necessary to succeed in conventional courtship rituals. Even in the early 70s, therefore, making a character a detective disqualified him from serving as a hero of the romance unless writers had a fillip like the two personae plot up their sleeves. *Old Sleuth,* however, turns this convention derived from the western into a device to emphasize the detective's principal virtue, he's nowhere but he's everywhere. A lot of this comes from French detective fiction. First and last, the novel emphasizes Sleuth's disguises: he appears first, at Merritt's bank, disguised as a well-to-do middle-aged country gentleman and in the last scene he doffs his whig to reveal himself as Loveland. In between, Sleuth appears in several other disguises, usually as some variety of old codger. This traces to Vidocq and, specifically, to Gaboriau's introduction of M. Lecocq in a variety of disguises. But there is some difficulty here. At one point or another people in the narrative realize that the old gaffer in the corner is Sleuth in disguise—Merrit realizes it at the beginning and Wiseman sees through Sleuth's disguise on the ferry and takes a shot at him on the dock.

While one part of Sleuth is anonymous, in disguise, the other part of him, again coming from the French tradition, is his wide-spread reputation. Everybody knows about Sleuth and considers him omniscient and omnipotent. Police officers, court officials, ship captains, to say nothing of criminals, immediately change their tune when they hear the name Sleuth. Here is the Americanization of the French tradition that the great detective need only mention his name and the guilty will tremble. Sleuth does do a bit of detecting in the novel. In its earliest form, sleuth is the track or trail of a person or animal. A bit later it came to be applied to tracking dogs as sleuth hounds. *Old Sleuth* changed that and made the term snyonymous with detective. And Sleuth does some tracking. Although there is not much precise geography in the story, aside from rough notions that we're on Staten Island or in New York, it does involve considerable running around. Further, in both cases when Minnie is kidnapped by Merritt's minions, Sleuth, "with the sagacity of an Indian" reads the scene of the crime and follows the trail.

Ultimately, though, we don't see much specific detection in the novel. Overlooking the multiplying of coincidences, Sleuth brings Merritt's crimes home to him not so much by supplying evidence as by the force of his personality and his reputation as a detective: Merritt capitulates and turns one third of his fortune over to Minnie largely because he knows that he is dealing with Old Sleuth. Although this motif has its sources in French detective fiction, it corresponds nicely to theory about establishing police forces. If, therefore, protective police prevent crime by being visible and scaring felons from their employment, then detectives by making their identity known frighten criminals into confession. This, in essence, updates the medieval notion that the evidence of one's crime is always present, but instead of trees or stones confronting the guilty, certain naive nineteenth century detective tales, like this one, create the myth that the detective in disguise is always present to astound the guilty and bring their crimes home to them.

In the pre-publication build-up, *The Fireside Companion* stresses the fact that *Old Sleuth* will be a mysteries and miseries novel. The first ad for *Old Sleuth* (on May 13, 1872) says that

It is a story of New York city life, and has largely to do with *fast* young men, and gives an insight into the life led in a city, which will startle a good many people. Mr. Pastor has been in a position to know more than most authors; and the story will be a record of facts more startling than fiction.

But *Old Sleuth* does not quite deliver the mysteries and miseries goods. To be sure, the second installment of the serial includes a mention of Eugene Sue and his description of cities, and there is a fairly detailed description of a gambling den in the same place. And, certainly, the last episode concludes with its *roman a clef* teaser: "As this is a real story we will allow our readers all to become amateur detectives..." We are not, however, really dealing here with a mysteries and miseries novel, because the plot of *Old Sleuth* depends largely upon the conventions of the serial romance. Never mind the mysteries and miseries of the city. Gaining the inheritance for the rightful heir motivates much of the plot. The characterization of Merritt, the villain, of his son, the potential rapist, of Wiseman, the murderous thug, as well as others, grow from traditional romance formulas. Likewise, building the novel on repeated instances of capture and escape, threats to virtue and life, go back at least as far as Hellenistic Greece. More than from the mysteries and miseries tradition, *Old Sleuth* draws material from the contemporary sensation novel, especially through the inserted histories of characters like the account of Mrs. Obitz's tragic past. Thus, advertising for the serial leans on sensation by emphasizing that "each chapter is a startling *tableau*" and that "each word of the conversation of his characters is fraught with *narrative* or *mysterious suggestions*."

Growing out of all its traditions, *Old Sleuth* washes most of its narrative materials with moral purpose. The history of Elmsely Merritt first teaches a lesson about the perils of gambling. Upon discovering the Bay Ridge corpse, Merritt's first impulses are honorable, but his ruination at the card table moves him to robbery and then to attempted murder. Merritt's history also shows the evils of money in that his passion to protect his riches moves him to cause all sorts of mischief to Minnie. Merritt Junior's character, gambler, thief and lecher, shows readers the depravity occasioned by sloth and inherited wealth. On the positive side, the history of Mrs. Obitz demonstrates how vice can be converted to virtue by exposure to goodness and innocence. And virtue gets its rewards. But all of it is bogus. *Old Sleuth* does not show what happens to either of the Merritt men after Minnie gets one third of their wealth. The moral lessons hold no claim to the readers' attention. The villains have occasioned kidnappings, attempted murder, false arrest and assorted other nasty things, but they simply fade out. So do most of the other elements of *Old Sleuth*, the mysteries and miseries, the quivering seconds of sentiment, the fleeting instances of danger. None of them remains at the end of the serial. The lovers are united, but assorted thousands of serial lovers are united in the story papers. *Old Sleuth* has filled up columns in nineteen issues of *The Fireside Companion* and that was its prime and overriding purpose.

That the hero of this particular serial had an impact on the development of popular fiction stems from the fact that his occupation as a detective was something comparatively new. More importantly, Sleuth's popularity came from the fact that he joins, for the first time, elements essential to make the detective a popular hero. Intelligence, expert knowledge, action and romantic attractiveness existed in the detective fiction before Sleuth, but they were always fragmented among characters. Acceptable detective characters were intelligent and expert, but they tended to be middle aged, like Burton and Gryce, or aloof participants in the world of other people's woes. Action and romance fell to the male lead, but, because of entrenched social prejudice, he could not be a detective. Sleuth combined the separate elements and that was something new. But Sleuth's popularity also resulted from Munro's persistent and expensive promotions and the fact that others wanted to get a piece of the action.

### *The Expressman and the Detective* by Allan Pinkerton, 1875.

In his preface, Pinkerton avers that " *The Expressman and the Detective*, and the other works announced by my publishers, are all *true stories*, transcribed from the records in my offices." Indeed, Pinkerton's works are about as exciting as transcribed records. Over the course of 278 pages in *The Expressman* Pinkerton renders an account of how his agents solved a $40,000 theft from the Adams Express Company in Montgomery, Alabama in 1858. Not that there was much solving to do; from the start, the Adams' Company suspected one of their agents, Nathan Moroney. The Pinkertons supply the proof that he did it. *The Expressman* recounts how detectives follow Moroney and his wife around the South, how they watch Mrs. Moroney once she moves in with her sister in Pennsylvania, how they have Moroney arrested and imprisoned in New York, and how they worm their way into the confidence of both husband and wife and find the money and procure confessions from them. To accomplish this, Pinkerton employed nine of his detectives (including Kate Warne, Pinkerton's first woman detective), not counting incidental help from Allan Pinkerton and other executives. Pinkerton ends his preface by saying "if the incidents seem to the reader at all marvelous or improbable, I can but remind him of the old adage, that 'Truth is stranger than fiction.' " In reality, however, the fact is that in *The Expressman* truth is duller than fiction. Here there is no hero, but a hero profession or a corporate hero. The close attention to the peripatetic action which could be riveting reads with the vivacity of a shareholders' report. Here the portraits of individuals possess little but superficial interest. And here the style jigs between obsessive refinement and incompetent buffoonery.

Although Pinkerton may have seen the welter of details as interesting, suspenseful and exciting, his books evoke none of these things. The book's chief aim was to further the image of the Pinkerton Detective Agency: they are, in some ways, prospectuses for prospective clients. It is one of the reasons that Pinkerton finds that all of the cities that his detectives visit are beautiful or charming spots: no Chamber of Commerce, or potential client, could take offense. Also, in *The Expressman* Pinkerton frequently includes descriptions of how anxious he is to please his clients: "Having thoroughly impressed on his mind the importance of the case and my determination to win the esteem of the company by ferreting out the thief." Pinkerton constantly keeps the executives of Adams Express informed about what is happening, and he even invites the president of the company along to watch his agents collar the stolen money. Along with this notice of the kind of personal attention that Pinkerton provides, *The Expressman* serves notice that solving crime does not happen overnight and it is not cheap. The case takes months and employs a squad of detectives. But they get the job done. Indeed the books serve as advertisement for corporate crime solving, for each of the agents works separately and reports to Pinkerton who sends out instructions and maps out each new initiative.

If Pinkerton's books have a corporate purpose, they also have a professional one. He wishes to say something about detectives in them. A bit of this concerns how detectives work. This boils down to the fact that they wear disguises (they come "from my extensive wardrobe, which I keep well supplied by frequent attendance at sales of old articles"), they shadow suspects while in these disguises and they also establish false identities so as to gain the confidence of suspects and elicit information from them. This is the chief burden of the books: showing operatives operating in disguise. There is no "scientific" detective work in *The Expressman*, no searching for clues and no building of logical structures. Insofar as the Pinkertons employ psychological detection, it is the job of the boss himself: in *The Expressman* through anonymous letters Pinkerton works on the culprits' emotions, and he publishes news of the Moroneys' tardy marriage so as to turn the hitherto friendly community of Montgomery against them.

Largely, though, Pinkerton views the current state of detectives in the United States as a sorry one. The detective in Montgomery, in fact, is one of the criminal's chums. In his second book, *Claude Melnotte as a Detective*, Pinkerton emphatically reviews the common reality of detectives:

One reason why the official detective is so often unsuccessful is that he is so well known. Even the small boys in the street, who regard him as a person endowed with supernatural powers, recognize him as he passes by and say: 'There goes the detective!' All the bar keepers know him, and have an extra 'smile' for him—gratis. In like manner he is 'dead-headed' at the hotels, theatres, restaurants and elsewhere, until he becomes, not only one of the best known men in town, but also, one of the greatest 'sponges' in the community. He dresses well, though a little loud perhaps, hob nobs with professional gamblers, and is often 'hail-fellow, well met,' with the thieves themselves. He is most likely their boon companion, and gets his regular percentage of the very 'swag' which he is hired to discover. If the losers are willing to pay more than the thieves can sell their plunder for elsewhere, the detective receives the money and returns the goods. In any event he gets his share. This whole class of detectives are ready to sell out or are already sold.

Pinkerton uses this reality as one of his premises. It is one of the reasons that he supervises his own people so closely. He does, nevertheless, have an exalted vision of what detectives can be which he voices near the close of *The Expressman*:

I had no doubts about what the results would be, but I should then have the proofs in hand to show my employers that the confidence they had bestowed upon me had not been misplaced; that the theory I had advanced and worked upon was the correct one; that my profession, which had been dragged down by unprincipled adventurers until the term "detective" was synonymous with rogue, was, when properly attended to and honestly conducted, one of the most useful and indispensable adjuncts to the preservation of the lives and property of the people. The Divine administers consolation to the soul; the physician strives to relieve the pains of the body; while the detective cleanses society from its impurities, makes crime hideous by dragging it to light, when it would otherwise thrive in darkness, and generally improves mankind by proving that wrong acts, no matter how skillfully covered up, are sure to be found out, and their perpetrators punished. The great preventive of crime, is the fear of detection.

But Pinkerton wants to do more than simply demonstrate that detectives are honest, or competent, or even the defenders of society. He wants the readers to understand that they are, or that he is, gentlefolk. Consequently, the style of *The Expressman* takes swings into the most outlandishly elegant diction, using, for instance, "risibles" instead of "laughter." The same motive moves Pinkerton to drop a little Scott here and a few lines of Burns there. His second book takes its title, *Claude Melnotte as a Detective*, from the character disguised as a nobleman in Bulwer Lytton's *The Lady of Lyons*. He wants readers to know that although he may have come from humble origins, detectives can be honest and diligent professionals possessed of special skills as well as devotion to justice, and that he, Pinkerton, is not only a business executive but a cultured man.

In retrospect, *The Expressman* chronicles ineptitude. When at the end Moroney unfolds his cleverness to a plant in the New York jail, the crime boils down to this: after he had stolen the money, he packed it in an old trunk and had it shipped to New Orleans to be then transshipped to Natchez. Later he took a tour of the South, picked up the trunk and brought it back to Montgomery where he stored it in the attic of his hotel. After her husband's imprisonment in New York, Mrs. Moroney went back to Montgomery, took the money from the trunk and hid it in her bustle. After transferring it to a more comfortable place, Mrs. Moroney took the money back to the Philadelphia suburb where she buried it in the cellar of her sister's house. Starting with Moroney's tour to retrieve his trunk, detectives watched every step that husband and wife take. They saw the trunk, they knew it was in the attic and they knew that Mrs. Moroney buried the swag in the cellar. The chuckleheads spent a good bit of the Adams Express Company's money gadding about the east coast when they should have simply searched the trunk in Montgomery or, at least, dug up the sister's cellar floor. But nobody seems to think of that. For Pinkerton the process of detection has far more value than the product.

This, along with the commercial bumpf and the inept writing, makes Pinkerton's books eminently forgettable. But they do bring something new to the detective story. Not only do they focus exclusively on the action of real detectives, they also depart from the heavy emphasis on sentiment which clogs most detective works of the period. In fact, had Pinkerton (or his writing agent) any competence as a prose stylist, the books would have a comic tone in many sections. *The Expressman* contains the narrative of one Simon Sugg's escape from a sheriff's deputy which Pinkerton includes only because he thinks it comic. He includes dialect passages because he found the speech of southern blacks humorous, just as he found their actions to be amusingly absurd (he describes two shoe shiners who divide the labor of spitting and shining). Pinkerton clearly sees detective Roch's put-on German accent and persona as extremely funny. He also finds several incidents in the plot to have their comic side: Roch scurrying after Moroney and his wife and detective Rivers running to Philadelphia when he can find no horse upon which he can shadow Mrs. Moroney. The illustrations bear this out. If we look at *The Dead Letter,* we find that the book version only carries six engravings, all of which render moments of intense emotion—Eleanor newly dressed in her widow's weeds and such like. Serial detective tales were limited to two or, at the very most, three illustrations (at the beginning of the run) and these commonly stressed the detective's appearance, usually in some clever disguise. *Old Sleuth* certainly does this. Pinkerton's first book has, by these standards, a lot of illustrations, thirteen of them. And none of them captures sentimental moments. A few of them portray detective events in the story: Pinkerton and the president of the Adams company watching their detectives recover the stolen money, for example. Most of them, however, capture moments of prime absurdity. Two men (one laughing and the other with mouth agape) looking at a third man (who is also laughing) holding a small dead dog by its tail, or Mrs. Moroney conking her brother-in-law over the head with a pitcher: hardly moments of piquant emotion or even straight description. The trouble is that the writing is so bad that it is difficult to tell when things are supposed to be funny. This is a bit easier in the second book where Pinkerton tells us that one of the reasons that he disguises his operative as a teutonic prince is to witness the absurdity of superficially republican Chicagoans. But in the later novels, humor dies off. Had Pinkerton been able to effectively fuse humor to the detective tale he may have substantially altered the genre. Innovation without competence, however, insures failure.

*The Leavenworth Case* by Anna Katharine Green, 1878.

Horatio Leavenworth lives in middle-class comfort with his nieces, Mary and Eleanore. Retired from business and widowed, he passes his time, with the aid of Trueman Harwell, his secretary, composing a book about his experiences in China. Everett Raymond, a junior member of the family's legal advisors, is called to the house with news that Mr. Leavenworth has been murdered, shot in the back of his head. Raymond walks into the midst of the inquest, meets the Leavenworth women, detective Ebenezer Gryce and sundry servants, etc. At the inquest, Harwell gives testimony insinuating that Eleanore is the murderess. Green presents her readers with various murder-related material: a room drawing and physical clues—the key to the murder room, Eleanore's handkerchief soiled with gunpowder and fragments of a burned letter. Gryce and Raymond also overhear one of the Leavenworth women addressing the other in accusing tones. For about half of the book Raymond bounces back and forth between the women who adamantly, melodramatically and repeatedly refuse to reveal the secrets that they hold. Henry Ritchie Clavering turns up in the second half and we learn that he is secretly married to Mary. This takes the principals into the countryside to investigate. Here they discover where the absconded maid, Hannah, is hiding, but before she can reveal anything she is poisoned. Back in the city nobody has any real evidence of anything, but there's now considerable prejudice against Mary, what with the secret nuptials, the fact that she's the main heir and that Mr. Leavenworth had a violent prejudice against Englishmen—Clavering being one of the race. Finally, Gryce falsely accuses Mary so as to be overheard by the suspects, and Harwell throws himself into the room and confesses. He did it because he secretly loved Mary.

The substance of *The Leavenworth Case* is Green's characterization of Horatio Leavenworth's adopted heirs, Eleanore and Mary. Just as Collins bases *The Moonstone* on Rachael's refusal to tell the world what she has seen, so *The Leavenwroth Case* runs on the refusal of the two cousins to tell anybody what they know. Raymond vibrates through the book, on one hand anxious for them to speak but on the other hand afraid of what their testimony will reveal. Green portrays the women's refusal to answer questions as mysterious, romantic and (in a twisted way) admirable, stretching women's power to say no into a tragic and heroic aspect of their characters. The irony is that the women do not know anything about the murder. Their secret is Mary's clandestine marriage to Clavering and Mr. Leavenworth's displeasure at its discovery. But what they know has very little to do with uncovering the murderer. It is simply a grand occasion for the melodramatic sentiment that marks *The Leavenworth Case* as a sensation novel. *The Leavenworth Case* consistently delves into the past to find the roots of melancholy and pathos in the present: thus Green inserts the history of Leavenworth's dead wife (essentially murdered by the cruelty of her first husband), the history of Mary's ill-fated courtship and marriage and concludes the novel with Harwell's account of his blighted and pathetic life. Green expects, as her chief object, to exercise and satisfy her readers' hair-triggered and hysterical emotions, a pattern she demonstrates in her drawing of her narrator, Everett Raymond.

Raymond, when he is not gasping or having palpitations, is a lawyer. Indeed, Green subtitled the novel "A Lawyer's Story." The usual assumption is that Green's interest in lawyers and the law came from her father, James Wilson Green, who was a lawyer. On one hand there is a great deal of incompetence here. Raymond, in the first place, goes to the Leavenworth house as a legal advisor to the family, but he does not, in fact, do this. Instead of seeing his clients, Raymond starts poking around with Gryce, the detective, even allowing the police to eavesdrop and harass Mary and Eleanore Leavenworth. Later in the book when Mr. Leavenworth's will is published, it's all news to Raymond. As a legal advisor, then, Raymond flops entirely. What Green seems to intend, however, is to use the enigmas in the novel as a show case for illustrating legal thinking. Whether she knew it or not, this emphasis on law as, essentially, a liberal art was a distinct movement in the 1870s: in 1873, for instance, Emory Washburn in *The Western Jurist* held that "the science of law was the science of mankind" and that lawyers "help solve the moral problems upon which the progress of law depends." In this sense, the novel presents us with Raymond thinking like a lawyer. Green, through Raymond, provides her readers with fascimilie letters, a plan of the murder room and, most importantly, lists of summaries and questions. When he can shuck his hyper-sensitivity, Raymond is a diligent, systematic and uncompromising thinker. His only problem is that he is repeatedly wrong in his suppositions about guilt, first inclining to center on Eleanore and then on Clavering. Raymond's mistakes occur because he is so emotionally involved in the case. They occur also because he has neither the means nor the technical expertise to unravel the crime.

The police do. In *The Leavenworth Case* Green introduces us to two police officers, Ebenezer Gryce and Q. Q is the leg man, the one who scurries around in disguise and finds out the answers to practical questions. Mostly he plays the role of a utility character. Gryce is the expert. Although not

a principal character, he is in many ways the least shop-worn character
in the novel. This is so because, instead of relying on her own imagination,
Green based her detective on some heavy borrowing from Dickens' Inspector
Bucket. Thus she makes him a hearty individual, afflicted at times by
rheumatism, who, like Bucket, has a comically disconcerting habit of fixing
his gaze upon inconsequential objects during a conversation. He is also,
like Bucket, the one who finally solves the case.

Green uses Gryce as a means of enabling Raymond to act as a detective
without having the responsibilities or less than acceptable social standing
of one of the force. She, in fact, provides some graphic passages reflecting
on the social position of detectives in the 1870s:

Mr. Raymond,...have you any idea of the disadvantages under which a detective
labors? For instance, now, you imagine I can insinuate myself into all sorts of society,
perhaps; but you are mistaken. Strange as it may appear, I have never by any possibility
of means succeeded with one class of persons at all. I cannot pass myself off for a gentleman.
Tailors and barbers are no good; I am always found out.

I can enter a house, bow to the mistress of it, let her be as elegant as she will, so
long as I have a writ of arrest in my hand, or some such professional matter upon my
mind; but when it comes to visiting in kid gloves, raising a glass of champagne in response
to a toast—and such like, I am absolutely good for nothing...But it is much the same
with the whole of us. When we are in want of a gentleman to work for us, we have
to go outside of our profession.

In spite of these social difficulties, Gryce possesses more practical
competence than anyone else in the novel. Part of this comes from his
policeman's knowledge of what goes on in his city. He knows, for instance,
that Clavering is watching the Leavenworth house when Raymond assumes
that he has taken ship for England. Part of it, however, comes from specialized
knowledge which he displays when he tracks down the source of the letter
discovered in the country village. Although Green could have based the
conclusion of the case on either of these areas of Gryce's expertise, she does
not. Instead she uses Gryce to squeeze the most possible melodrama out
of the case by having him falsely accuse Mary Leavenworth of the crime
in the presence of several listeners so as to force the murderer into confessing.

*The Great Bank Robbery* by Julian Hawthorne, 1887

The Novelist meets The Journalist in the street. To renew their
acquaintance, they dine and then go to watch a popular horse tamer. At
dinner the Journalist discusses professional criminals. At the horse tamer's
they watch several difficult horses being broken, but then one temporarily
escapes and threatens to plunge into the spectators' gallery. The Novelist
is intrigued by a mysterious woman who confronts the wild horse, seemingly
thrilled by this exposure to danger. Later the Journalist begins to tell the
Novelist the story of this Mrs. Nelson: her aspirations to be a social leader
and the collapse of her husband's business. Then the Journalist refuses to
relate the remainder of her history. His interest piqued, the Novelist goes

to police headquarters and talks to Inspector Byrnes who lets him have free run of the documents relating to the October 27, 1878, robbery of the Manhattan Savings Institution.

Hawthorne bases a large portion of the narrative on facts verifiable by reference to Byrnes' *Professional Criminals of America*; he admits, however, "that I am unable to state whether Inspector Byrnes has ever heard of the existence of such a person as Mrs. Nelson." The Novelist determines to turn the official documents into a connected narrative which follows. Mrs. Nelson, out of frustration for her husband's loss of money as well as an unnatural craving for excitement, forms a friendship with James D. Grady, ostensibly a diamond merchant but actually a prominent receiver of stolen goods and criminal entrepreneur. She helps Grady obtain information about the interior of the Manhattan Savings Institution which Grady's hirelings proceed to burgle. They have suborned one of the watchmen and they kidnap the other. In about an hour on Sunday morning of October 27, 1878, they enter the vault and force several of the bank's safes, getting clean away with $2,747,700. The rub is that they got only $11,000 in cash; the rest was in securities.

Enter Inspector Byrnes:

This was a tall and well built man of perhaps thirty five years of age, with a face expressive of quiet but penetrating intelligence, and a bearing that denoted power, self-confidence and reserve. He was neatly and unobtrusively dressed, and looked like a prosperous man of business of the higher class.

In this chapter, "A Man With Eyes," Byrnes surveys the scene of the crime. He questions suspects and has some of them shadowed, including one of the watchmen, Shevelin. The first lead comes when detectives discover that one Mr. Smith has some interest in the crime. They shadow Smith to Chicago and a detective takes the job as Smith's secretary only to discover that Smith is engaged in writing a book about crime and has collected criminal memorabilia—including what he believes to be one of the stolen securities. Mrs. Nelson then leaves New York for Washington, for she intends to lobby against the bank's efforts to have a bill passed in Congress which would allow the duplication of the stolen securities—thereby recouping almost the whole loss and negating any chance for the thieves to sell the securities back to the bank. On the train, an incognito detective talks to her about his knowledge of police gossip about the robbery; he confronts her with her duplicity, Inspector Byrnes materializes and Mrs. Nelson signs a confession about her part in the planning of the robbery. Byrnes then arrests Shevelin and questions him for a number of days, avoiding *habeas corpus* by holding him 24 hours, releasing him and immediately arresting him on another minor charge. Shevelin finally turns state's evidence and reveals the names of the others who broke into the bank vault. Grady packs up and determines to skip town, taking Mrs. Nelson with him. Although fascinated by his criminality, Mrs. Nelson wants no part of Grady as a constant companion and tries to poison him. He tries to kill her but she escapes, and, because of the intense situation, Grady dies of a heart attack. Then the book ends without a return to the frame story.

*The Great Bank Robbery* is a thoroughly bungled book which one would do well to avoid. Hawthorne fumbles the plot not only by failing to complete the framework, but, more importantly, he is confused about the book's exact purpose. The only sure thing is the book's glorification of Inspector Byrnes, and, in retrospect, not much glory attaches to either the robbery (the crooks only got $11,000 in cash, and the bank and Congress thwarted any attempt to sell the securities back) or the solution. Byrnes did not personally arrest any of the criminals.

At the beginning of *The Great Bank Robbery* Hawthorne includes a dialogue between the Journalist and the Novelist on the difference between average persons and the professional criminal. The Journalist contends that the criminal's life is a pretty happy one:

> Now the soul of the criminal (don't forget it's the profession I am talking about) never gets handcuffed. He always means to get off, and half the time he does. He never stops hoping, for there are too many reasons for hope...Being a professional the dread of social obloquy can not touch you. You not only don't care for it, you're proud of it; for the more they hate you, the greater is the compliment to your power and capacity. You are no hypocrite—and all you have to do is to plot and contrive, and when the time comes, to act. You are constantly matching your wit and resources against those of law and society: you attack, you parry, you retreat, you out-fraud. There's no time for ennui—your blood is always on the jump!

So first we have this romantic view of crime and criminals. But then Hawthorne follows this up with Mrs. Nelson, whom he portrays as a diseased thrill-seeker, a social aberration whose lust for excitement drives her to crime. Although her social standing and her sex prevent her arrest, after the robbery we see her as an alluring and, therefore, dangerous example of perversion. And then with Grady, we get a bit of sociological background. In the chapter "A Graduate of the City" Hawthorne colors in a bit of the history that led an able youth into crime. But what of those who actually burgled the bank: Ellis, Coakley, Young Hope, Old Hope, Bill Kelly, Johnny Dobbs, George Mason and the rest? While Hawthorne arranges his narrative so as to shift focus between criminals and detectives, Mrs. Nelson and Grady receive all of the attention. The actual perpetrators are an addendum scooted in in the last chapter. So what is the novel's perspective on criminals? It is a mish-mash of Bulwer Lytton's picture of romantic, happy thieves, a portrait of tragic and dangerous psychology, a bit of city-bashing sociology, along with terse criminal records which Byrnes did better in *Professional Criminals of America* (which contains photos and dossiers of 6 of the bank burglars) the year before.

The plot echoes the same confusion: Hawthorne cannot decide just what to describe. He begins the book as if to contrast the guilt of the normal citizen involved in crime with the life of the professional criminal. Then he plunges into what seems to be a sensation novel plot detailing the unnatural urges of Mrs. Nelson, along the lines of *East Lynne*. Next comes a description of the discovery of the burglary at the Manhattan Savings Bank, but the description of the detection becomes fragmented while the plot follows other interests. Hawthorne almost introduces a red herring with Mr. Smith the amateur criminologist and the bunco trick played on him. (The souvenir security he buys is not really one from the burglary.) This is, however, only part red herring; it is also part admonition to amateurs not to confuse the police by meddling. Rather than purposefully shifting from description of detectives to description of criminals, we are left with a muddle with large gaps. We catch only glimpses of the police working relentlessly to capture the criminals, and see almost nothing substantial of the criminals' lives after the crime. Here the author cannot decide what is the most interesting: describing the mechanics of the commission of the crime, the details of detection, the sociology of criminals, the psychology of pursuit, or the psychology of escape. Bits of people, superficial details of places and events are all Hawthorne provided. Part of this came from simple ineptness—readers should, after all, demand consistency and there is little of it here. Part of this, though, came about because Hawthorne partly abandoned the old sensation novel method of portraying crime and criminals without having a pattern for how to deal with crime, criminals and detectives in a more realistic manner.

Although his is a decidedly small part in the narrative, the portrait of Inspector Byrnes is in some ways the least bungled part of the novel. Byrnes does play a small part; he lets the novelist look at police records, he appears at the scene of the crime, he questions suspects, he appears to witness Mrs. Nelson's confession and he takes Shevelin's confession. In Byrnes, however, Hawthorne presents the first respectable, socially secure detective in American fiction. He looks "like a prosperous man of business of the higher class." Not only do police officers admire Byrnes ("the police officers on duty greeted him with manifest satisfaction"), but so does the public at large. All agree that "this was New York's greatest detective." From the beginning of the book he is a celebrity. The Journalist speaks admiringly of his Rogues' Gallery and Byrnes generally receives the attention of a devoted public; he, in fact, has a museum holding relics of his triumphs— including the handcuffs used on the kidnapped watchman from the Manhattan Bank. Obviously one of Byrnes' strengths is his sense of to whom and about whom to talk:

But, in his public capacity, he recognizes but two classes in the community—those who have been convicted of offenses against law and order, and those who have not. Of the former he is ready to speak as freely as is consistent with official prudence and etiquette; of the latter he can not be induced to say anything, save in the way of ordinary comment and remark.

Byrnes has added public relations to the traditional reassurances about the detective's discretion. Withal, Hawthorne carefully points out that Byrnes respects the forms of the law here as well as with the *haebus corpus* business with Shevelin. Nevertheless, Byrnes has "a bearing that denoted power." Indeed he exudes a sort of omniscience: "he would be a rash man who should venture to assert that there is anything in New York that the inspector does not know." When the Journalist goes to Byrnes in the narrative and suggests that he watch Grady, the reader receives the impression that Byrnes already knows this and has his nets out. But Byrnes is no armchair detective. As soon as he arrives at the bank he gets down to business: "It was his present duty to study the confusion which the thieves had left behind them, and endeavor to deduce from it some traces of their identity." Even this busy-work can be expertly, even magically, done if done by Byrnes: "Inspector Byrnes, by nature and training, was fitted for it to an extraordinary degree;" "so can an efficient detective divine, from the manner in which a safe has been attacked...something pointing to the identity of the operators." In summary, we learn that "Sound common-sense and unfathomable subtlety have seldom been more effectively combined than in the person of the New York inspector."

It is, perhaps, too bad that the New York inspector was chronicled first in a book with neither subtlety nor common-sense.

After pushing through these five novels we need to ask ourselves about their significance, and the significance of the first twenty years of American detective fiction. The answer to the first part is easy: none of these novels is significant as literature. Further, none is significant in beginning major enduring traditions for American detective fiction. They are not, however, entirely negligible, for they highlight some of the problems in the evolution of American detective fiction.

Part of the reason that they do not begin enduring traditions for detective fiction lies in the fact that they fail as literature. They fail as literature first of all because of the inability of the writers as stylists. The prose in these books ranges from purple to neutral to incompetent—the most incompetent style coming from whoever wrote the Pinkerton books where the comic intent and the expression rarely match up. *The Leavenworth Case* contains the most pulsating, overwrought prose. In no case do we find fluent, realistic and effective prose. We also find virtually no real vernacular speech. Servants and foreigners have particular diction, talk funny, but the principal characters speak, by and large, the vanilla diction of the late nineteenth-century middle class. Therefore, although the narrator's voice is, by and large, efficient, when characters speak, they expose themselves as being artificial and priggish. And this is particularly evident in these early detective works when characters speak of love—which they do with some frequency.

Unlike writers dealing with detection at about the same time in Europe, like Gaboriau and Collins, American detective works were not very long novels. They cannot, therefore, properly sustain more than one purpose. And that purpose most often is that of the sensation novel, or, more specifically, that purpose revolves around the tragedies and triumphs of love. With the exception of *The Expressman and the Detective*, all of these books deal with sex: *The Dead Letter* involves the widowed virgin, the unrequitted virgin and the slandered lover redeeming his name and finding a mate; *Old Sleuth* contains the hero's love trial of saving the woman in order to achieve her as a reward; *The Leavenworth Case* again contains the unrequited lover, the agony of the lover's suspicion as well as the love trial; and *The Great Bank Robbery* uses as one of its confused focuses the admonition against women's unnatural urges. Wilkie Collins says that *The Woman in White* demonstrates "What a Woman's patience can endure and what a Man's resolution can achieve." This pretty neatly sums up the main purpose of most of the early detective works in America.

None of these books responds to the real crime and violence which appeared in the society of the time. They contain, indeed, comparatively little violence. Partly this occurs because they have little to do with cities, real cities. Each of the books takes place at least in part in New York, but none conveys the sense that the metropolis is the Sodom of the East. More people live and do business there, that's all. The books which include professional criminals (*The Dead Letter, The Expressman and the Detective, Old Sleuth* and *The Great Bank Robbery*) convey little sense of the existence or nature of a criminal class. By and large, again because of the roots in the sensation novels, American detective fiction dwells on the failure of morality as the principal cause of crime: the cousin's sloth and lust for money in *The Dead Letter*, the lust for money in *Old Sleuth* and the lust for excitement in *The Great Bank Robbery*. In *The Leavenworth Case* the failure of morality receives some background, but this simply emphasizes pathos which also stems from the sensation novel. Because of the attention to individual moral failure, these early novels either do not draw attention to civil processes attendant upon crime or the culprit escapes civil punishment for his deed: in *The Dead Letter* the murderer simply gets banished, the villain only has to make restitution in *Old Sleuth*, and Byrnes never uses Mrs. Nelson's confession in *The Great Bank Robbery*. One important reason for this rests with social snobbery; wealthy families solve their own problems and wish, at all costs, to avoid the scandal of arrest and trial. Rich folks' delicate sensibilities need to be protected. Part of it also relies on two deep-seated religious notions, conversion and punishment by conscience. Evil-doers don't really escape. Exposure leads either to conversion or to a barren life torched by guilt.

In part because of their focus on emotion, the novels do not use detectives as main characters. *The Dead Letter* and *The Leavenworth Case* both introduce detectives to provide expert guidance to fortify the efforts of the romantic male lead. The same holds true with *Old Sleuth*, even though the detective is the romantic lead in disguise. Strangely enough, the two most celebrated detectives of the period, Pinkerton and Byrnes, are not the principal characters of the books which feature them. Writers of the period simply could not fashion a way of making detectives fit into their antiquated plots. Consequently the detectives are, for one reason or another, outcasts. Partly they are outcasts, as in the case of Gryce, because they do not come from the proper class. The social prejudice against detectives, however, is not an obtrusive theme: Mr. Burton in *The Dead Letter* is at home with all classes of people, Pinkerton hob-nobs with corporation presidents, and both Sleuth and Byrnes are sought-after celebrities. Given the world of these books, American detectives received a good bit more social acceptance than the "use the servants entrance" attitude in mid-century British fiction. If their manners, speech and class do not separate these American detectives, their profession does.

The most prominent feature of fictional detectives of this period which sets them apart from others is the aura of power that authors give them. Omniscience and omnipotence spring to mind. In the case of *The Dead Letter*, the detective (and his daughter) literally possess occult powers. Although more concrete, the other detectives differ from ordinary characters in either knowing more, or seeming to know more. Byrnes has all of the secrets of New York at his finger-tips; Gryce makes the narrator seem a booby in the extent of his knowledge; Sleuth not only knows all, he is everywhere; and Pinkerton moves detectives and criminals about the chess board of the eastern United States. This air of power and omniscience becomes the dominant attribute of the detectives of this period. Once readers look underneath this aura, however, the detective's power reduces to some limited and specialized motifs. Although solving the crimes in *The Dead Letter* and *The Leavenworth Case* requires some small specialized knowledge particular to detectives (the backwards letter, peculiarities of paper, etc), the detectives in these and other early works largely find people: their success depends chiefly on tracking and eavesdropping. In some cases they rely on an extensive and anonymous network of "shadows." In others, Sleuth and Pinkerton, they depend on disguise. These early detectives specialize not so much in precise knowledge of the material world, which is the case in Gaboriau, as they do in finding people. It is a toss-up whether Burton's trip to California or Pinkerton's crooks' tour of the eastern seaboard holds the mileage record. Thus while the authors say that their detectives' powerful intelligence sets them apart, the books say that their abilities to read a trail and to endure train-lag set them apart.

If the fictional detectives stand apart from the other characters in the books, they do not stand apart from the police. Rather than being mavericks, these early American detectives operate in cooperation with the police. The police suggest the services of Burton, Gryce and Byrnes are metropolitan police officers and the police hold Pinkerton and Sleuth in high esteem and give them every aid and assistance. Unlike Poe and Gaboriau, American detective fiction does not yet emphasize the stupid policeman or the animosity between private and official detectives. Neither are they egregious lawbreakers. The fact is that in most of these books the readers and the detectives know the identity of the villains long before the confronting accusation. Some of this has to do with authors' creation of melodramatic suspense, but some of it has to do with following the forms of law, the requirement of proof. Pinkerton and Byrnes demonstrate a punctilious observation of the letter of the law concerning warrants, arrests and detention. Even in those cases in which the culprit escapes civil justice, the detective does not rely simply upon his own judgment: Burton puts the matter to the jury of the family before letting the murderer go free. These detectives, all of them, emphatically protect and serve not their own but the standards of their societies.

In capsule, then, these early novels made the detective an important character in fiction, but not a main character. Although they did not emphasize it, they established a pattern of action above reason, and they created the detective as one apart from the others in the world of the story. They, however, made little connection with the real world of crime and violence in America. Most importantly, these early writers did not create a literary form which would allow the detective to become an actual hero.

# Chapter 3
# Contexts
# 1890-1917

Between 1880 and 1900 New York City's population grew from less than two million to nearly three and a half million. Atlanta, Buffalo, Columbus, Cleveland, Detroit, Indianapolis, Milwaukee, Omaha and Toledo more than doubled their population. In 1810 there were 19 cities in the United States with populations over 100,000; in 1880 there were 50. Immigration reached an all time high. And the cities of the period in many ways were awful. New York City's Eleventh Ward was, *The Growth of the American Republic* tells us, the most crowded spot on earth, far surpassing the population density of Bombay, India. In *American Notes* Kipling, after visiting Chicago, said, "Having seen it...I desire urgently never to see it again." Baltimore, Boston, Chicago and San Francisco all burned to the ground around the turn of the century. In the depression that lasted from 1893 to 1898, four million workers were unemployed. Percy Grant, in *Everybody's Magazine* wrote in 1901:

> Cities have been called ulcers. They swell and fester on the surface of human population, which is healthy only by its sparser distribution. They are full of filth, poverty and vice. They breed criminals. They graduate thieves, murderers and panderers as naturally as universities graduate scholars.
>
> This is not the worst. Cities not only produce vice and crime; they also consume virtue. More horrible than a disease, they appear like diabolical personalities which subsist upon the strength, health, virtue, and noble aspiration produced in the country. A city is a Moloch; the fagots of its fires are human bodies and souls.

While preachers like Grant condemned the cities, others, like Jacob Riis (with books like *Battle with the Slums*, 1902), realized that America could not return to its rural past and, therefore, had to come to terms with its unpleasant present. Nevertheless, even without the burden of crime, life in America's cities at the turn of the century was nasty, brutal and short.

But things were not so bad in Newport and Cape May. Because the growth of law had not caught up with the growth of the country's economy, the rich got indescribably richer. Indeed they had their own testament to justify the heaping up of wealth: William Graham Sumner's 1883 *What Social Classes Owe Each Other*. Sumner warned that "If we do not like the survival of the fittest, we have only one alternative and that is the survival of the unfittest. The former is the law of civilization; the later is the law of anti-civilization." Although the Sherman Anti-Trust Act passed in 1890, conglomerates and cartels were the rule of the day. In 1899 nine American industrial combinations—Standard Oil and the like—were capitalized to the tune of over $50 million each. And a lot of people danced to that kind of tune: U.S. Steel, Pullman and other corporate giants exerted a great deal of control over local, state and national affairs. Yet one U.S. Senator called Vanderbilt "the most censurable" of Civil War profiteers, Jay Gould got his start by selling counterfeit shares in the Erie Railroad, and Rockefeller started his road to riches with money he had embezzled from a produce business in Cleveland. Characteristic of the age, A.S. Mercer's *The Banditti of the Plains* (1892) describes Wyoming's Johnson County War between cattlemen and homesteaders and makes clear that the real bandits of the plains were the cattle barons. Crime?

Crime is whatever society chooses to call it. A wave of concern for crime, old fashioned crime, hit the country at the turn of the century. In 1904 S.S. McClure took to the editorial columns of his magazine and wrote a nine page editorial on "The Increase of Lawlessness In The United States." He begins by saying that "At present there are four and a half times as many murders and homicides for each million of people in the United States as there were in 1881." McClure cites news items from New York, Chicago, Indianapolis, Pittsburgh, Charleston and San Francisco to color this thesis, and includes lists of comparative statistics to hammer the facts home.

Americans were, once again, worried about their lives and property. Beginning with the founding of the Jewelers' Security Alliance (for retailers) in 1883 and the Jewelers' Protective Union (for manufacturers) in 1893, businesses combined to protect themselves against criminals, often putting private detective agencies—Pinkertons at first—on retainers. From 1894 to 1909 members of the American Bankers' Association displayed signs warning that they were protected by Pinkerton's. Life in America seemed to be more dangerous than ever: a *New York Tribune* article in 1903 cites a police estimate that 20,000 people in the city regularly carried pistols. The Sullivan law in New York established strict regulations for carrying firearms, but even its supporters saw that it had little impact on reducing the number of guns on the streets. Life seemed not only more dangerous but more violent. The commonness of lynching is suggested by the number of anti-lynching articles to appear in contemporary magazines. Street gangs, long a feature of nineteenth century city life, became particularly virulent in the last part of the century. When Pike Ryan, the leader of New York's Whyos, was arrested, he carried a printed price list of the gang's services: these ranged from punching, for $2.00, to "Ear Chawed Off," for $15.00, to murder ("Doing the Big Job"), for $100 and up. Winchester introduced the sawed-off shotgun in 1898 by offering for sale a weapon with a twenty inch barrel for police use in riot control. Within twenty years two American Presidents, Garfield and McKinley, were assassinated. So were a number of public officials, police chiefs and mayors, across the country. East or West, America was not a safe place at the turn of the century.

The difference between Garfield's assassin in 1881 and McKinley's in 1901 shows a new element in American crime. A disgruntled civil servant shot Garfield; an alleged anarchist shot McKinley. At the turn of the century American public opinion, never mind Mr. McClure's statistics, saw organized crime, anarchists and mafiosi, as well as the frontier, to be the chief threats to public safety.

In the early 1880s Johann Most brought the notion of anarchism to American labor unions. Anarchist publications frequently recommended violence against what they saw as an unacceptable state of things: in 1884 Albert Parsons in *Alarm* wrote, "Working men of America, learn the manufacture and use of dynamite—a weapon of the weak against the strong, the poor against the rich. Then use it unstintedly, unsparingly." When a striker against McCormick Harvester threw a bomb that killed seven and wounded many more in 1886, Joseph E. Gray of the Cook County Criminal Court rounded up eight anarchists and four of them were eventually executed. None of the eight was at the scene of the bombing. Early in the new century bombings in Colorado and Idaho connected to labor unrest and the I.W.W. During a labor dispute the *Los Angeles Times* building blew up in 1910. Throughout the period the press saw anarchists with bombs behind every bush: *Pool's Index* catalogues seventy four periodical articles on anarchists between 1887 and 1902, including "The Physiognomy of Anarchists" by the celebrated Italian criminologist Cesare Lombroso. Most labor troubles of the period—the Homestead strike, the strike in Cripple Creek against mine owners, and the 1894 Pullman strike—were tarred with the brush of anarchism. The police could round up anarchists and juries could condemn them, but because of the frequent irrationality of these official acts, American labor developed a picture of the police, and especially private police like Pinkerton's, as criminal agents of criminal industrialists.

To some it seemed that at the turn of the century the West was coming east. Western crime, of course, began before the 1890s. It had its own particular character, involving the figure of the gunslinger, and its own flair for notoriety. Jesse James gave an interview to a reporter from the St. Louis *Dispatch* in 1874, John Wesley Hardin's autobiography appeared in 1894, and Emmett Dalton, of Dalton Brothers fame, came out with his *Beyond the Law* in 1916. The dime novel and the newspaper acquainted eastern readers with Billy the Kid, Jesse and Frank James, Sam Bass, Butch Cassidy, the Sundance Kid and all the rest. It made exciting reading, but at the turn of the century Americans began to fear that the lawlessness of the west was not simply diverting entertainment. It was a threat to the entire country. *The Great Train Robbery*, the first American film successfully to tell a story, intended to focus these fears. Thus *The Edison Catalogue* of 1904 advertises the film this way:

This sensational and highly tragic subject will certainly make a decided "hit" wherever shown. In every respect we consider it absolutely the superior of any motion picture film ever made. It has been posed and acted in faithful duplication of genuine "hold-ups" made famous by various outlaw bands in the far West, while the East has been recently shocked by several crimes of the frontier order, which will increase the popular interest in this great head-line attraction.

This added to the notion that contemporary crime was different.

Just as *McClure's* editorialized about crime in 1904, so did *Collier's*, in a three part series by Broughton Brandenburg. Brandenburg knew what caused crime—foreigners. Thus in the series, entitled "Our Imported Criminals," he wrote:

What two years ago was termed 'a wave of alien crime' has swelled to an appalling tide. The incoming millions of Europe threaten to give a new and deplorable color to our public morals. Meanwhile the police stand helpless and baffled before cold-blooded daylight murders, kidnappings for ransom, blackmail and extortion, and kindred outrages.

The immigrants who received the most attention from Brandenburg and from the press in general were from Italy. "The Dagoes did it," are supposed to have been the dying words of New Orleans police chief David Hennessey in 1890. Nine years earlier Hennessey as a detective had captured Giuseppe Esposito, believed to be the leader of the New Orleans Mafia. The public largely ignored the eruption of the Tong Wars which began in Chinese communities in California and New York in the 1880s, but it did not ignore the Italians. If it wasn't anarchists behind every bush, it was the Black Hand or Camorra or Mafia. Feelings ran high. The nineteen Italians who were arrested for Hennessey's murder were lynched in the parish jail and Italy broke off diplomatic relations for a time. A sample of the xenophobia that swept the country comes in *The Baltimore News'* comment that "The Italian immigrant would be no more objectionable than some others were it not for his singularly blood-thirsty disposition and frightful temper and vindictiveness." Although it was a national paranoia, most of the Mafia scare centered in New York where even the legendary Chief Byrnes became involved in a Mafia case only to have the jury free the accused, Vincenzo Quarteraro; Byrnes then announced that Italians could "go ahead and kill each other."

Between 250,000 and 300,000 Italians lived in New York, forming their own cities within a city. "All these places," reported Italian Counsul Giovanni Branchi, "were virtually without police supervision with the exception of the regular Irish policeman at the corner of the street, who did not care a rap what Italians did among themselves so long as they did not interfere with other people." It was not until the first decade of the twentieth century that New York Police Commissioner McAdoo established an Italian Department, a handful of officers under Sergeant Petrosino. The Italian Department had to cope not only with criminal associations brought to this country from Europe, but also crime spawned by the failure of civic order in the United States; blackmail and extortion formed the basis of most of their cases. Petrosino's assassination while on a fact-finding trip to Italy in a small way shows what these officers were up against.

But foreign born criminals were not the only ones engaged in wholesale extortion. The police in many American cities were, too. In 1891 the Society for the Prevention of Crime elected Rev. Charles Parkhurst its president. Founded in the 1870s, the Society had little impact until Parkhurst initiated the first Valentine's Day massacre. In 1892, on February 14, Parkhurst took the pulpit in his Madison Square Presbyterian Church and lit into "the polluted harpies that, under the pretense of governing this city, are feeding day and night on its quivering vitals...a lying, perjured, rum-soaked, libidinous lot." When public, press and politicians demanded more than strong language, Parkhurst, and private detective Charles Gardner toured the seamiest parts of the city and in March, 1892 he preached on the same topic, but with affidavits as his text.

Out of the furor caused by Parkhurst came the Lexow Investigations of 1894, which revealed some of the corruption of Tammany Hall politics. Chief among the culprits were policemen. Not only were policemen, owing their jobs to politicians, involved in wholesale election fraud, but the whole system stank. Ranking police officers bought their posts (one Captain Creedon confessed to paying $15,000 for his promotion to captain), and even patrolmen paid the politicians—at $300 a job. To recoup these expenses, the New York police systematized extortion: one madam testified that she had paid an aggregate of $30,000; policy shops paid $15, saloons $20 and pool rooms $300 a month. Everybody paid off the police. Teddy Roosevelt, who became one of the four New York Police Commissioners in 1895, observed that "I have the most important and corrupt department in New York on my hands." Roosevelt, prowling the streets at night, found that few patrolmen actually patrolled their beats. Persistent corruption, city and state politics as well as Roosevelt's own temperament doomed his efforts to reform the New York police: he kept the office for only a year.

Corruption was not unique to New York: the Andrews Committee, Philadelphia's counterpart to the Lexow Committee, demonstrated that a Republican-run government could maintain a police department as corrupt as Tammany Hall's in New York. One of Lincoln Steffens' real finds was the "big mitt ledger" which contained the daily accounts of police graft in Minneapolis. When Colorado Governor Waite attempted to remove the Denver Fire and Police Board for their refusal to enforce the law, the members refused to be fired. Waite called out the militia and, as Ben B. Lindsay recalls:

There were riflemen in the towers and in the windows [of City Hall]...; and on the roofs of houses for blocks around were sharpshooters and armed gamblers and the defiant agents of the powers who were behind the Police Board in their fight. Gatling guns were rushed through the streets; cannon were trained on the City Hall; the long lines of the militia were drawn up before the building.

Only the arrival of Federal troops, dispatched by President Cleveland, prevented bloodshed. As for Chicago, Eddie Jackson, a pickpocket, recalled that at the 1893 World's Fair in his city, "The arrangement with the police was a 'regular take weekly' of $250...The returns were good. It was a poor week without $1500 for my end." Eventually in Chicago, as in New York, a public investigation (in 1911) showed corruption from bottom to top in the police department.

There was also brutality. The Lexow commission found that in police stations "prisoners purportedly under the law's protection were brutally kicked and maltreated—almost in the sight of the judge presiding in the court." One of the highest officers in the New York police department in the early 90s was Inspector Alexander "Clubber" Williams, an officer renowned for hitting first and then asking questions. Although no one has pinned this down, in the 1890s an old practice got a new name, the third degree, and Jacob Riis wrote that even the celebrated Chief Byrnes "would beat a thief into telling him what he wanted to know." From his aerie at Harvard, Hugo Musterberg wrote in *McClure's* in 1907 that "The dazzling light and the cold water hose and the secret blow seem still to survive, even if nine tenths of the newspaper stories of the 'third degree' are exaggerated." In the last quarter of the century Americans invented the blackjack (the first OED citation is from 1889), soon to become one of the policeman's best friends. A substantial portion of the public, however, didn't mind the use of and threat of force by the police: Henry George in *Social Problems* (1883) put it this way:

> ...let the policeman's club be thrown down or wrested from him, and the fountains of the great deep are opened, and quicker than ever before chaos comes again. Strong as it may seem, our civilization is evolving destructive forces. Not desert and forest, but city slums and country roadsides are nursing the barbarians who may be to the new what Hun and Vandal were to the old.

Barbarians or criminals, this view held, must be countered by the only thing that they understand, force.

From the '90s onward waves of reform hit many urban police departments, but they often had little impact. Tammany's Boss Crocker said "Our people could not stand the rotten police corruption. They'll be back at the next election; they can't stand reform either." S.S. McClure in his piece on "The Increase of Lawlessness" includes in his summary arguments the questions: "Can a body of policemen engaged in blackmail, persecution, and in shielding law-breakers make a community law-abiding? Can a body of policemen engaged in criminal practices prevent others from committing crimes?" Nobody said yes. But nobody knew quite what to do.

It was not just police forces that fumbled with the problems of crime in the United States. Following the English system, American communities early on adopted the system of elected coroners to investigate suspicious deaths. The elected corners in New York between 1898 and 1915 included not only elected politicians but also barbers, saloon keepers, and a milkman, as well as others unfamiliar with medicine. Jurgen Thorwald in *The Century of the Detective* states that in New York between 1868 and 1890 "out of every one hundred uncertain or suspicious deaths, in only eight cases was any autopsy performed." Boston replaced elected corners with medical examiners in 1877, but other cities were slow to follow. A 1914 report in New York maintained that

the elected coroner in New York City represents a combination of power, obscurity and irresponsibility which has resulted in inefficiency and malfeasance in administration of the office...So far as the activities of the coroner's office in New York City are concerned, infanticide and skillful poisoning can be carried on almost with impunity.

It was only in fiction that Craig Kennedy set up to practice scientific detection at the turn of the century—it took New York City quite a bit longer. The City did not replace the system of coroners with qualified medical examiners until 1918.

It was in many ways a paradox. At the same time that the unparalleled corruption of American police forces became known, criminology made its first real advances. At the end of the nineteenth century Europeans began to try to find means to cope with the crime and criminals spawned by modern society. Most of the new techniques and theories made their way to Britain and eventually America, but neither country led the way in either criminology or forensic medicine. While European Universities established chairs and departments of forensic medicine in the nineteenth century, American universities stalled until Harvard's institute for legal medicine (1932) and the department of forensic medicine at NYU (1936). But what was it that got European scientists and police officials so worked up?

The first meeting place of science and police work was with the whole business of identification. Police and jurists throughout the nineteenth century longed for an easy way to identify people, to describe them as unique individuals, and also to identify potential criminals before they actually took to crime. At first phrenology promised to be the answer: to provide a way of determining people's character by examining the formation of their skulls. As late as the 1880s phrenologists testified in court in the United States, but their testimony produced mixed results. In the 1885 trial of Maria Barberi in New York, for instance, the phrenologist for the defense, Dr. Hrdlica, maintained that the evidence of the defendant's skull proved her to be a lunatic. He was then shown unlabeled charts of the heads of President Cleveland, George Vanderbilt and the presiding judge and claimed that the charts were those of abnormal individuals. Not a lot of points won here. While Hrdlica was demonstrating the failings of phrenology in court, the press ran drawings of the defendant's ears and asked the question, "Is she degenerate?" In 1885 this was more relevant than the shape of her skull.

In the 1880s, asking about the shape of someone's ears, or nose, or lips, or jaw meant more than aesthetics. These were some of the things marked off as significant by Cesare Lombroso in his *L'Uomo delinquente* in 1876. Riding a Darwinian ripple, Lombroso held that criminals were throw-backs to earlier stages of human development; instead of evolving, as Victorians would have it, to perfection and civilization, the criminal was a biological degeneration to earlier forms of anthropoid. Criminals committed crimes because they weren't quite human. Quickly Lombroso became the authority in Europe about crime and criminals. His works were translated into French, German and then English. Not only did they have a great impact on continental thinking about crime and criminals, they had some influence in America: as late as the 1920s S.S. Van Dine could have his hero cite Lombroso as current, top-drawer thinking about people and crime. Not only did some of Lombroso's works appear in this country, but biographical articles and books (for instance, Hans Kurella's *Cesare Lombroso, A Modern Man of Science* in 1910) pictured him as the expert on man and crime. Not everyone, though, agreed with Lombroso, and at the turn of the century a number of American writers took up opposing points of view. It was not biology, argued people like Jacob Riis in *How the Other Half Lives*, that caused degenerate people, but degenerate living conditions (tenements, lack of education and so on) that made people criminals.

Whether or not you could judge people by the cut of their ears, modern police forces had to be able to identify them, had to be able to distinguish the practiced felon from the innocent citizen. The American rogue's galleries mentioned earlier used photography to identify criminals. Following up on this, William A. Pinkerton contributed his agency's extensive file of photos to serve as the basis of the National Bureau of Criminal Identification established by the International Association of Chiefs of Police (of which Pinkerton was a board member) in Chicago in 1897. Even before the chiefs set up their Bureau, however, it became apparent that photographs were not enough to identify criminals. Alphonse Bertillion in 1883 introduced his system of twelve standard measurements (including head length and width, middle finger, left foot and forearm) and founded what he called the science of anthropometry. Americans quickly took to this, and in 1889 the American Bertillion Prison Bureau published Bertillion's *Instructions for Taking Descriptions for the Identification of Criminals and Others*. In 1894 Ida M. Tarbell wrote a piece for *McClure's* on scientific criminal identification as practiced in France, using photographs supplied by Bertillion himself. But the new science of anthropometry had a short run, for in the mid 1890s several people in Britain more or less simultaneously discovered fingerprints to be an infallible method of identifying people. Although American law enforcement continued to use Bertillion measurements, fingerprinting quickly came to America, with the St. Louis police being the first American force to switch from Bertillion measurements to fingerprints in 1904. In fact, the Leavenworth Penitentiary provided an ultimate proof of the utility of fingerprints when a clerk discovered two prisoners with the same name, Will West, the same Bertillion measurements, remarkably similar identification photos, but different fingerprints.

From mid-century, European medical science sought to aid in the detection of crime. The most notable work in English was Taylor's *The Principles and Practice of Medical Jurisprudence*. By the end of the century, toxicologists could identify the presence of many mineral and vegetable poisons, and criminal cases in America sometimes hinged on medical evidence. By 1898 scientists had a test to differentiate human blood stains from animal blood stains. All that this meant was that expert chemists knew what to do, until Austrian Hans Gross, the most practical author of the period, collected and systematized police science for workers in the field: his *Criminal Psychology: A Manual for Judges, practitioners and Students* came out in Boston in 1911. Although the U.S. contributed little to these areas of scientific criminology, it made a significant contribution with the work of Charles E. Waite and Calvin Goddard who, essentially, invented modern ballistic science in the 1920s.

Bringing science to the aid of the police was a popular idea. To follow up on his editorial "The Increase of Lawlessness," S.S. McClure turned to the universities for help. He hired Hugo Musterburg, Professor of Psychology at Harvard University, as a commentator on crime. In 1907 and 1908 *McClure's* published Musterburg on "The Third Degree," on "Hypnotism and Crime" and on "The Prevention of Crime." American interest in disciplined thinking about crime accelerated in the early years of the twentieth century, and led to the National Conference on Criminal Law and Criminology held in Chicago in 1909. This conference, in turn, led to the establishment of the American Institute of Criminal Law and Criminology. Thus, "scientific" and scientific thinking about criminals and crime detection of the past twenty years now had a home in America. American police and criminologists had access to state-of-the-art theory and practice. But it did not make a lot of difference on the streets.

Even though there were, no doubt, many honest and conscientious municipal police officers and detectives, the massive publicity about political corruption obscured their service and achievements. The only official detectives to get good press were agents of the federal Secret Service. The Secret Service existed from 1860 as a branch of the Treasury Department to enforce those laws coming under the aegis of the Treasury. After McKinley's assassination the Secret Service assumed the job of protecting the President. Literature and the press of the period celebrated Secret Service agents, especially in their dealings with counterfeiters. Nevertheless, a superficial reading of America at the turn of the century gives the impression that private detectives could and should take over the job of confronting crime. People and organizations with money turned to Pinkerton's or Burns' detective agencies. By the turn of the century the nation had looked at its experience and had evolved the myth of the great detective. The seventies had Allan Pinkerton, the eighties had Thomas Byrnes, and the new century had William Burns. The flaws of these men were manifest. Pinkerton prolonged the Civil War though his incompetent estimates of Confederate strength. Byrnes kept crime out of New York's financial districts simply by arresting any suspicious person seen on their streets. Burns tried to intimidate jurors when his client Harry F. Sinclair, oil magnate, was on trial for contempt. But their successes were spectacular: Byrnes did keep

Wall Street free from crime, Burns exposed land fraud and civic corruption. All of these hero detectives, moreover, knew about self-promotion. Pinkerton had his own narratives, Byrnes was the hero in Julian Hawthorne's books and Burns wrote *The Masked War* (1913) and, with Isabel Ostrander, *The Crevice* (1915). Burns, in fact, had a connection with another kind of hero detective: his conversations about American crime and detectives with Arthur Conan Doyle formed the inspiration for *The Valley of Fear*.

While Byrnes and Burns and Allan Pinkerton's sons were advancing their own reputations, American periodical publishing changed radically. New technology caused a lot of this. By the turn of the century hand-set type was a thing of the past: printers could now use Mergenthaller's linotype. In 1886 the rotary press replaced the flat bed press and paper flew through the presses. Ives invented what is called half-tone engraving in 1886, and the camera replaced the engraver at the print shop. The cost of illustrations fell dramatically, and their frequency in publications rose just as dramatically. And there was advertising. Because railroads reached everywhere, there was now a national marketplace. Companies began to realize this in the 1880s, but the real burst of national advertising came in the 1890s: Quaker Oats, Uneeda Biscuit, Van Camp's Boston Baked Beans, Pears Soap, King C. Gillette's razor, Dr. Lyon's Tooth Powder and many other products all used national advertising. Professor Mott tells us that during this period, Eastman Kodak spent $750,000 a year for ads. Manufacturers and publishers alike discovered in the 1890 that people actually liked advertisements.

Before the 90s Americans had three choices when it came to periodical literature. They could read newspapers, which now came out daily. They could read literary magazines, or they could read family story papers. Between the literary magazine and the family story paper there was little middle ground. Literary magazines were serious in their fiction and non-fiction: they were consciously and decidedly high-brow journals. The family story papers thought of themselves as the voice of the middle class, but their vision of middle-class culture ran to tendentious moralizing (deportment was probably the most popular editorial theme), namby-pamby commentary on current events (*The New York Ledger* particularly liked to say that animal protective societies were okay but we ought to think about people first) and dopey fiction. Consequently neither hit the mark of really appealing to real middle-class taste.

Magazines that did appeal to middle-class taste appeared in the 1890s. The pattern for these new magazines came from England where *The Strand* led the way. *Collier's, Cosmopolitan, McCall's, McClure's, Munsey's* along with a revitalized *Saturday Evening Post*, all did something new. William Archer, in 1910, said of these new magazines that "there is nothing quite like them in the literature of the world—no periodicals which combine such width of popular appeal with such seriousness of aim and thoroughness of workmanship." Archer called them "cheap magazines," and indeed that was one of their innovations. In October, 1893 Munsey tried a grand experiment in his magazine: he sold it for a dime a copy—less than it cost to print—hoping to make his profit from advertisers, not from readers. It worked, and quickly all of the other popular magazines learned the lesson and lowered their prices to ten cents. These magazines boomed in the 1890s: *McClure's* began in 1892 with a circulation of 8,000; two years later its circulation was 250,000.

The new magazines gained much of their popularity because they combined qualities of the newspaper, literary magazine and the illustrated paper. Unlike daily newspapers that quickly move from today's sensation to tomorrow's, the magazines covered larger stories. *Collier's* issue of May 28, 1898 was the Cuban Number, and carried numerous photos by Jimmy Hare. Senator Beveridge of Manifest Destiny fame gained much of his reputation from the *Saturday Evening Post*. The first issue of *McClure's* carried an interview with Edison and an article about Alexander Graham Bell. *Collier's* paid reporter Richard Harding Davis extravagantly for his articles on the Russo-Japanese War. Jack London's prose and sixteen pages of pictures covered the San Francisco Earthquake of 1905.

Like the literary magazines, the new magazines also carried a considerable amount of fiction, serials (the Fu Manchu stories appeared in *Collier's*) but more and more short stories. They saw fiction, in fact, as a sign of their respectability. When an 1895 editorial in *The Independent* argued that literary periodicals did not lower their price because "they will wish to maintain that higher, purer literary standard which succeeds in securing the best but not the most numerous readers," S.S. McClure shot back that his magazine carried Stevenson, Kipling, Gladstone, Doyle as well as Howells, Stephen Crane, Owen Wister and Edward Everett Hale. *Collier's* carried work by Kipling, Robert Chambers, Hall Crane, Frank Norris, F. Marion Crawford, Edith Wharton, Anthony Hope and Jack London. Howells served briefly as joint editor of *Cosmopolitan* in 1892. Indeed, Howells commented that "in belle-lettres at least, most of the best literature now sees the light in the magazines, and most of the second-best appears first in book form." The new magazines also carried lots of illustrations, chiefly photographs. Exotic places from China to Cuba, famous people and notable events all appeared in photographs.

But the new magazines did something more. Although newspapers were quick to expose scandal and corruption in American life, they had only a local perspective and the press for tomorrow's copy kept them from thorough study and investigation. Not so the magazines. *McClure's*, with others in hot pursuit, invented what Teddy Roosevelt called "muckraking." Josiah Flynt started the parade when he and Alfred Hodder began their series "Notes from the Underworld" in August 1901 for *McClure's*, followed the next year by Flynt's more factual series "The World of Graft." Ida M. Tarbell wrote her series of articles "The History of the Standard Oil Company" after four years of research and $50,000 from S.S. McClure. McClure also sent Lincoln Steffens on a jaunt across the country to gather material for the articles that became *The Shame of the Cities*. An anonymous detective was the author of a series exposing New York's graft in *Cosmopolitan* in 1905. The following year the same magazine took on the U.S. Senate, beginning with "The Treason of the Senate." Samuel H. Adams hopped from *McClure's* to *Collier's* and took with him his research exposing the patent medicine industry. *Everybody's* sent reporter Harvey O'Higgins to Denver to collaborate with reformer Ben Lindsay on what became *The Beast* (1909). *Leslie's* took on railroad accidents, *Everybody's* went after the New York Life Assurance Company and the Beef Trust. In the first decade of the century muckraking became a standard feature of most American journalism.

American magazines at the turn of the century had obvious interests in crime, police and detectives. S.S. McClure's concern about American lawlessness reflects one side of the contemporary attitude toward crime, but Hutchens Hapgood's *The Autobiography of a Thief* (1903) as well as Josiah Flynt's work show writers willing to observe criminals without overt moralizing. At the same time, a fascination with crime, especially foreign or exotic crime, persisted. Melville Davisson Post did a six part series, "Extraordinary Cases," in the *Saturday Evening Post* in 1911 and 12, and in the next year Marie Belloc Lowndes contributed "Great French Mysteries" to *McClure's*. For the first time, writers emphatically labeled as criminals government officials and indifferent corporations. The police: journalism had little good to say about them. In *Notes from an Itinerant Policeman*, Flynt says

Until the general public takes an interest in making police life cleaner and in eliminating the professional offender and the dishonest public servant from the problems which crime in this country brings up for solution, very little can be accomplished by the police reformer.

One hope that the magazines saw was in scientific detection. Ida M. Tarbell did a two part series for *McClure's* in the mid-90s, but the real emphasis on science comes after the turn of the century. *Current Literature* of 1911 carried an article entitled "Why the Great Scientist Will Supersede the Great Detective." In 1912 *Collier's* ran a piece on "Scientific Sleuths" by A. H. Gleason, and the chief advocate of the scientific story, Arthur B. Reeve, wrote "Five Rattling Detective Adventures: The New Method of Detectives Who Have Turned Scientist" for *The World's Work* in 1913. Private detectives had their place, too. *Collier's* published an article in 1911 on "Private Detective's Work." On a more ambitious scale, Harvey O'Higgins, Dana Gatlin and Arthur B. Reeve wrote a series of articles, "Detective Burns; Greatest Cases" that stretched from 1911 to 1913 in *McClure's*. Even Chief Byrnes recovered from his Lexow set-back and before his death in 1910, Jacob Riis and Lincoln Steffens both wrote about him with some awe.

While these new middle-class magazines burgeoned, reaching out for a new audience and new subjects, Harper Brothers was not sitting on its hands. They, of course, had their high-hat literary magazine, *Harper's New Monthly Magazine*, but they also published a middle-class journal, *Harper's Weekly Magazine*. When *McClure's*, *Munsey's* and the rest took off in the early 1890s, Harpers followed the crowd, making their weekly look like the other successful magazines with news items, photos, features, columns and, of course, fiction. *Harper's Weekly* was, if anything, a bit more on the masculine side than the other magazines, with lots of articles and pictures about the navy, about horses and about sports. During the early 90s, *Harper's Weekly* also paid some attention to crime. It paid particular interest to the mafia business in New Orleans: the cover on March 28, 1891 shows Italian prisoners being killed in the parish jail and an accompanying editorial says that "It is certainly an extraordinary fact that a conspiracy of foreign criminals has so completely overawed and paralyzed society in New Orleans that the city could be saved to order and law only by a temporary resort to barbarism." Later they ran a cover picture of New York police chief William Murray and noted his retirement and replacement by Inspector, now Chief, Byrnes. During the same period *Harper's Weekly* ran fiction by Kipling, Henry James, Lilian Bell, George Jessop and J.M. Barrie, but no crime fiction. This briefly changed in 1893.

Sherlock Holmes had appeared in book form in the United States before 1893: Lippincott published both *A Study in Scarlet* and *The Sign of the Four* in 1890. As in Britain, however, the Holmes novels did not quite catch on. Harpers brought out the first series of Sherlock Holmes short stories, *The Adventures of Sherlock Holmes*, in book form, in 1892, but these never saw periodical publication. *Harper's Weekly* brought Sherlock Holmes to American magazines on January 14, 1893, with the publication of "The Adventure of the Cardboard Box." Within the year, they ran eleven Holmes stories from *The Memoirs of Sherlock Holmes* series. Maybe it is a strange juxtaposition: on February 11, 1893 the readers of *Harper's Weekly* got "The Adventure of the Yellow Face" and, at the same time, an anti-Tammany editorial; in November, after all of the Holmes stories had run, there is an editorial opposing Boss Croker and, on the cover November 11, a picture of the assassination of Chicago's mayor. American violence and corruption contrasted to British reason and competence. But maybe the juxtaposition is not so strange after all. *Harper's* led off the Sherlock Holmes series with "The Cardboard Box," which is not only one of Doyle's more gruesome tales (Miss Susan Cushing receives two freshly severed human ears through the mail), but also one that mentions Poe prominently. They followed this up with "The Yellow Face," a story with an American background, turning on miscegenation. These pieces may have been more appropriate to America of the 1890s, and, therefore, more publishable, than Doyle's first series which leads off with Holmes chasing around trying to save the bacon of a plump Bohemian aristocrat.

For some reason, probably financial, *Harper's Weekly* published all of the stories from *The Memoirs of Sherlock Holmes* except "The Final Problem." S.S. McClure acquired the story about Holmes' supposed death and published it in his new magazine in December, 1893. *McClure's* was very taken with Doyle. In 1893, before "The Final Problem" ran, the magazine featured Doyle in the "Human Documents" section, a section of brief biographies and photos of famous contemporaries. After running the "last" Holmes story, *McClure's* included an interview with Doyle, the author's reflections on reading, and several of his non-Holmes stories. Indeed, before 1900 they published eleven of Doyle's stories, but, of course, no more Sherlock Holmes. Sherlock Holmes did not inspire *McClure's* to go headlong into the detective fiction business. Nevertheless, the magazine displays a hearty new interest in real detectives after publishing "The Final Problem." First, there was a mini-series by Ida M. Tarbell in the spring of 1894 about French criminology: "The Scientific Method in the Identification of Criminals," and "A Chemical Detective Bureau." Late in the same year readers found an article about "How Allan Pinkerton Thwarted the First Plot to Assassinate Lincoln." This piece led to a series of seven articles in 1894-5, "Stories from the Archives of the Pinkerton Detective Agency." Just as Doyle's fictional detective inspired an interest at *McClure's* in real detectives, the accounts of real detectives may have taught the journalists at the magazine to act like detectives. Starting with Flynt and Walton's "True Stories from the Underworld," (which became *The Powers that Prey*), and becoming more evident in Flynt's "The World of Graft," *McClure's* published journalists who, in fact, acted as detectives: journalists like Ida Tarbell with her research for her "History of the Standard Oil Company," and Lincoln Steffens with his sniffing out the *Shame of the Cities*. In the early twentieth century, after muckraking at *McClure's* slowed down, the magazine went back to imported detective fiction, publishing R. Austin Freeman in 1910 and 1911. Virtually repeating its earlier pattern, the magazine moved from fiction to fact: from publishing Dr. Thorndyke to publishing an extended series on real detective work in "Detective Burns' Greatest Cases" written by Dana Gatlin and two writers, O'Higgins and Reeve, who, at the same time, were publishing detective fiction in other magazines.

In general, American magazine publishers did not rush to detective stories after the 1893-4 publication of the Holmes stories. It took almost another decade for detective stories to begin to really sink into the trade. This time, around 1910, it seems, they took hold. Partly they took hold because the second time Holmes appeared in American magazines, (in the stories collected as *The Return of Sherlock Holmes*), they were bought by *Collier's*. *Collier's* published thirteen new Holmes stories from 1903 to 1905. Although *Harper's Weekly* and *McClure's* were aggressive magazines, *Collier's* was a far slicker journal: it had a larger format, it had colored pictures on its covers and it had the fabulously popular Gibson Girl. When the Holmes stories appeared in *Collier's*, the magazine made much of them, with teasers running in issues before publication and with colored drawings of the detective on the cover of the issue.

At about the same time that *Collier's* ballyhooed Sherlock Holmes, the American magazine industry began to view the detective story as separate from other brands of fiction. Detective stories got their own heading in *The Readers' Guide to Periodical Literature* in 1905, and a bit later magazines began running rudimentary criticism of detective stories: "The Detective

Story's Origin" appeared in *Harper's Weekly* in 1910 and *The Nation* featured a piece on "Detectiveness in Fiction" in 1912. Popular magazines now began to run detective stories, often American detective stories, with some regularity: the year after *Collier's* published stories from Doyle's next collection of Holmes stories, from *The Last Bow*, they introduced readers to Harvey O'Higgins' boy detective, Barney. In 1911, in the way of competition, *Cosmopolitan* ran Arsene Lupin from abroad and started a series of Arthur B. Reeve's stories that would last until the end of World War I. Likewise, in 1911 *The Saturday Evening Post* introduced Melville Davisson Post's Uncle Abner. *Lippincott's* added Carolyn Wells to the parade of American detective writers in 1912. The detective story had found a home in popular magazines.

One of the reasons that detective stories found a home in American popular magazines is that many of them were written by journalists and editors. Unlike Britain, where the turn of the century detective story drew writers from diverse walks of life, from physician to clergyman, most turn of the century detective writers in this country had some connection with journalism. Edwin Balmer, who wrote the Luther Trant stories with William MacHarg, became the editor of *Redbook*. Samuel Hopkins Adams was an editor at *McClure's* and then *Collier's*. Reeve, before he invented Craig Kennedy, worked at various editorial jobs around New York. Harvey O' Higgins wrote for *McClure's*. Hugh C. Weir, creator of Madelyn Mack, as was Jacques Futrelle was a journalist. Indeed, the most famous journalists of the day wrote fiction about crime. Hugh Green includes a story by Richard Harding Davis, probably the best known reporter of the day, in his *The American Rivals of Sherlock Holmes*, and Lincoln Steffens, a close second in the fame department, wrote some short crime fiction, including "Dan McCarthy, Captain of Police" (1901).

That so many American detective writers during this period were journalists means several things. First of all, it was a break from the past. Professional fiction writers dominated the American detective story before the turn of the century. This was not only the case with the hacks who cranked out hundreds of pieces of detective fiction for the story papers, dime novels and detective libraries, but it also extended to Hawthorne and Green: all of these people wrote fiction to make their living. Hawthorne, in fact, in *The Great Bank Robbery* sets up an opposition between the Novelist and Journalist. Next, the movement of journalists to the detective story in the early twentieth century suggests that it was a form that prolifereated from the top down: people in the publishing industry decided to write and publish detective stories rather than detective stories rising from independent writers. It was, in part, a created phenomenon. Additionally, the link between detective stories and journalists means that the writers brought with them a specific background of current events as well as an inclination toward investigative reporting, muckraking. Finally the infusion of journalists in the early twentieth century had certain effects on the literary style of detective and crime fiction. During this period newspapers and magazines began to pay attention to making a style which communicates with precision. All of these things helped to shape American crime fiction of the period.

If many of the writers of the period were journalists, the newspaper person is also a favorite character in their detective and crime stories. Doyle made his narrator a physician and so did Freeman. The only prominent newspaper person in British fiction of the period is the newspaperwoman who narrates Orczy's Old Man in the Corner stories. On this side of the Atlantic, the newspaper reporter-narrator became something of a favorite character: Futrelle has his Hatch, Reeve has Jameson and Hugh C. Weir has Nora. Each one is a reporter who has formed a relationship with the genius detective, who chronicles his or her triumphs and who puts up with the detective's vagaries. The reporter as narrator makes more sense than the physician as narrator: physicians are supposed to be out curing the sick and not tagging along with eccentric detectives, but this is precisely the thing that the reporter is supposed to do. Flynt and Walton, indeed, picture their narrator as a scribe, one who simply writes down what he sees. By the time we get to Adams' Average Jones we essentially have the reporter as detective hero, for although Jones may not literally be a reporter, he certainly uses his friend's newspaper as a resource. Jones' researches, in fact, bear more than a bit of similarity to those done by a conscientious journalist about to do a job on a robber baron.

While the detective stories written at the turn of the century in Britain were consciously apolitical (in "The Reigate Squires" Watson tells us that there will be no "politics or finance" in the Holmes stories), this was not the case in the United States. The period opens, in fact, with two books that specifically aim to disturb readers about the *status quo* in America: The Randolph Mason stories and *The Powers that Prey*. Turn-of-the-century writers who took up the more conventional detective story often wrote pieces about politics. Reeve's "The Campaign Grafter" and Adams' "The One Best Bet" and "B-Flat Trombone" tackle corrupt politicians whom the detectives not only catch in crooked shenanigans but also force out of the business. These conventional detective writers also frequently went after big business. Adams does this more than most, but other writers like Balmer and MacHarg go after the corrupt business and business deal. Here there is not a great deal of difference between what muckraking journalists were doing in the real world and what detectives were doing in the world of fiction.

One of the connections between journalism, crime and detective fiction can be found in science. Popular magazines at the turn of the century often trumpeted the achievements of modern science and technology, featuring men of science like Edison as well as the inventions of the new technology. Early on, Ida Tarbell wrote French applications of science to crime solving. By the early twentieth century, American magazines began to extol the promises of scientific detection. From 1911 to 1913 *Current Literature* and *Collier's* and *World's Work* all showed readers how science would replace old-fashioned detection. They reflected the actual advances which were taking place in police science as well as the period's general fervor for and faith in science. Even without the foreign model of R. Austin Freeman's scientific detective and scientific tales, American authors would probably have come to science on their own. Arthur B. Reeve, of course, is the fountainhead of the American scientific story, but there were other writers who also emphasized the detective as the scientist. MacHarg and Balmer's Luther Trant is a psychologist back when psychologists were considered scientists. Francis Lynde's detective's name, Scientific Sprague, illustrates his inclination. Even detectives who are not principally scientists occasionally act like them: Average Jones solves some cases with his knowledge of science and Professor Van Dusen in one story even messes around with radium.

Science plays a particular role in our detective stories. We can see this is what happened to psychology. Americans recognized psychology as a branch of knowledge much earlier than did the general public in Britain, and our detective fiction reflects this. MacHarg and Balmer as well as Reeve wrote detective stories based on psychology. They do not, however, emphasize psychology's capacity to explain human motives; instead they see it as a science which produces instruments to discover and capture the guilty. This was a detective fiction's general treatment of science: science produced gadgets that made crook-catching easier. MacHarg and Balmer tell their readers of marvels like the pneumograph, the chromoscope, the kymograph and the plethysmograph. Reeve talks of the detectoscope, the telegraphone and the telautograph. These marvels enhance detectives' skill: they not only help with mundane things, like enabling detectives to hear conversations when they are not present, but they also empower detectives to see into the human bosom, to read the physical signs of mental activity. Although the gadget stories seem dated today, they played well in their own time. Indeed, they were often fictional accounts of actual scientific discoveries and technological innovations that were featured in the same magazines in which they were published.

If the scientific stories were contemporary, they also show detective fiction applying blinders to itself. Demonstrating clever science in a detective story usually means basing it on a clever and sophisticated crime—South American arrow poison, things like that. Although most American scientific writers tried to make their fiction relevant (including, as Reeve does, things like the Mafia) their fascination with science often overwhelms any depiction or concern for real crime—the smash and grab, the hold-up, the bank robbery and the like. The fascination with gadget science thus often makes many turn of the century writers forget about the sort of thing drilled at by Flynt and Walton, the character of the criminal, or emphasized by Jacob Riis, the society that makes people into criminals.

In many ways American detective stories of the period differ from those written in Britain which began to play up the entertainment and, in fact, the game value of the detective story. American stories of the period took off from the muckrakers, but instead of viewing the complete social picture they followed up on vague socialist notions and assumed that crime came from the top down, from the corrupt politician or monopolist or other forms of money and power hungry humanity. Get them, the implication goes, and other kinds of crime will wither away. In this, the writers lost the knowledge held by every police officer: that some people, high or low, will maim or kill over a word; that some will steal for the joy of possession, or for the excitement of the simple act of stealing.

If reality does not distinguish them, one of the marks of stories of the period is energy. With the exception of the grouchiness of Professor Van Dusen, all of the detectives seem to vibrate, they have so much energy. Kennedy springs into action at a moment's notice, Average Jones darts off with almost boyish enthusiasm and Madelyne Mack bustles about so fast that her companion can hardly keep up with her. No more armchair detectives here. Almost every case means going out and dashing after solutions to the perplexing situation created by crime. In part this reflects the age, with its trains, airplanes and, especially, motorcars. Motorcars provide part of the plots for several of the writers. Although most of the cases occur in New York, there are now fictional detectives in Boston and Chicago. In all cases they are not content to sit on their duffs. Average Jones travels to Baltimore for "The Man Who Spoke Latin." Madelyn Mack goes to Boston for the case of "Cinderella's Slipper," and Hatch even manages to leverage the Thinking Machine to scout things out in suburban Boston. The energy of the detectives also reflects, in a way, the ardor and urgency to combat crime, to get things cleared up as quickly as possible. There is not a lot of time to sit around gabbing, trying to sort out who committed the crime: since science offered its help, there was no need to do things the old-fashioned way.

Coupled with the energy, is the fact that social status is no longer a problem for detectives. Turn-of-the-century stories present the police as almost an irrelevance, because the upper classes have taken over the business of catching criminals. Average Jones, Madelyn Mack and the rest all have impeccable social credentials; they are so impeccable, in fact, that they are a license for the kind of unorthodox behavior that they use to solve crimes. In most cases, however, the passport to social status in the detective story is not one's inherited wealth but one's education and profession. Largely due to the scientific story, when the expert (whether chemist or psychologist) sweeps in, murmurings about the intrusion of lower class snoops go out the window. The private investigator no longer approaches the client hat in hand; the situation now is reversed.

A lot of this came about because of Sherlock Holmes. The Holmes stories undoubtedly had an impact on American detective story writing. They had an impact, first of all, in terms of form. Before Holmes most American detective tales were novel-length. After Doyle's switch to short stories, American fiction switched as well. In most cases, though, American short stories learned to avoid the traps that Doyle too often lays for himself. Doyle liked the inserted narrative, the sentimental blast from the past that explains the enigma in the present, a pattern he adopted when he used Jefferson

Hope and an excursion to Utah to explain things in *A Study in Scarlet*. Perhaps because American short detective stories came later, perhaps because science often plays a significant part and perhaps because Americans have a longer tradition of short story writing, turn-of-the-century pieces in this country stay on target more precisely than Doyle's do. Doyle's adoption of the Watson narrator, however, was taken up quickly and thoroughly in this country: many of the writers of the period used it. The other formal notion that turn of the century writers adopted from Doyle was the notion that the detective story showcased, first of all, reason, but also cleverness. In Professor Van Dusen's "two plus two," Kennedy's scientific lectures and in so many other cases, detective writers mirrored Doyle in saying that the detective story demonstrated rigorous and reasoned thinking. Be that as it may, both Doyle and American writers of the period also wanted to show readers that they were clever, and the answer was, very simply, something that they had not thought of but yet that they would admire as being innovative, and, in a word, clever.

Most detectives created after Sherlock Holmes, whether British or American, respond to him in one way or another. The idea of the genius detective clearly influences our detective stories. Here, as in Britain, however, the idea of genius has specific contemporary connections. Instead of the moody outsider used by Poe and British writers like Bulwer Lytton, the genius needs to produce tangible evidence of brain power. The detective story, especially the detective story with a scientific bent, allows for this kind of demonstration of genius. Further, it makes connections with thoroughly documented geniuses like Edison to validate the character's *bona fides*. Likewise, the notion that the genius has the licence to be a pain in the neck—to show off by means of deduction demonstrations, to ask questions and not answer them, to dive into moods of stony withdrawal, etc.—comes from Doyle. Largely, though, American characters display less hauteur in this department than do their British peers.

If the detective story at the turn of the century became the playground for eccentric genius, it gave scope to other kinds of character eccentricities. This response to Holmes in Britain gives us blind detectives, female detectives, clerical detectives, and so on. In this country the turn of the century produced eccentrics, but not so many. Hugh C. Weir, Rinehart, Green, Reeve and others added women detectives to the roll of crime fighters. O'Higgins gave readers his charming boy detective, Barney, and Post contributed his historical backwoods detective, Uncle Abner. The principal focus, though, was on male detectives who did not make a fetish out of their peculiarities.

None of this means that the old order had passed away. While Post and Flynt tried to take the wraps off of the hypocrisies of American views of crime, the detective story libraries and dime novels continued. Nick Carter and Sherlock Holmes were contemporaries. Crime fiction, then, became even more multi-layered than it had ever been, with fiction for children and fiction for adults, with stories for low-brow taste and stories aimed at middle-class readers, with tales written to divert and tales intended to teach, with detectives whose skills are those of the frontier scout and detectives who read the periodic table at breakfast. Although crime fiction did not achieve the kind of visibility that it held in the nineteen twenties and thirties, there came, nevertheless, to be a fair amount of it published. Although some of it struck a pessimistic, even alarmist, note, the crime fiction of the period still maintained the notion that, properly handled, crime need not be a threat to Americans or to America.

This view could not last long in the twentieth century.

# Chapter 4
# Texts
# 1890-1917

As the nineteenth century was ending and the twentieth century beginning American detective fiction almost came into its own. It moved out of the ghetto of the story paper more emphatically into the world of regular fiction. By the early '90s, *Putnam's* advertised a series called "Stories of Mystery and Crime" including, from the last period, *The Leavenworth Case* and introducing Melville Davisson Post and Ottolengui as important writers. We can see a move away from the link between sensation and detection in *Putnam's* blurb for Richard Dallas' *A Master Hand*, which says that "there is no emphasis on the horrors of the deed, but the reader's entire attention is held to the detection of the mysterious murder." Not all of the fiction bears this out, but some of it goes outside or inside of detection to consider vital social issues.

As we go from the 90s into the next century, the dominant shape of fiction changes from the novel into the short story; this corresponds not only to the introduction to America of the Sherlock Holmes tales, but also to the emerging prominence of the powerful middle class magazines. Literary style, too, escapes from sentimental bondage. We can see two styles take over: first a mannered style heavily dependent on irony and then a lighter, journalistic style open to serendipitous humor. Detective fiction during this period may generate important ideas but it still does not produce important literature. It is enough that detective fiction improved vastly from its sometimes less than dignified beginnings.

### *The Man of Last Resort, or The Clients of Randolph Mason*
### by Melville Davisson Post, 1897.

"The Governor's Machine:" The young Alfred Capland Randal departs Harvard for the west, determined to find fame and fortune by organizing a political machine: "The East offered no theatre for his talents; it was closely organized; its political machinery was too strong for him to hope to oppose it." With him go "two of his college associates, a stranded gambler, called for convenience 'Billy the Plunger,' and an old Virginia gentleman named Major Culverson." After numerous scrapes, Randal becomes governor of a Southwestern Commonwealth, and the Major becomes Auditor and the gambler becomes Secretary of State. Near the end of Randal's term, he becomes anxious to return East to marry the girl he left behind. It turns out, however, that the gambler has been into the state's treasury and has lost $50,000 to nasty and unscrupulous opponents. Randal is about to kick in his life's savings, and thereby blight his future, when the gambler goes to Randolph Mason. Mason advises him to induce the nasty and unscrupulous opponents to loan him $50,000 for the purposes of speculating in oil stock. They take the bait, loan the money and sign a contract. Billy fills up the treasury and refuses to pay off the loan; they take him to court but the court refuses to enforce the contract, because "when one lends money to another for the express purpose of enabling him to commit a specific unlawful act [i.e. speculation, construed here as gambling], and such act be afterward committed by means of the aid so received, the lender is *particeps criminis*, and the law will not aid him to recover [the] money..."

"Mrs. Van Bartan:" A young woman marries a young wastrel with expectations of wealth from his mother. The mother cuts them out of the will. The young Mrs. Van Bartan appeals to the lawyer for her mother-in-law whom she, in reality, loves. He consciously allows the will to be made as invalid—letting the bequest read "to St. Luke's Episcopal Church" which is neither an individual nor a corporation—and the estate goes to the son and daughter-in-law. The lawyer, however, is ruined and departs for Japan.

"Once in Jeopardy:" Brown Hurst burns down his business in Chicago for the insurance money and corrupts the investigator, Robert Gilmore, with whom he becomes partners. Moving to West Virginia, they set up as industrialists and plan to insure Hurst's life and fake his suicide. Gilmore, partly because of Hurst's indifference to the woman he married to receive the insurance money, makes the thing real, and murders Hurst. Randolph Mason contrives to have a detective accuse Gilmore to an incompetent deputy sheriff, in the absence of the sheriff. The case comes quickly to trial and Gilmore is acquitted. The sheriff returns and has real evidence of the murder, but they cannot try Gilmore because of the prohibition of double jeopardy.

"The Grazier": There is a pool of oil under the land of a generous but improvident West Virginia cattleman. The oil company has bought up his debts and is making foreclosing noises. Mason's advice is to lease the land and the oil rights to separate, non-resident individuals, so as to tie up the oil company in court proceedings and prevent foreclosure until the grazier can benefit from the oil revenues and release himself from his debts.

"The Rule Against Carper": Carper has embezzled funds. At this point he has attenuated the legal proceedings as far as possible. He is in for it, and muses on his misspent life. Then he thinks of Randolph Mason and goes to his house. About to enter, he encounters two physicians and overhears "It is a bad case of acute mania...I gave him two hyperdermics of morphine, and he is still raving like a drunken sailor." Shorn of this last resort, Carper returns home and picks up a pistol to commit suicide.

Unlike earlier detective or crime fiction, Post wrote the Randolph Mason stories for a cultured audience. Although sometimes tortuous, his style is generally cultivated, leisurely and leans toward the comic or the ironic. Here is a small example from "The Governor's Machine:"

'Bumgarner,' [the Chinese servant whom the Major has rechristened] he said softly, 'you are a frightful example of man's neglect. You have been trained by a Massachusetts Yankee. Ergo, your lack of knowledge is sublime. Bitters you might put in a plebeian gin fizz, and be happy thereafter. Bitters you might put in a high ball of whiskey, and live thereafter. But bitters in a julep, *magnum sacrum!* and the gods would crush you! Bumgarner, you are an awful throbbing error, and you have had a providential escape from death.'

By strict construction, neither these stories nor those contained in Post's first Randolph Mason book, *The Strange Schemes of Randolph Mason,* are detective fiction. The detectives who appear in them are purely incidental characters. Post's first detective was Uncle Abner, who appeared in the *Saturday Evening Post* beginning in 1911. But the Mason books are significant for American detective fiction not only because they treat crime but also because they treat the law.

Post, a lawyer himself, ostensibly presents these stories as case studies. To each piece he prefixes a list of legal precedents. "The Governor's Machine," for instance, starts with:

(See the learned opinion of Mr. Justice Matthews in the case of Irwin vs. Williar, 110 U.S. Reports, 499; the case of Waugh vs. Beck, 114 Pa. State, 422; also Williamson vs Baley, 78 Mo. 636; 15 B. Monroe, Ky. Reports, 138. See also, in Virginia, the case of Machir vs. Moore, 1 Grat., 258).

In the rather extensive Preface to *The Man of Last Resort,* Post reports that "a few gentlemen of no inconsiderable legal learning, and certain others to be classified as moral reformers" objected to his first Randolph Mason volume, maintaining that Post went about things the wrong way. What he was about, Post says, was "to point out a few of the more evident inadequacies of the law and a few of the simpler methods for evasion that are utilized by the skillful villain." While some readers might think this a dangerous course, in a democracy "If the law offers imperfect security and is capable of revision, the people must be taught in order that they may revise it." So Post writes the Randolph Mason stories in order to enable the law to bar skillful villainy. Not quite.

In the Preface Post makes clear that the most skillful villains are not those hauled into court but robber barons and corrupt corporations:

It must be borne in mind, however, that more gigantic and more intricate methods for evading the law and for appropriating the property of the citizen are available. The unwritten records of business ventures and the reports of courts are crowded with the record of huge schemes having for their ultimate purpose the robbery of the citizen. Some of these have been successful and some have failed. Enough have brought great fortunes to their daring perpetrators to appall that one who looks on with the welfare of human society at heart.

Evil prospers, the citizen suffers and the law provides no relief: the law allows and promotes skillful villains and neglects human welfare. Post ends the Preface by saying that he "has finally come to believe that the ancient maxim, which declares that the law will always find a remedy for a wrong, is, in this present time of hasty legislation, not to be accepted as trustworthy."

Enter Randolph Mason, the unlikely Robin Hood. In *The Strange Schemes*, Post describes Mason:

> Looking at the face of Randolph Mason from above, the expression in repose was crafty and cynical; viewed from below upward, it was savage and vindictive, almost brutal; while from the front, if looked squarely in the face, the stranger was fascinated by the animation of the man, and at once concluded that his expression was at the same time sneering and fearless.

When Mason speaks he is brutally blunt. Replying to Gilmore's admission that he has waited too long to seek council in "Once in Jeopardy" Mason says "It is the characteristic error of the witless." But Randolph Mason rarely appears in these stories. The characters consult him, certainly, but Post often does not describe the interview. Post gives us hints about Mason, hints that ultimately posit a romantic character, a titan driven mad by the cynicism of his profession. But Mason is not so much a character as a force.

He is a force aiding what is right. In Post what is right means, first of all, punishing, or at least thwarting, what is wrong. Impersonal corporations and political parties cannot be punished, but they can be kept from having their way. This is the case in "The Grazier" where Mason's advice keeps the oil company from nipping Rufus Alshire's property and in "The Governor's Machine" where the commercial vultures, First Class Crawley and Hiram Martin, lose their ill-gotten gains to the Governor's forces because of Mason's council. Mason's advice keeps the big boys from winning. In "Mrs. Van Barton" and "The Rule Against Carper" Post shows punishment being visited on the corrupt: Mrs. Van Bartan wins her mother-in-law's fortune but ruins her first love and devastates her future, and Carper faces suicide having thrown away love, honor and honesty. Mrs. Van Bartan and Carper have ruined themselves and the legal system has been a mere adjunct to this ruination. In neither of these stories does Mason offer legal advice—indeed he cannot in "The Rule Against Carper."

In Post, what is right also means supporting and upholding goodness or innocence, no matter how tenuous that goodness or innocence. Starting from the purest example, Rufus Alshire is a paragon: Post describes him as something out of Anglo-Saxon legend, huge, generous and competent in those things befitting a man. His generosity has landed him in trouble and Randolph Mason's advice saves his land. Then there are the scallywags in "The Governor's Machine": Randal, the Major and the gambler. These men have had some reasonably harmless adventure and fun out of their lives and they demonstrate continued willingness to share one another's troubles: they could have simply blamed the loss of the state's treasury on the gambler and left him to suffer for it. When Mason provides their legal wrinkle, he rewards this, as well as the Governor's love for the girl he left behind. The most mixed case is that of Gilmore: Gilmore is a confessed murderer whom Mason liberates from the law's hold. Yet Gilmore is more weak than vicious. Hurst is the tempter, an evil genius who intends to desert his wife and continue in his unregenerate ways. But all along what Post has been writing about is not law and lawyers and courts at all. In response to the assertion that "this murderer cannot be punished," the last statement in "Once in Jeopardy" speculates that it will come, perhaps, "when the gentleman shall have passed the melancholy flood with that grim ferryman..."

Post's importance is not in writing about a detective, but in writing about the law, in some ways the most important issue in American detective fiction. What is the law in the United States and who makes it? The Puritan colonists thought that the law was written in the scriptures, that God made the law. British Common Law dominated the early years of the American Republic, and Blackstone taught the nation's lawyers that judges and the history of judicial decisions made the law. Jacksonian Democrats emphasized that elected legislatures, following the will of the electorate, made the law. At the turn of the century, journalists held that the rich and their lackey politicians made the law. There was quite a crowd in the business of making law in the United States, without even mentioning Thoreau or the unwritten and situational notions of law in the West. Post bases the Randolph Mason stories on the belief that the great jumble of law and law-makers does not always have the welfare of human society at heart, and that they will not always find a remedy for the victims of crime or vice or greed. But a special individual with special knowledge can do this, even though it costs him dearly.

### *A Conflict of Evidence* by Rodrigues Ottolengui, 1893

Two detectives, Tom Burrows and John Barnes, from Boston's Pilkington's Detective Agency, arrive in Lee, New Hampshire to track down one Walter Marvel who has threatened John Lewis, the uncle and guardian of his sweetheart, Virginia Lewis. Meeting a man who claims to be Lewis' long-lost son, the detectives arrive at the Lewis house only to find a murder: apparently John Lewis has been shot and has fallen into the fire. Barnes, the more experienced of the two, teaches Burrows, a kind of probationary detective, some rudimentary lessons. Virginia Lewis does some suspicious things which they observe, they scrutinize the network of footprints in the snow (map included) and shadow Virginia when she goes to mail a letter. Following the letter, Barnes finds Walter Marvel about to leave the country, but persuades him to return to Lee. At the inquest, both Virginia and Walter's sister confess to the murder, partly to defend Walter and partly because a lot of people had been scurrying around the Lewis' grounds shooting off pistols on the night of the crime. Detective Burrows, in spite of his inexperience, follows a trail that leads him to discover Walter's pistol and the charred remains of what seems to be a disguise. Walter is arrested:

But Walter is not guilty and Barnes knows it; he upbraids his student for his independent efforts, orders him off the case, and when neither Burrows nor his superiors in Boston will move on this, Barnes quits Pilkington's and sets off to find the real murderer. He performs a reenactment of Walter's version of what he did that evening and finds evidence that clears him. Discovering a secret room in the Lewis house, Detective Barnes discovers a written confession and the body of the real John Lewis. In his confession, Lewis tells of his sister's marriage and desertion by her husband (a relative of Walter Marvel). The sister, who believes her husband to be lost forever, discovers that he has been appointed to a diplomatic post in Paris, so she, her baby daughter and Lewis go to Paris for a reunion, but her husband has remarried and repudiates her. So Lewis and his sister have Marvel arrested for bigamy and jailed. Marvel swears vengeance, the sister dies and Lewis moves from Richmond to New Hampshire, setting up a trap and alibi in case Marvel shows up. He dyes his hair and beard, invents a fictitious son and has a secret room built in his house. Marvel does appear, Lewis kills him, disfigures him in the fire and assumes the identity of his own fictitious son. Overcome with guilt as well as the knowledge that Barnes is going to find him, Lewis commits suicide. Barnes, however, arranges testimony to the grand jury which keeps all of this covered up so that Virginia and Walter can live happily and in peace.

Well, sure, parts of this do stretch our credulity, like the murderer disguising himself as his son and nobody catching on. Being a dentist, Ottolengui could have forged new ground at the autopsy by simply looking at the corpse's teeth, but he didn't—all the physician does here is to probe the two bullet wounds in the body. And sure, parts of the novel wear the tatters of others. The courage of one woman and the hysteria of another suggest an ambience of the sensation novel, and resolving the crime by inserting a historical narrative comes from Gaboriau, whether directly or through imitation of Doyle's Sherlock Holmes novels (which are, themselves, imitations of Gaboriau). *A Conflict of Evidence* is not, however, a totally derivative book, for it shows some new directions and concerns, some of which are quite contemporary and a few of which may be genuinely American.

Although *A Conflict* does look into the troubles in the course of true love, it is not, a sensation novel. Ottolengui may include men and women courageous in love, but he focuses the novel on the actions of his two detectives. Indeed, his use of two actual detectives shows some originality. At the turn of the century writers in Britain and America looked for ways to make the detective problem into a detective novel. The traditional solution to the problem lay in concentrating on the domestic problem of the main characters and making the detective a subsidiary, though important, character. This, almost inevitably, led to one of the lovers acting as an amateur detective, aiding and peering over the shoulder of the real detective. This is certainly the essence of *The Dead Letter* and *The Leavenworth Case* as well as a number of British novels. But when writers thought about removing the love interest, they had to face the fact that dwelling solely on a detective problem often does not provide enough material for a novel. They had to add more than problem, solution, explanation of solution. One answer to this was using the old formula of the stupid police, where the police arrest the wrong person and the detective needs to put it right. Ottolengui takes this formula, but he up-dates it: neither of his detectives is stupid or prejudiced or lazy. They successively come up with convincing material proof. What Ottolengui has done here is to plump up the old detective versus police rivalry, but, additionally, he delivers an early variety of the multiple solution story—the one in which readers are offered one convincing solution after another. He has found one way to bulk up the detective problem and to keep it in the foreground at the same time.

Ottolengui presents another reasonably fresh element in *A Conflict* in the nature of the problem itself. Earlier stories provide crime problems that fall into two categories: there is the mystery where there are no clues whatsoever at the scene of the crime, the solution to which necessitates plunging into the past and probing people's lives. Then there is the straight-forward problem, where the clues at the scene of the crime simply need to be read by an expert like M. Lecoq. Anthropologically, the one links up to the sensation novel and the other to a stage when the public wanted to learn about the methods and methodology of police work. Ottolengui mixes things up and presents real puzzlers. Why does the body have two wounds and only one hole in the nightshirt? (Because Lewis disposed of Marvel's clothes and dressed him in one of his own nightshirts, but had to make a bullet hole in that.) Which of the many people running around outside shooting off their pistols really killed Lewis? (None of them.) In addition to presenting what amounts to enigmatic clues, Ottolengui specifically calls his readers' attention to some of the detective work as they proceed through the book. Thus, when he introduces a diagram of the house and environs, Ottolengui speaks directly to his readers:

> That you may well understand the deductions which the detectives reached, from the study of the grounds, it will be best for you to follow closely a description of the place with the assistance of the accompanying map.

The problem is that none of the crowd gallivanting about in the yard has anything to do with the murder. Ottolengui, nevertheless, does give us some genuine clues, not: the most significant of which is that Lewis' mastiff is extremely friendly to the allegedly long lost son. But what gives here? The omniscient narrator encourages us to pay attention to evidence and then calls our attention to chimeras. This is unlike most contemporary detective story practice; nineteenth century detective tales rarely invite the readers' participation in solving the crimes—the Sherlock Holmes stories certainly do not. Ottolengui here employs a technique that did not become common until the Golden Age of the detective novel.

It would be nice if Ottolengui were consciously ahead of his time in the craft of the detective story. His playing with clues and his introduction of two detectives, however, springs from other causes. Chiefly it comes from his notions about evidence. At the turn of the nineteenth century, there was some real public concern about circumstantial evidence. In the late 60s and early 70s, *The New York Ledger* ran pseudo detective tales like "Did they Hang the Wrong Man?" "Circumstantial Evidence. My Friend's Story," and "Circumstantial Evidence." American detective fiction, in fact, keeps coming back to discussions of circumstantial evidence up through the Philo Vance stories of the 1920s. This reflects certain almost inevitable changes in real trials. Beginning in 1865 with the publication of Taylor's *The Principles and Practice of Medical Jurisprudence* a new element entered as evidence in criminal investigations. Science and expert testimony, it seemed, were far superior to the testimony of witnesses. They established guilt beyond doubt, something quite significant to the increasingly anonymous citizens of the late nineteenth century when it was impossible to know the character or antecedents of defendant, judge or juror. This, of course, eventually lead to the scientific detective story of the next decade, but Ottolengui does not quite make it that far. *A Conflict* begins with a strong emphasis on the weakness of circumstantial evidence. Detective Barnes' fame rests on the fact that he always goes very slowly so as to avoid its pitfalls. Barnes, in fact, early on gives a short dissertation on circumstantial evidence:

> We are considering a case purely on circumstantial evidence. I have all my life made a specialty of such, and I divide it into three grades, according to the logical deduction which it indicates. The first of these I call a "circumstantial possibility." For example, had the wound in this case been differently located, it might have been a "circumstantial possibility" that it was a suicide. Second we have a "circumstantial probability," such as I have here and will explain. Third, the "circumstantial proof," where the attendant facts leave absolutely no room for doubt; in my experience a rare thing.

*A Conflict* almost goes the next step from circumstantial evidence to scientific proof. In his efforts to prove young Marvel innocent, Barnes needs to verify Marvel's claim that he threw his disguise along with Virginia's locket into the river. Folks drag the river but cannot find the clothes, but Barnes makes up a bundle of clothes the same size and weight as Marvel's, waits for the same time of day and throws them into the river at the same point Marvel claimed to have used. And he finds the evidence. With this procedure Ottolengui probably follows the convention of the reenactment of the crime made popular by *The Moonstone*, and he specifically couches it as an experiment. The problem that Ottolengui has, however, is that he seems unaware of the last few decades' development of police science: there are lots of footprints, but one thinks of photographing or making casts of them, and the autopsy, as mentioned earlier, is cursory even by the standards of the 90s, and this only touches on a few of the bloopers in the novel.

Indeed, Ottolengui combines hints of a different kind of story along with naive and old-fashioned notions about the detective. When Barnes follows Virginia Lewis to town the first time, we learn that he carries a fake beard along with him to use as a disguise. With this looped over his ears Ottolengui will have us accept that no one recognizes his detective. Come on. And the murderer passing himself off as his own son doesn't pass muster either. Even though Ottolengui has largely pushed sentiment off center stage, he cannot get rid of it altogether. One of Detective Barnes' chief qualifications is that "he had a heart, and this very fact, though unrecognized by his superiors, made him the keenest man in the employ of the Pilkingtons." Ottolengui makes this fact serve the story, for Barnes' heart makes him determined that the innocent should not suffer by false accusation. He cannot, however, make the inserted dollop of sentiment in Lewis' confession serve the story. Ottolengui put it in because he accepted that because great detective writers like Gaboriau and Doyle did it, that readers actually wanted pathos and romantic revenge in their detective stories. They actually did not, but that was for others to prove. But they proved it by doing some of the same things that Ottolengui did.

*The Powers that Prey* by Josiah Flynt and Francis Walton, 1900
"In the Matter of his Nibs:" A rural big-whig who periodically comes to the city to let his hair down is robbed of his money and watch. He complains to the chief of police and flaunts his political connections. The chief calls in the town's principal crooks and tells them to find the thief, or else. To ensure the continued cooperation of the police, the crooks track down the thief.

"A Bill From Tiffany's:" Motivated by his fiancee's hunger for money and status, a detective pressures a former criminal to act as an informer on one of his friends. A crime is solved, the criminal sent to prison and the reward is granted to the detective. The criminal later escapes and murders the informer.

"The Revenge of the Four:" A consortium of con men and pickpockets descends on Cornville, Ohio, and, with the cooperation of local police and politicians, they clean out the citizens.

"The Order of the Penitents:" A detective takes bribes from prisoners to make their lives in captivity easier. For a fee he helps a prisoner escape, forces him to reveal the location of his hidden booty and then rearrests him and sends him back to jail.

"The Prison Demon:" A detective frames a member of the underworld in order to take away the man's wife. The convict learns of this, asks for a conference with the detective and murders him. He is convicted of this murder but judged insane and degenerate and kept as a sort of living exhibit at the prison.

"The Great Idea:" Crooks decide to back the election of a reform administration. One of their number becomes the new chief of police and they have a field day.

"Found Guilty:" Because of a grudge he bears for a member of the underworld, a policeman frames the man for a murder he did not commit. The real killers fall out and shoot each other, and one of them confesses to the policeman that he committed the murder. The policeman suppresses the confession and the innocent man goes to the electric chair.

"On Sentence Day:" An old offender narrates the story of a young man of good family who goes wrong. He is in and out of jail until tutored in the ways of crime, whereupon he becomes a prosperous and slick crook.

"Peggie Niven:" A cross-dressing bandit sticks up a man who turns out to be down on his luck and gives him $5.00. Years later, the man has struck it rich and has his pocket picked by the same criminal. He wants to let her go free, but a busy body insists that the pickpocket be taken to court. More years pass and the original robbery/charity victim is about to be ruined by the busy-body, but the original criminal intervenes to save him.

"A Dead One:" Although a successful and prosperous professional criminal through his mid-life, the rigors of prison and police take their toll and this member of the underworld ends his life living in an English slum in order to escape the continued persecution of the American police.

The stories in *The Powers that Prey* originally appeared in *McClure's Magazine* and in some ways forecast the appearance of muckraking. Josiah Flynt Willard had lived among various citizens of the underworld, from tramps to criminals, and Alfred Hodder (i.e. Francis Walton) later was an aide to William Travers Jerome, a reform District Attorney. Both men had the credentials to describe the life of the underworld and the way that the upper world impinged upon it. They self-consciously assume the character of scribes, the term used in several of the stories—most notably in "On Sentence Day" and "A Dead One," where the narrator records the stories of old cons. The individual pieces shed a new light on "the criminal class," but this is not quite muckraking. For one thing, the characters in the stories and the narrators themselves assume that things are the way that they are and will not change: the muckrakers exposed facts with the notion that exposure would help to make things better, but Flynt and Walton don't expect things to be better. Part of the control of the book comes from their concept of the Powers That Prey. The authors describe a world composed of The Powers That Rule and The Powers that Prey. These powers exist and conspire together in the upper world and the underworld simply mirrors this: the monopoly boss, the political boss, the criminal boss. Flynt and Walton do not accept reform as one of their objects and so they occasionally deal in pathos, but most often they deal in irony. Describing the inhabitants of penitentiaries as penitents, for example, underlines the corruption of officials and the course of criminal scholarship embarked upon by inmates.

Although the stories in *The Powers that Prey* are separate pieces, they do contain two continuing characters: Ruderick MeKloud (who appears in "In the Matter of His Nibs," "The Revenge of the Four," "The Great Idea" and "On Sentence Day") and Charley Minick (who appears in "A Bill From

Tiffany's" and "The Order of the Penitents"). MeKloud and Minick come to represent significant aspects of the criminal and the detective. Through MeKloud, in fact throughout the book, the authors take aim at contemporary criminological concepts of "degeneracy." "The Prison Demon," for instance, shows a man driven to murder by simple and understandable human motives (his wife and child have been appropriated by the policeman who has framed him) yet the prison authorities "consider him the kind of criminal that Professor Lombroso suggests might fitly be put out of the world." MeKloud is not a monster of any stripe, no demon or degenerate. He lives by running various cons, but, especially, he survives because he recognizes the realities of his world—do a good smart job and give the police their cut. In practically every story the writers emphasize the essential humanness of criminals, that they act upon completely understandable motives and in many cases they do the things that any person would do. As a rule, however, once a person has a record as a criminal, he or she becomes a victim of the powers that prey—the police.

Charley Minick is a detective. Flynt and Walton do, indeed, portray extremely vicious police officers: Detective Ackeray in "The Prison Demon" and Captain Brigstock in "Found Guilty," because of their own personal corruption, devastate the lives of better men than themselves. Minick isn't as bad as that. Minick, a man of average competence and little ambition, has a wife whose social climbing pushes her husband to use the only tools available to detectives. Here the only consistent crime-fighting tool that the police possess is the knowledge of criminals' identities. Hardly far fetched, the knowledge of criminals' identities made Inspector Byrnes' reputation with his idea of the dead line (any known criminal who crosses a line drawn around Wall Street was immediately arrested) and William J. Burns makes much of knowing ex-cons in *The Crevice*. Thus, the detection in "In the Matter of His Nibs" shows no pointless trips to Jersey to inspect "the scene of the crime," no long interviews with reporters about suggested clues, and no "keep the wires hot." When his wife gets unbearably offensive, Charley Minick simply goes out and puts the screws to the cons and ex-cons. Even though in "A Bill from Tiffany's" this process causes one good man to be killed because Minick has forced him to squeal, the authors do not portray Charley as a particularly bad cop. He simply plays the role cast for him with occasional efficiency, just as MeKloud plays the role cast for him.

*The Powers that Prey* has a less appreciative attitude toward other forms of police work. There is, of course, the condemnation of the morally dishonest policemen in "The Prison Demon" and "Found Guilty." "A Dead One" focuses on police brutality when the retired offender compares English and American Police:

I ain't stuck on England or the coppers here, but the coppers can't cut up with a bloke here the way they do in the States. 'Course they hammer me every now an' then when they take me to the station house, but that's just a habit they've got into. You see the people over here won't let 'em do any hammerin' in the streets, an' as they've got to get exercise somehow, they do the hammerin' at the station house. They ain't so wise as our coppers, but they ain't so crooked either.

Most often, *The Powers that Prey* focuses on the crookedness of "our coppers." Here the first rule is connections. From one side, the police, as seen in "In the Matter of His Nibs," stir themselves to action principally when crime has affected the rich and powerful. From the other side, to ensure their success, criminals need to square the politicians and the police. The two stories that take place in Cornville, Ohio ("The Revenge of the Four" and "The Great Idea"), embody Flynt and Walton's Introduction to Practical Graft. In "The Revenge of the Four" we meet Mayor Adolph Hochheimer:

His apprenticeship in high politics began when he constructed his first block of tenement houses with thinner walls and less commodious apartments than the law commands; he was obliged to "square" the building committee...He was obliged to "square" everybody and keep them "squared," and they showed an equal facility in taking on the required shape and in losing it again.

The con men who descend upon the lambs of Cornville know full well that "the politicians 'a got the state by the throat, an' you know as well as I do, that where they get their graft in guns [criminals] can too." They also know the going rate charged by the police for permission to practice in Cornville: "Some of 'em has come up a little in their commission charges, but most of 'em are askin' twenty per cent., same as usual." And they take the "hoosiers" for all that they have. By the time of "The Great Idea," a reform candidate offers himself to the electorate of Cornville. Jumping on MeKloud's "great idea" the underworld rigs the election so that the reform candidate wins. In a passage that reflects on New York reform governments and police commissioners, like Teddy Roosevelt, the criminals discover

that a town is never so gullible as when Reform attempts to tell it that it "shan't."...Pocketbooks were, perhaps, no more numerous than in Mayor Barwood's day, but they "came up easier"...The new police force could no more tell when a pocket was being picked; they couldn't even tell when one was picked, unless they found the "weeded leather" on the ground...It is also to be remarked that they [criminals] were not called on to pay a percentage of their winnings to the "wise."

Although *The Powers that Prey* pictures criminals either sympathetically or romantically (as in "Peggy Nivin"), pictures average citizens as "hoosiers" and pictures police in, at best, an unwholesome light, the authors realize that there is more to crime, criminals and police in America. Their simple thesis about the inevitable divisions between the powers in society at first blush suggests the necessity of a type of leveling, say socialism. But *The Powers that Prey* deals very little with wealth as power: the politician almost inevitably possesses the power in the stories. This rottenness in America grows out of another source. The people care very little about enforcing the law. In "Found Guilty" one of the criminals reflects on the differences between Europe and America:

> You remember that gun in Berlin trying' to make a get-away after he'd picked the Moll's pocket, an' how the whole street sprinted after him? That's the way they do things on this side—the crowd is in sympathy with the copper an' not with the gun. In the states they give a gun a runnin' chance, an' let the copper do the chasin'.

A nation of people who will not sprint after the pickpocket will hardly sprint after the politician. These are the facts in *The Powers that Prey*.

*The Thinking Machine: Being a True and Complete Statement of Several Intricate Mysteries which Came Under the Observation of Professor S.F.X. Van Dusen, Ph.D., L.L.D., F.R.S., M.D., etc.* by Jacques Futrelle, 1907.

"The Problem of Cell 13:" Van Dusen wagers that he can escape from any prison. He does this by tying a thread from his unravelled socks to a rat, sending the rat with a message tied to it to a friend outside through a disused pipe and drawing various items through the pipe into his cell. He then shorts out the prison's electricity and escapes when his accomplice enters with the repair crew from the electric company.

"The Scarlet Thread:" A valet attempts the life of a stockbroker and accidentally kills a maid by blowing through the pipes for illuminating gas, thereby extinguishing the flames and letting gas enter the rooms. To see whether his victim is asleep the valet ties a small mirror to the rope on the flag pole and lowers it so as to peer into the stockbroker's windows. A thread from the bathrobe he wears sticks to the flag rope and with this Van Dusen discovers the method. He discovers the murderer by weighing the characters and motives of those connected with the case.

"The Man Who Was Lost:" A man with amnesia shows up at Van Dusen's rooms and asks for help in discovering his identity. The Thinking Machine diagnoses the amnesia as having been induced by drugs. He has Hatch squire the patient around Boston hoping for some association, and he traces the man's money to a Montana bank. A woman turns up claiming to be the wife of Van Dusen's patient, but she isn't and she is arrested. By collecting some small bits of information Van Dusen discovers that his patient is an officer of a Montana bank who has been victimized by the bank's embezzling president.

"The Great Auto Mystery:" Two rich young men go joy-riding in the country with a well-known actress. After they stop and then continue their journey, they discover that the woman in the car is seriously wounded; she died in a doctor's office and it's discovered that she has died of a knife wound. Days later one of the young men faints in the street, Hatch brings him to Van Dusen's and he takes up the case. He discovers that the body in the car was not the actress but a young woman who committed suicide in the car because of her despair over her abortive elopement: the automobile clothing, goggles, mask and so on, have prevented proper identification.

"The Flaming Phantom:" Reporter Hutchinson Hatch visits an allegedly haunted house and is convinced that it is really haunted. After others fail to debunk the ghost, Van Dusen acquires some background on the family and visits the house. He discovers that a dissolute relative has been playing ghost by using phosphorus and mirrors. The professor also discovers the hiding place of the family jewels which had been a mystery for a generation.

"The Ralston Bank Burglary:" After the Ralston Bank has been robbed, Van Dusen is called in. The one clue is a handkerchief scented with violet perfume. Van Dusen sniffs the staff and then searches them, only to find some of the stolen money in the bank president's coat. After Hatch does some errands, Van Dusen exposes the bank president's secretary as the inside contact of the burglars.

"The Mystery of a Studio:" A young woman disappears from her lodging and Hatch discovers that she was the model for a famous painting. Van Dusen arranges for Hatch to search the painter's studio where he discovers the woman's gloves and veil. The painter, whose mind is increasingly unbalanced, is shot by an intruder and hospitalized. He escapes from the hospital and Hatch and Van Dusen rush to the studio. Here they find the young woman's fiancé, who was the intruder, wounded, and the painter locked in a closet where he has kept his model chloroformed.

The Thinking Machine stories appeared first in Boston's *American Journal Examiner*.

Arthur Conan Doyle found one of his American imitators in Jacques Futrelle. Futrelle clearly bases his hero on the pattern of the genius detective. Although Futrelle tells his stories in the third person, Hatch is clearly Dr. Watson. Like Watson, Hatch has an open and somewhat impetuous nature, and his profession as a news reporter involves him with the world of people and events which he in his small way tries to figure out—Futrelle allows Hatch small discoveries but denies him any of the big ones. Hatch admires Van Dusen not so much because he provides scoops for the reporter but because he tolerates Hatch's presence and allows him to see the products of the genius at work. In appreciation for this privilege Hatch becomes not only the agent who brings Van Dusen some of his cases but also his lackey, running errands to get this and find out that. He is a notch above Detective Mallory, whom Van Dusen tolerates only because of his power of arrest, but only a notch. The kind of sucking up to genius displayed here moved Bret Harte to begin his Sherlock Holmes parody by having Watson say: "with the freedom of an old friend I at once threw myself in my familiar attitude at his feet, and gently caressed his boot..."

Professor Van Dusen shares a number of attributes with Holmes. His rooms and his housekeeper point back to Baker Street and Mrs. Hudson; his usual occupation is messing about in the small laboratory in his rooms. Van Dusen's most Holmesian attribute, however, lies in his insistence on reason and the power of the mind. "Two and two always make four" and "nothing is impossible" serve as passwords to Van Dusen's presence. He insists that Hatch examine his language and his descriptions in order to rid them of prejudice and fuzzy thinking. What Futrelle has done is to abstract Doyle's superficial stress on reason and make it the basis of his character. Van Dusen, Futrelle would have us believe, is the closest one can come to being just a brain. He does not give much physical description of his detective, but he always mentions that Van Dusen wears a size 8 hat. Futrelle also shows Van Dusen's brains with the academic degrees strung out after his name: if one degree gave Frank Baum's scarecrow brains, imagine Van Dusen. Upholstering his hero with the trappings of genius, Futrelle, in the tradition of Poe, portrays a person uncomfortable in the everyday life. Van Dusen is a misogynist: "There was one thing on earth he was afraid of— a woman" ("The Ralston Bank Burglary"). He cuts himself off from the normal affairs of the world: "I never read the newspapers" ("The Ralston Bank Burglary"). He lives so much in his own world and by his own standards that he has little patience with others and his relations with others come down to either lectures or abuse. Like Baroness Orczy's Old Man in the Corner (who tells tales to a newspaper reporter and who appeared in British magazine fiction in 1901 and in book form in 1905), Van Dusen is uncivil, condescending and downright grouchy. Unlike Orczy's Old Man, society accepts and honors Van Dusen because he has accomplished something. Futrelle mentions inventions and discoveries without specifying them, but Van Dusen's chief importance as far as the stories are concerned is his solution to crimes.

Futrelle gives a scientific gloss to his stories by appending all of the degrees to Van Dusen's name, by telling us that the hero messes around with chemical apparatus in his rooms and by creating the illusion that science plays an important part in the cases. The science is an illusion first of all because Futrelle doesn't take the trouble to understand much about science. In "The Great Auto Mystery" Van Dusen tells the assembled witnesses that "I had, I may say, too, examined his head minutely. I have always maintained that the head of a murderer will show a certain indentation." This isn't even Lombroso, it's phrenology which was discredited a generation before Futrelle wrote. In "The Ralston Bank Burglary" Van Dusen tells us that the burglars loosened the bars in the window with a chemical but doesn't tell us what it was; in "The Man Who Was Lost" the criminals induce amnesia with another unspecified chemical. This hardly passes as science. That everybody assumes in "The Great Auto Mystery" that the actress is the dead woman, in spite of the fact that the actress is blonde and the dead woman a brunette, demonstrates that Futrelle draws a world which has very cavalier notions of precision.

Futrelle creates the illusion that his stories present rational problem solving by calling his hero "The Thinking Machine," by repeating "two plus two always equals four" and through his structure. The stories always end in the Thinking Machine's lecture about how he solved the tangled up case. They are about logic because Van Dusen says so: "It is the chaining together of fact after fact; a necessary logical sequence to a series of incidents, which are, separately, deeply puzzling" ("The Man Who Was Lost"). All of this emphasis on logic and thinking is, nevertheless, illusion, and sometimes Futrelle lets the veil slip, as in "The Man Who Was Lost:"

> There are shades of emotion, intuition, call it what you will, so subtle that it is difficult to express them in words. As I had instinctively associated Harrison with Bell's present condition I instinctively associated this woman with Harrison.

Futrelle may have his character spout off about logic, but he clearly perceives the heart of detective stories as illusion or trickery, or, at his best, as playing with his readers.

The clearest example of this is in "The Problem of Cell 13." Here readers fall for Dr. Ransome's "You mean you could actually think your way out?" and assume that Van Dusen intends to escape from prison unaided. Yet Van Dusen escapes only because Hatch helps him pull off a rather mundane escape in disguise. With all of Futrelle's stories the facts of the conclusion fit the facts of the case because the author arranges them to do so and not because of irrefutable logic. But there is nothing wrong with this; it's what Doyle and most of the other detective writers of the period did.

At his best Futrelle does pretty well. He was an able stylist capable of adding humor and irony through his writing. The pattern he chose for his stories is not as stodgy as the intellectual blush seems to imply. It goes like this: either someone applies to Van Dusen or Hatch goes to Van Dusen with an unsolvable problem; the Thinking Machine visits the scene of the crime and finds things; he sends Hatch off to find other things; someone is arrested or Van Dusen seems to be on the wrong track; Van Dusen assembles the principals, he recapitulates and then explains the solution. This formula had room for some suspense, some comedy and for a surprise ending, and that is about all that readers usually expected from a turn of the century detective short story.

### *The Circular Staircase* by Mary Roberts Rinehart, 1908

Rachael Innes, her town house being renovated, rents a country estate, Sunnyside, and moves there with her nephew, Halsey, niece, Gertrude, and maid, Liddy. The owner of the house, a banker, Paul Armstrong, is vacationing in California with his wife and step-daughter, Louise. Early one morning, Arnold Armstrong, the black sheep son, is found shot at the bottom of the circular staircase in Sunnyside. Then the action really starts. Gertrude Innes' intended, Jack Bailey, is briefly arrested in connection with the collapse of Armstrong's bank, so Gertrude sulks around the house. Next, Miss Innes discovers Louise Armstrong at the lodge suffering from an unidentified malady. Finally, word comes back from California that Paul Armstrong has died from a heart attack. When Louise Armstrong recovers she tells Halsey that she cannot marry him and that she will marry the somewhat sinister Dr. Walker. A child with an unknown background turns up being boarded at the home of a townswoman.

Then things begin to happen at the big house. Unknown intruders bump through the house at night: they stick a ladder up the laundry chute, burrow a hole in the trunk room and even run iron bars through the plaster walls. To defend against these things, Miss Innes, on Halsey's suggestion, hires a gardener named Alex to help guard the place. She also joins forces with Mr. Jamieson, a detective, who later brings other detectives to help out. At this point, Halsey disappears, having been kidnapped and thrown into a freight car headed out of town. Through information from tramps, they find Halsey in a far-off hospital. Jamieson and Alex go to the town cemetery and dig up Paul Armstrong's grave and discover that the body in the coffin is not Paul Armstrong's. Miss Innes goes to the hospital to visit the Sunnyside housekeeper who is dying from blood-poisoning. Mrs. Watson tells of how her sister secretly married Arnold Armstrong, and after having been deserted died giving birth to a son. Mrs. Watson has kept the child in a home, but has forced Arnold to support him. She brings the child to town hoping to influence Arnold, but he begins to abuse her. She, it turns out, shot him at the foot of the spiral staircase. After returning home, Miss Innes starts thinking about secret rooms and finds one. She enters the room where Paul Armstrong has hidden the money he has stolen from his bank, but the door snaps shut. Armstrong then enters the house, but Alex and others spot him. He slips into the hidden room, Miss Innes screams and the others discover them, but in escaping Armstrong falls down the spiral staircase and dies. The murder is cleared up, the embezzled funds are found and the young people can pair off: Halsey gets Louise who has been forced to reject him by her step-father, and Gertrude gets Bailey who had been at the house disguised as Alex the gardener. Miss Innes concludes the narration with wistful memories of the excitement of the events at Sunnyside.

Rinehart wrote *The Circular Staircase* as "a semi-satire on the usual pompous, self-important crime story." In this she obliquely participates in a popular movement to parody Sherlock Holmes. Here, as abroad, parodies largely took the form of short stories, the kind of hit and run best suited to satire and parody: Mark Twain, O. Henry, Bret Harte and Stephen Leacock all wrote parodies of detective stories. Frenchman Maurice LeBlanc moved parody to long fiction in his later Arsene Lupin tales, but he needed to add elements of the rogue and gentleman crook to his hero to stretch satire out to book length. Rinehart's satire in *The Circular Staircase* shows principally in the notion of a middle-aged spinster and not the professional detective making most of the discoveries; this does not mean, however, that the detective is altogether negligible, for Jamieson seems to know what goes on most of the time, and Rachael Innes comically begrudges him credit for his accomplishments in her narration. But the detection part of *The Circular Staircase* is only "semi-satire" and, no matter who gets the credit, Rinehart does not really satirize detecting or detectives *per se*, as do most of the Sherlock Holmes satires and burlesques of the period. Instead, in calling the book a "semi-satire," she confuses satire with comedy, for the book is a comic detective novel and not a satiric one.

The comedy resides mostly in Rinehart's portrayal of her narrator. Rachael Innes possesses indomitable balance and good humor. She faces trouble with servants, her nephew and niece's romantic dilemmas, murder, kidnapping and repeated noises in the night without turning a hair. The events in *The Circular Staircase* provide others with occasions for brooding, hysteria and assorted varieties of the heebie jeebies, but Rachael Innes never loses her pluck, and the contrast is one of the bases for comedy in the novel. The other basis for humor is Rinehart's drawing of Miss Innes' upper middle-class "spinsterish" character: her irritation that her servant wants a gown in a color that will look frightful, her vexation with servants, her knitting slippers and so on. Although Rinehart invents some amusing situations— like Miss Innes in her dressing gown searching the roof for evidence—there are no knee slappers in the book and much of the comedy turns on class, race and sex prejudice. If much of its humor is dated or timid, *The Circular Staircase* marks a significant change: with few exceptions, like Pinkerton's *The Expressman and the Detective*, American crime fiction in the nineteenth century was either morally emphatic or analytical, or both. Rinehart took a murder mystery, as well as traumas of love, and treated them in a light, comic manner. And *The Circular Staircase* became a very popular novel. It became popular because it never asks too much of its readers: there are bits of suspense, terror and pathos but they never last very long, just as there are bits that invite analysis which don't last very long either. The author simply wants to entertain her readers, and had she possessed a sophisticated background and education she could have written something like the Golden Age novel.

This, of course, causes some trouble. If Rinehart presages the light tone of the golden age novel, does she handle the material in the same manner as the writers of the 1920s and 1930s? Does she work the writer-reader game of hiding and finding clues to the "puzzle" presented in the narrative? In her autobiography, Rinehart refers to *The Circular Staircase* as a "logical crime novel," and several times in the course of the narrative her narrator calls the crime problem a "puzzle." In spite of these appurtenances, however, *The Circular Staircase* does not do the kinds of things that writers of the Golden Age did to their readers. First of all, the solution to the murder of Arnold Armstrong does not come from the careful following of clues and reasoned evaluation of evidence: it comes from the death-bed confession of the housekeeper which reveals a substantial body of facts unknown to the readers and the persons in the world of the book. Likewise Rinehart presents no clue to suggest that Paul Armstrong is not dead until Alex and Jamieson dig up his grave. The only area that readers can really think about is the business of unknown people rooting around in the house looking for the secret room. But here readers mostly depend on groundless conjecture. Rather than giving her readers clues, Rinehart gives her readers questions. The novel overflows with questions: chapter eight, for instance, contains

28 questions. Most chapters, after the fashion of serial writers, end with questions, and throughout her narrative Miss Innes inserts clumps of questions at critical junctures. In addition to depending on questions to sustain the atmosphere of mystery, Rinehart uses tidal technique: she introduces a situation and then surges forward, intimating things about the future, and then recedes back into the present of the narrative. Thus early in the book, the Armstrong's lawyer tries to get Miss Innes to give up her lease on the Sunnyside:

'We had better wait and see if they wish to come,' I said. 'It seems unlikely, and my town house is being remodeled.' At that he let the matter drop, but it came up unpleasantly enough, later.

What Rinehart no doubt intends by calling *The Circular Staircase* "a logical crime novel" is that when readers reach the unmasking at the end everything is consistent and that the end explains all of the enigmas in the rest of the book. But that does not make it a reader-writer game like the Golden Age novels of the late 1920s.

In spite of some of its modern appearances, *The Circular Staircase* in many ways looks back to the sensation novel. Rinehart just lightens the tone and turns the emphasis from generating pathos to encouraging excitement, thereby anticipating the thriller. *The Circular Staircase* does, nevertheless, rely on stock sensation novel motifs. There is the hidden domestic history of Arnold Armstrong, for a starter. Most significantly, the progress of the investigations in the novel runs up against the simple refusal of people to testify: Halsey and Gertrude do not lie (Rinehart wanted the book to be moral enough for her sons to read), they just say that it's none of anybody's business. Here we have the twin nineteenth century conventions that the rich are different (why not lock them up as material witnesses? Because they are rich and, besides, one of them is a woman). Miss Innes, as well as the authorities, indulge Halsey and Gertrude, and consequently make things worse for everybody. This is the course of most sensation novels, because the true kernel of the story is not the solution to the mystery but the celebrating of the trials and triumphs of not one but two sets of lovers. Given this as a reward, it made little difference to readers that nobody recognizes Jack Bailey when he shaves his moustache and returns as Alex the gardener. Likewise, it was altogether fitting to this kind of readers that the law does not detect and punish the criminals. Paul Armstrong was a grasping money-fanatic, and Arnold Armstrong was a dissolute wife-abuser and providence simply rids the world of them. Mrs. Watson, whom circumstance and evil placed in an impossible position, clears her conscience and dies in the hospital. The account holders in Armstrong's bank get their money, Bailey's reputation is cleared, the lovers have each other and nobody, neither the detectives nor Miss Innes, has had a substantial hand in the detection of the disposal of the evil people.

*Average Jones* by Samuel Hopkins Adams, 1911.

"The B-Flat Trombone:" A.V.R.E. Jones discovers that a wronged husband has planted a bomb in a corrupt politician's easy chair and plans to detonate it with the vibrations caused by a street trombone player. Jones finds the culprit but he also forces the politician to withdraw from the mayoral race.

"Red Dot:" The Beef Trust attempts to murder a chemist who is about to expose their nasty practices. Average discovers the intended use of poisonous Red Dot spiders and forces the robber baron responsible to flee the country.

"Open Trail:" A fake patent medicine tycoon hires Average to find his son who has gone off to Mexico looking for gold with two con men who intend to rob and murder him. Average arrives in Mexico in time, saves the young man and his money. He not only keeps some of it back, knowing that the tycoon will try to cheat him, he leaves the son in Mexico to be made into a real man instead of a purposeless wimp.

"The Mercy Sign:" An Armenian assassinates a Turkish diplomat by shooting, through a blow-pipe, poison gas into his hotel room. He reveals at the end that he sought revenge upon the diplomat for the atrocities he had committed in Armenia.

"Blue Fires:" A *Moonstone* take off, a sleep-walker takes a necklace from another's hotel room. After Average tracks him down, the necklace turns up in the pocket of his dressing gown.

"Pin Pricks:" In order to obtain a legacy, a blind man tries to drive the other heir insane by sending him messages spelled out in pin holes. Average forces him to relinquish his claim to the fortune.

"Big Print:" While watching con artists set up a fake meteorite scam, a young boy falls from his tree and is knocked unconscious. The husband and wife confidence company take him along with them. Average tracks them through notes they had made for advertising their fake meteorite.

"The Man Who Spoke Latin:" To dupe a Baltimore bibliophile, a con man pretends to have met with an accident which has caused him to revert to his ancient Roman manifestation: he can only speak Latin. Average not only exposes the fraud but discovers that he was after a letter from Bacon mentioning Shakespeare.

"The One Best Bet:" Average prevents a gambling czar from assassinating the governor.

"The Million-Dollar Dog:" Sylvia Graham will inherit a fortune if she takes care of a dog until its death. Her villainous uncle murders the dog and hides its body, but Average introduces carrion beetles into the house to find it.

Average Jones, after emerging from Hamilton College, falls under the peculiar conditions of his uncle's will. His uncle, Adrian Van Reypen Egerton, late mayor of New York, stipulates that the principal to be taken over by him [Average] at such time as he shall have completed five years of continuous residence in New York City. After such time the virus of the metropolis will have worked through his entire being. He will squander his unearned and undeserved fortune, thus completing the vicious circle, and returning the millions acquired by my political activities, in a poisoned shower upon the city, for which, having bossed, bullied and looted it, I feel no sentiment other than contempt.

His friend Waldemar, a newspaper editor, diagnoses Jones' problem as boredom and suggests that he partake in the "Adventure of Life." Specifically he challenges Jones to try to track down fraudulent advertisers in newspapers: "Within six months, if you're not sandbagged or jailed on fake libel suits, you'll have a unique bibliography of swindles. Then I'll begin to come and buy your knowledge to keep my own columns clean." Jones, thus begins his life as the ad-visor investigating ads. Peculiar ads like:

WANTED—A venerable looking man with white beard and medical degree. Good pay to the right applicant.

and

WANTED—B-flat trombonist. Must have experience as street player. Apply between 8 and 10 P.M.

These ads serve, at the beginning, as a way of giving Jones a part in the Adventure of Life: they bring him into contact with zany and dangerous situations. By the time of "Blue Fires," Adams tells us, "A detective he now frankly considered himself; and the real drudgery of his unique profession of Ad-Visor was supportable only because of the compensating thrill of the occasional chase..." As he develops expertise in advertising, however, Jones uses ads to solve cases. Knowing the lingo helps Jones solve the kidnaping in "Big Print;" in "Red Dot" he sees the ad warning residents not to frequent certain spots before the first frost, and this serves as a clue about the poisonous spiders. He advertises for the particular skills associated with the problems and because he knows the journalistic outlets so well he can find carnival performers, milkmen, envelope erasers, and so on. So advertising gives Average something to do, it serves a civic purpose of helping to keep the trade clean, and it helps him solve crimes at the beginning, middle and end. It plays another role as well. Most earlier detective stories use the clue in its original sense, a string to be followed. Clues fit naturally together and, when found, give the detective the culprit. Adams introduces the notion of wildly diverse clues which became popular in certain circles of Golden Age writers. A strange ad, a performance on antique instruments, knowledge of naval weaponry combined with facts about those people connected with the case yield the solution of "The B-Flat Trombone." Indeed, this is Adams' main reason for inventing Average's club, the Cosmos Club, which limits its membership to those having widely varied, eccentric and esoteric knowledge. Others would become famous for this kind of clue ten years later.

Others would also become famous using the same style that Adams used in the Average Jones stories. First of all, when Jones speaks to a purpose, he drawls, puts on the attitude of "a youth bored with life." Added to this, he talks funny. Here is a passage from "The Man Who Spoke Latin:"

'Hello, Bert,' returned the Ad-Visor, looking up at the faultlessly clad slenderness of his occasional coadjutor, Robert Bertram. 'Sit down and keep me awake till the human snail who's hypothetically ministering to my wants can get me some coffee.'

'What particular phase of intellectual debauchery have you been up to now?' inquired Bertram, lounging into the chair opposite.

'Trying to forget my troubles by chasing up a promising lead which failed to pan out. Wanted: a Tin Nose, sounds pretty good, eh?'

'It is music to my untutored ear.'

Facetiousness, puns, overstatement: in short, comic diction much like that of P.G. Wodehouse. This was, however, before Wodehouse had invented Bertie and Jeeves and at about the same time (1910) that he wrote the first Psmith book, *Psmith in the City*. Much of Adams' comic style seems to come from his fondness for college slang: he refers to Average's college experiences fairly often (in "B-Flat Trombone," "Blue Fires," "The Man Who Spoke Latin," and "The One Best Bet"). The stories, in face, seem to be Adams' attempt to recreate the zest for living, the fun and the intellectual pursuit of an idealized college life.

Average, in his detection, employs those things that he picked up in college. Francis Bacon's distinction between words and things helps Average find the somnambulist in "Blue Fires;" Euclid, "one of the greatest detectives of all times," provides the geometry that solves "One Best Bet." Indeed, Average Jones' detective abilities are those gained from a liberal education: "You have one rare faculty, Jones," his favorite professor told him. "You can, when you choose, sharpen the pencil of your mind to a very fine point." Thus, combining his own specialized knowledge with the encyclopedia of the members of the Cosmos Club, Jones uses disciplined and focused thinking to solve the problems of crime.

The problems of crime in Adams' stories are sometimes the problems of graft and corruption. Adams was, after all, an important muckraking reporter and editor. He may not have been Steffens or Tarbel, but his articles on patent medicine frauds were a significant contribution to American journalism and life. The Average Jones stories are, if you will, sort of a muckraker's holiday. Several of them turn on corrupt politicians: "B-Flat Trombone" shows a crooked politician prevented from running for office, "One Best Bet" deals with an assassination attempt on an honest governor and a corrupt judge appears in "The Million Dollar Dog." Adams has few kind words for policemen: "The police (with the characteristic stupidity of a corps of former truck-drivers and bartenders, decorated with brass buttons and shields and without further qualification dubbed 'detectives')..." "Red Dot" describes the Beef Trust's attempt to murder a chemist who is about to expose their corrupt practices. "Open Trail" brings Average into contact with a patent medicine millionaire. "The Mercy Sign" conveys outrage in the Turkish slaughter of the Armenians.

But a number of the stories have little to do with political or social consciousness. "Blue Fires," "Pin Pricks," "Big Print" and "The Man Who Spoke Latin" have little to do with larger issues. In fact, if we except "Pin Pricks" (which deals with a criminally deranged mind), Adams concentrates on events which do not have serious consequences.

What all of this means is that almost ten years before they appeared in England, Adams assembled the parts of the Golden Age story: witty dialogue, disparate facts, the truly sophisticated amateur, the emphasis on thinking without a lot of mumbo jumbo, all focused on a case that has few mortal consequences. It may be, then, that the Golden Age detective formula is yet another product that can be labeled Made in America.

*The Silent Bullet. The Adventures of Craig Kennedy Scientific Detective* by Arthur B. Reeve, 1912.

Craig Kennedy's Theories: "It has always seemed strange to me that no one has ever endowed a professorship in criminal science in any of our large universities." "Today it is the college professor who is the third arbitrator in labour disputes, who reforms our currency, who heads our tariff commissions, and conserves our farms and forests—why not professors of crime?" "But as for running the criminal himself down, scientifically, relentlessly—bah! we haven't made an inch of progress since the hammer and tongs method of...Byrnes." "I am going to apply science to the detection of crime, the same sort of methods by which you trace out the presence of a chemical, or run an unknown germ to earth."

"The Silent Bullet:" Those involved in market manipulation shoot a stock broker. Kennedy discovers that the bullet made no noise because of a silencer, enlarged photos of the bullet carry marks of the fabric of the coat through which it was shot and the chairs in Kennedy's lab are "wired under the arm in such a way as to betray on an appropriate indicator in the next room every sudden and undue emotion."

"The Scientific Cracksman:" An heiress about to lose her prospects cracks a safe with an electric drill to alter the will; awakened by the noise, her grand uncle dies of shock. Kennedy uses his knowledge of the latest criminal practices, photography, a blood-pressure cuff and a word association test.

"The Bacteriological Detective:" To benefit from a tycoon's will, a typhoid-carrier is introduced into the house and the tycoon dies. Kennedy prevails by finding fingerprints and detecting the presence of disease from a person's handwriting.

"The Deadly Tube:" To obtain a divorce, a husband exposes his wife to radioactive material and blames a physician using x-ray therapy. Kennedy uses a microphone to overhear a confession.

"The Seismograph Adventure:" A medium murders a wealthy woman with a mixture of morphine and bella donna. Kennedy knows that bella donna conceals symptoms of morphine poisoning and uses a seismograph to detect an accomplice making the spirits' raps.

"The Diamond Marker:" A jeweler is murdered by a man who pretends to have invented a way to create diamonds in an electric furnace. As well as recognizing the symptoms of cyanogen poisoning and knowing about thermit, Kennedy once again uses a microphone.

"The Azure Ring:" A market swindler murders a couple about to be married with a poison ring loaded with curare. Kennedy knows about the newly fashionable poison.

"Spontaneous Combustion:" To gain an inheritance, a relative murders and burns the upper portions of the victim. Kennedy proves that spontaneous combustion cannot be, and then uses the precipitin test to distinguish human blood.

"Terror in the Air:" A rival inventor uses electricity to disable an experimental airplane. Kennedy uses only a compass this time.

"The Black Hand:" The Black Hand has kidnapped the daughter of a famous tenor. Kennedy discourses on ricin and uses his microphone.

"The Artifician Paradise:" A rival faction in a Latin American revolution dopes a leader of the opposition with mescal. Kennedy restarts the victim's heart with electricity.

"The Steel Door:" The police raid a high-class gambling den. Kennedy discourses on gambling systems, finds a magnetically controlled roulette wheel and uses an oxy-acetylene torch to cut through the steel door.

The stories in *The Silent Bullet* originally appeared in *Cosmopolitan* from December 1910 to November 1911.

Reeve developed a pattern for the Kennedy stories and pretty much stuck to it: the client comes to Jameson and Kennedy's apartment, outlines the dilemma and asks for help. Kennedy and Jameson visit the scene carrying some apparatus which bewilders Jameson. Kennedy disappears into his laboratory and has all of the suspects assemble in the lab-lecture room. He gives a lecture citing authorities: "An author of many scientific works, Dr. Lindsay Johnson, of London, has recently elaborated a new theory with regard to individuality in handwriting" ("Bacteriological Detective"). He also does some sort of demonstration, like shooting a silenced pistol in "The Silent Bullet." For the sake of variety and action-excitement, Reeve includes tales that take place outside of the lab ("Terror in the Air;" "The Black Hand;" "The Artificial Paradise;" and "Spontaneous Combustion"). But the essentials are the same.

The Craig Kennedy stories fit two international developments in detective fiction. They are, first of all, reactions to the casual use of science in Doyle and his predecessors, who often bound up their stories with "poisons unknown to science" rather than doing even the most cursory search for accuracy. Reeve, therefore, follows the lead of R. Austin Freeman and his Dr. Thorndyke stories, which demonstrated that readers can be just as interested in the careful process of detection as they are in its sensational outcome. Craig Kennedy also responds to the creation of American criminology as separate from sociology which happened in the first decade of the twentieth century: Jameson fights a losing battle with Kennedy in "Craig Kennedy's Theories" when he argues "College professors for the sociology of the thing, yes; for the detection of it, give me a Byrnes." Kennedy argues that sociologists "still treat crime in the old way, study its statistics and pour over its causes and theories of how it can be prevented." The crime scientist, Kennedy says, runs the criminal down "scientifically and relentlessly." In some ways this argument simply reproduces the notions about preventive and detective police of the last century. Kennedy also maintains that the United States lags woefully behind Europe in this regard: "We are children beside a dozen crime-specialists in Paris, whom I could name."

In this, Reeve ties himself to the late nineteenth century development of the university in this country as well as the love-affair between American and German higher education. Kennedy is a university professor; the laboratory and lecture-room are to Kennedy what 221B is to Holmes. He also carries the color of the German academic tradition. Whereas British scientific detectives frequently find that the demonstration itself is enough, Kennedy does not. He must not only demonstrate the thing itself but also must cite the authorities—insofar as Reeve felt readers had the patience for hearing authorities cited. Further, Reeve conceives Kennedy as an argument for specialized graduate study—that American universities establish chairs of crime science. The second two stories in the volume touch on education. In "The Scientific Cracksman" the burglar seeks to alter the will of John G. Fletcher, Steel Magnate, so as to prevent his fortune from going to establish "a great school of preventive medicine." Kennedy solves the case for his friend and colleague, John G. Fletcher II, "Blake professor of bacteriology at the University" who becomes dean of the new graduate college. In "The Bacteriological Detective" Kennedy prevents an unscrupulous attorney from changing a will so as to receive a million dollars to establish the "Bisbee School of Mechanical Arts."

Reeve, however, was no scientist. Unlike R. Austin Freeman who actually tested some of the experiments and proofs in his stories, Reeve drew his science from contemporary magazines and newspapers. In "The Scientific Cracksman" Reeve simply looked back into *McClure's* October 1907 issue and read Hugo Musterberg's account of "the new psychological method" of timing the lapse between question and response in order to detect which key words cause the subject most stress. "The Seismograph Adventure" relies on the fact that belladonna masks some of the symptoms of morphine poisoning, a fact uncovered by Isaac White of *The New York World* in the 1892 Anna Sullivan poisoning case. "Spontaneous Combustion" relies, ultimately, on the precipitin test devised by Bordet (1898) and Wasserman (1900), but probably specifically relies on a 1902 French murder case where the test disproved the defendant's assertion that the blood on his clothes came from a rabbit he was carrying.

Reeve, though, was not a mere lay recorder of the march of science against crime. Many of the stories emphasize method: "I intend to disregard everything that has been printed, to start out with you as if it were a fresh subject and get the facts at first hand" ("The Azure Ring"). Kennedy practices scientific method, going from specific to general, but Reeve does not emphasize this beyond noting it. Reeve was more importantly an advocate for new technology. In "The Deadly Tube" and "Terror in the Air" Kennedy defends forward-looking scientists (a radiologist and an aeronautical engineer) from those who would misuse science for their own purposes. "If this suit goes against you," says Kennedy in "The Deadly Tube," "one of the most brilliant men of science in America will be ruined." Kennedy, likewise, exposes scientific humbugs, from the obvious target of the spiritualists in "The Seismograph Adventure," to the villain who seeks to establish spontaneous combustion as the cause of death in "Spontaneous Combustion," to the fake diamond-maker in the story of the same name. It is not quite muckraking, because Reeve does not give Kennedy the passion or Jameson the brains to be a muckraker. It does, however, attach to the era's inclination to link crime to more than delimited personal motives and to make the detective more than someone who simply proves the guilt of individuals.

Reeve does not limit himself exclusively to scientific crimes and criminals. The most conspicuous example of this is "The Black Hand" which Reeve modeled on the recent extortion threats against tenor Enrico Caruso. "The Artificial Paradise" concerns a populist revolution in the Latin American land of Vespuccia with Kennedy and Jameson's sympathetic with the revolutionaries agains the corrupt old regime. In "Steel Door" Kennedy volunteers to help the New York police raid a high class gambling den, and in "The Silent Bullet" the murder involves "The System's" attempt to manipulate stocks. Even "The Azure Ring," the most domestic of all of the stories, involves swindlers and con artists. So, if all the stories do not advance or defend science, they advance or defend certain social issues, thereby departing from the last era of American detective fiction which cannot see very far beyond the domestic.

But there is not a lot of fire in the Kennedy stories. They are all, of course, Sherlock Holmsey. Kennedy's clients tend to be less helpless than Holmes' (only two frightened young women in the book: "The Bacteriological Detective" and "The Artificial Paradise") and being mostly professionals (physicians, attorneys, policemen) establish him more firmly as a consultant than does Holmes' procession of weak and helpless clients. The story patterns come from Doyle as do the character patterns. Walter Jameson, a newspaper reporter, is the Watson narrator; he is not only virtually no help in the cases but far more naive and blindly servile than Watson.

Craig Kennedy is the genius detective, by Holmes out of Thorndyke. He is something of a paradox, being both more personable than Holmes and more stodgy. His superficial warmth comes largely from Reeve's constant use of the first names Craig and Walter. Using first names is an indelible sign of American culture and fiction which establishes an atmosphere of democracy. In spite of Jameson's evident dullness, the fact that he and Kennedy are on a first name basis means something. But it does not save the stories. The scientific appliances and gymnastics do not make the stories fail, their author does. Reeve writes the Kennedy stories as principally dialogue, purposeful, get to the problem and solution dialogue. He gives his readers little about the people or places that Kennedy and Jameson encounter. Readers rarely feel atmosphere or anything else in the stories except get to the science. Danger, mystery, adventure, these seldom figure in Reeve's characters or plots. We all know Sherlock Holmes and, believe me, Craig Kennedy is no Sherlock Holmes.

*The Crevice* by William J. Burns and Isabel Ostrander, 1915.

Pennington Lawton, "the supreme power in the financial world of the whole country," dies of an apparent heart attack after a mysterious and tempestuous late night meeting. His daugher, Anita, hears part of this meeting. Several days later her minister, Dr. Franklin, tells Anita that in spite of his immense wealth her father died insolvent, and that three of her father's friends, Mr. Rockamore, an English promoter, Mr. Mallowe, the president of Street Railways, and Mr. Carlis, the political boss of the city (which is sometimes New York and sometimes Illington), have volunteered to be her benefactors and protectors. Anita has ineffectual suspicions which she shares with her fiancé, Ramon Hamilton. After an attempt on Hamilton's life they call in detective Henry Blaine to sort things out. Blaine sets one of his bright young men, Guy Morrow, on the trail of Burnell, a forger who has a connection with the case; Blaine finds Burnell and sets up to watch him but falls in love with Burnell's daughter. Turning to Anita's sole asset, the charity which she has established to assist unemployed women, Blaine places "girl spies" in the offices of Anita's three protectors. Hamilton then goes and gets himself kidnapped. Blaine uncovers more forgeries, the forger disappears from Morrow's view and the "girl spies" are discovered and fired. Anita discovers a phial of poison in her father's favorite chair, and so it turns out that he was poisoned. The three conspirators try to get Blaine off the case by causing labor unrest in a distant city, accompanied by that city's fathers' appeals to Blaine for help. Through a physician, Blaine discovers the whereabouts of the kidnapped Hamilton and rescues him. Blaine, after practicing a bit of badgering, not only tells Rockamore that the jig is up, but reveals his knowledge of Rockamore's secret murders of members of his family in his native England. Rockamore commits suicide. Carlis storms into Blaine's office, rants and raves and after unsuccessfully offering Blaine a huge bribe he confesses. Mallowe falls apart and confesses. Anita gets her father's fortune, and she and Ramon are soon to be married. As Blaine leaves he sees "Just a man and a maid, sunshine and happiness, youth and love—that, and the light of undying gratitude in the eyes they bent upon him."

William J. Burns: premiere detective, Secret Service Agent, Chief of the F.B.I. under Harding, founder of the William J. Burns National Detective Agency, the man who helped the Department of the Interior uncover vast land fraud, the man who cleaned up graft in San Francisco and sent Boss Abe Ruef to prison, the man who helped solve the murder of Herman Rosenthal which temporarily cleaned up the New York Police Department, the man who gave Arthur Conan Doyle the ideas for *The Valley of Fear*. What tales he could have told. But here he didn't. Instead he teamed up with Isabel Ostrander and produced a second-rate thriller, rather than giving his readers a real look into what must have been Burns' very exciting and interesting world.

In Britain, Guy Boothby, Sax Rohmer, John Buchan and Edgar Wallace solved the difficulty of making a detective problem into a novel by inserting it into a story of mixed action, adventure and sentiment. The thriller is in many ways an up-to-date sensation novel. Instead of centering on the domestic melodrama of lovers separated, threatened and tortured by circumstance and their own emotions, thrillers reduce the emotional travail to bite-sized pieces and change the nature and scope of the threats. They move out of the domestic realm into a world where villains menace not only individuals but countries. Thus the detective is not a mere follower of clues and protector of a family, he becomes the implacable foe of the Master Criminal and the savior of civilization. Instead of a plot of sentiment with detective excursions, the thriller plot includes recurring instances of capture and escape, success achieved and undone; it runs around for three hundred pages and wraps things up in seven.

This just about covers what Burns and Ostrander do in *The Crevice*. They make their villains giants who possess unlimited and overwhelming resources; they filch Lawton's empire with ease, and almost everyone is in their pay from thugs like Paddington the crooked detective who does a lot of their dirty work, to Anita's pastor whom they bamboozle into becoming their tool. In typical thriller fashion, *The Crevice* contains not one but loads of crimes and criminals. The plot joins a number of thrilling threads: the dangers to Anita and Hamilton, the discovery and loss of Burnell, the developing love of Guy and Burnell's daughter, to say nothing of the work to defeat the plot to steal Lawton's fortune. And it takes quite a man to tie all of this together and rescue all that is decent. Never mind that the premise of the novel is incomparably confused and mutton-headed: it is not likely that the estate of "the supreme power of the financial world of the whole country" can turn on two forged documents—neither of which is a will. But premises rarely bother thriller writers, or, to be fair, many thriller readers.

For our purposes, *The Crevice* represents what must be the ultimate inflation of the detective. Henry Blaine is not simply another gumshoe picked out of the telephone directory. When Hamilton recognizes that he cannot cope with the dangers and mysteries associated with the loss of Lawton's fortune, he tells Anita Lawton that

'There is only one man in America to-day, who is capable of carrying it through successfully. I shall send at once for the Master Mind.'

'The Master Mind?'

'Yes, dear—Henry Blaine, the most eminent detective the English-speaking world has produced.'

Hardly occasional, this kind of puffery continues throughout the whole novel. Blaine is "the man of decision," "The great investigator," he possesses "inscrutable imperturbability," and his smile has "struck terror to the hearts of the greatest malefactors of his generation." It goes on and on. This guy isn't just good. He remembers the mug and *modus* of every crook. He serves not only great individuals, but states as well. He even knows chapter and verse about foreign crimes and criminals and helps out Scotland Yard when he has the time and inclination. Withal, Blaine is not snob. Although he has a regiment of agents, he takes it upon himself to burgle Mallowe's office. In spite of having served the rich and powerful, Blaine has real sympathy for the little person. He understands Burnell's plight and lets him go free. Mostly he appreciates love, the love of Anita for her father and husband-to-be, as well as the developing love of Guy Morrow and Emily Burnell. Underneath it all, Blaine is a romantic:

I, who make my living, and shall continue to make it, by unearthing malefactors; I, who have built my career, made my reputation, proved myself to be what I am by detection and punishment of wrong-doing—I wish with all my heart and soul, before God, that there was no such thing as crime in this fair green world!

As silly as much of *The Crevice* is, the novel does contain some interesting sidelights on the developing conventions of American detective fiction. The authors place some stress on their detective's mental acumen. Some of this shows in pure professional expertise, like Blaine's ability to spot forgeries and recognize the hand of the forger by examining the document.

On a somewhat higher plain, the authors stress Blaine's ability to reason. They demonstrate this by following a convention as old as Poe which appears with some frequency in early twentieth century detective writing in Britain, ciphers. The novel introduces, and reproduces, two different ciphers which Blaine explains as he deciphers them. The Master Mind, nevertheless, does not solve the case by means of fancy reasoning. We can, I suppose, see the detective as an organizational genius; *The Crevice* does show Blaine running a large and complex organization and deploying and controlling his resources. This seems much like Pinkerton's picture of himself in *The Expressman and the Detective*. But it is neither the genius nor the executive who straightens things out in *The Crevice*. Shadowing, eavesdropping, and most importantly, knowing the faces and histories of criminals solve the case. These, too, are the traditional skills of the detective in American fiction.

Blaine, moreover, introduces what will become another convention of the American detective. All of the earlier detectives we have seen, especially Pinkerton and Byrnes, operate with at least superficial respect for all of the niceties of the law. Blaine (and apparently Burns) does not. Forget that he suppresses evidence and frees a few law breakers—all detectives in fiction do that—Blaine, however, burgles Mallowe's office and then has his agents break into Burnell's shop and steal his forger's kit. He accepts breaking the law for the higher good as simply another facet of his occupation.

Burns and Ostrander were among the first American writers to recognize that the American city provides a background as suitable for thrillers as Europe with its gothic sites. Blaine works in a city gripped by corruption. Never mind why the Master Mind doesn't clean this up; he lives in a world controlled by Carlis, the political boss. From police and judges down to the functionaries in the land office who file the bogus deeds, Carlis owns the city. To appreciate the ambiance of the novel, we need to have firmly in mind that money and political power mean an awful lot in this world. Anita Lawton and Ramon Hamilton have neither money nor political power. But they have Henry Blaine. Hardly a tilter after windmills, Blaine understands that brains and vigor and patience will deflate the arrogance of the mighty and reveal them for what they are.

At the turn of the century American detective fiction made its first real advances. From the 1860s through the 1880s detective stories in book form appeared only occasionally. By the turn of the century detective fiction had become a recognized genre, even though, with hindsight, contemporary notions of the precise nature of detective stories were loose and confused. And it became a respectable genre at that: detective fiction moved out of the ghetto of cheap fiction into the legitimate world of middle-class readership. Editors of respectable middle-class magazines like *The Saturday Evening Post* and *McClure's* accepted that detective stories were legitimate enough to run in their journals and publishers like Putnam's began to assemble mysteries into an advertisable group. Part of the reason for this was the notion that if the English can do it, it must be okay. The American publication of the Sherlock Holmes stories did much to elevate the status of the form in this country. We need to recognize, however, that although Doyle did contribute to the popularity of the detective story in this country he did not introduce the detective to America. There were numerous detectives, both official and private, in American fiction before the arrival of Sherlock Holmes. Additionally, American authors at the turn of the century did not simply slavishly imitate Doyle. Coincident with the introduction of Sherlock Holmes, American writers hammered out themes unique to this country.

For one thing, American detective fiction at the turn of the century is more relevant than Doyle or earlier American detective fiction. With a few exceptions, the Sherlock Holmes stories deal with limited domestic problems and mysteries that the detective can solve. They have nothing to do with the real problems of crime and detection in Victorian London, a city with a significant crime problem, and they view law and justice with middle-class complacency. Post and Flynt obviously differ here: their stories about crime and detectives served them principally as means of focusing on social and political dilemmas which they perceived to be threats to the republic but which had no real solution. Even in much more clear-cut detective stories, authors like Reeve (with "The Campaign Grafter") and Adams took problems in politics to be their proper domain, something that Doyle consciously avoided.

On the whole, fictional detectives in America deal with problems far more real and relevant than those presented in British detective fiction, and American writers recognized the place of the new science of psychology in their fiction long before British detective writers did. Sure, they still use old chestnut motivations like inheritances, but they also bring in problems of stock swindles, bank failures, trust bullying and the mafia. These are far more real situations than those in the Holmes stories: in "The Red Headed League" Doyle's focus is on zaniness rather than the reality of the bank robbery and his tales about foreign terrorists, like the KKK or the Mormons, have little connection to reality. American detective writers were not as genre-bound as their British contemporaries; their background in muckraking journalism or the general atmosphere of muckraking influenced them. Excepting Post and Flynt, the American detective writers at the turn of the century did not fuse muckraking and detective fiction very thoroughly—other demands, often detective story demands, dominate their fiction—but it did help to make their stories reflect more accurately the contemporary American scene: airplanes, trains, automobiles, political bosses, get rich quick artists, unscrupulous money men. Flynt, Futrelle, Adams and Burns all set their fictions in modern American cities and some of them begin to bear a faint resemblance to real cities in America at the turn of the century. Not so with Doyle who more or less consciously time-locked all of the Sherlock Holmes stories in the London of the 1890s.

Not only does American detective fiction reflect some of the reality of turn of the century life, it frequently has a purpose beyond entertainment. Detective story readers, particularly in the twentieth century, do not like to admit that they read for entertainment. Early in the century, readers took up the justification that reading detective stories develops the mind: grinding away at trying to solve the problem in a detective story is an exercise in logic. I don't think that this is true; further, authors did not intend their stories to be exercises in logic (or trickery) until the 1920s. At the turn of the century what Doyle and Freeman and others intended was to present fictional demonstrations of genius at work, and then to assemble consistent materials to justify the solution and establish the illusion that readers could have solved it for themselves when they couldn't. Futrelle, and, to a lesser extent Reeve and Adams, take this approach to their fiction. They present an enigma, a wonderful solution and then the explanation of that solution. Readers are supposed to be delighted in watching the geniuses at work.

Except that in American fiction of this type, there is sometimes a bit more than the simple display of genius. For one thing, genius is a bit different in this country; it partly depends on education. Average Jones links some of his solutions to principles he learned at Hamilton College. Futrelle adds Ph.D., LL.D., F.R.S. and M.D. to Van Dusen's name, and Craig Kennedy is a professor. What degrees does Sherlock Homes have? Where did Father Brown attend seminary? What university is Thorndyke affiliated with? In Britain it doesn't make much difference, but at the turn of the century in the United States with the expansion of universities, it does. For another thing, American crime fiction often displays a great deal of ardor. Post and Flynt clearly have a message which dictates the shape of their fiction. But even with more conventional writers, American detective fiction often does more than present a brain teaser or demonstration of genius. Reeve wants to show a genius at work, but he also wants to make a point about the paucity of resources in this country for the scientific detection of crime: indeed, he was invited to help establish a national detection laboratory during World War I. Adams wants to show us a quite different kind of genius at work, but he also wants to make a case for the ennobling power of work versus bourgeois idleness as well as a case against the corruption of governments and corporations.

But what about the more hum-drum authors like Ottolengui? What do they provide beside watching somebody uncovering clues and using his head? Well, Ottolengui warns readers about the nature of evidence, that one must not simply accept a set of facts without carefully searching for all of the facts. And this is something connected to all detective fiction at the turn of the century and has a special relationship to the evolution of the scientific detective tale. Neither the law nor the rulings of judges establish the nature of evidence, the findings of juries do. Fingerprints, for instance, are simply fingerprints until juries accept that they provide proof positive of identity. Whereas juries used to hear the testimony of people, something they were used to doing every day, from the middle of the nineteenth century they were faced with an increasing number of increasingly complex scientific "proofs." The Crippen jury, for instance, based its judgment on expert testimony of a small piece of pickled skin. What turn of the century detective stories did was familiarize readers with scientific proofs. They also helped to establish the image of the expert, and this was particularly important in the United States where suspicion of intellectuals runs deep. Most significantly for us, they established the detective as a competent, careful and expert professional. In America writers did this by turning away from the mysterious powers associated with the detective in the nineteenth century, by allying him with science and scientific method and by showing him to be independent from the corrupting forces of money (in the form of powerful people and corporations) and power (in the form of corrupt government).

Popularizing new scientific proofs and legitimizing the professional detective, however, take second place to the increasing attention in these books given to the nature of the law. Both Post and Flynt insist that the law in America has gone sour, has become the tool of anyone who can buy a judge or a legislature. These works of the 90s simply lament this fact, but in different ways the writers of the first decade of the twentieth century do something about it. Adams, Futrelle and Reeve introduce the genius who can remedy the stupidity of police and courts by the application of superior intelligence and the production of irrefutable logic. In the urbane settings of their stories, much like the urbane settings in contemporary British fiction, this approach works. But not so in Burns who knew first-hand how police and judges and legislatures could be bought. Burns reestablishes skepticism about whether the law and justice represent the same thing. His detective, therefore, commits illegal acts in order to make justice prevail.

This is not to say that at the turn of the century detective fiction grappled powerfully with the realities of American crime and detection. It did not. Post and Flynt come the closest to dealing with essential problems, but they, too, are limited. Post concentrates mainly on white collar crime without acknowledgement of violence and brutality while Flynt's attempted objectivity in portraying those who are preyed upon edges toward a pathetic or romantic portrayal of criminals mixed with a one-sided, albeit understandably one-sided, view of police officers. Further, none of these writers (possibly excepting Flynt) treats violence. In spite of the fact that firearms enter into most of the writers' works—indeed in *A Conflict of Evidence* just about everyone in New Hampshire carries a pistol—there is virtually no gun-play after the commission of the crime. Criminals docilely accompany detectives. Other than in Burns, where there is a bit of shoving and pushing, these books render no physical violence.

Writers of this period render no physical violence because they did not have the language for it. In the books of this period we can see several kinds of style, but none of them is capable of describing either criminals or violence. Publishers at the turn of the century held strong opinions about the use of slang. They virtually banned its use except for local color or dialect characters. Likewise, acceptable sentence structure tended toward the use of lengthy sentences full of semi-colons and subordinate clauses. The most that writers could accomplish using this kind of language was irony or comic effects. We, therefore, see almost all of the writers engaged in this. Post and Flynt describe their vision of the world limited by a style which cannot show what they wish to say. It is not surprising that in the twentieth century writers like Rinehart, Futrelle and Adams use comic effects in their prose, because comic prose was acceptable, whereas slang, raw simple sentences and short paragraphs were seen as being sub-literary. In terms of portraying the real person who inhabit the world of crime and detection, readers would have to wait until the 1920s for the evolution of a new kind of American prose which could accurately render these things.

They, however, did not have to wait for new narrative forms, because at the turn of the century there exist, in germ, three kinds of detective story, all new. One feature of the fiction of this period is the radical surordination of the sensation novel. Although Ottolengui, Rinehart and Burns touch on the sacrifices and trials of love in their novels, these are not the principal focus. The other writers avoid the sensation novel partly because it was alien to their taste, but also partly because they wrote short fiction and short fiction cannot contain much beyond a detective plot. Once the sensation novel had been minimized, the question was what was going to replace it. The simplest transition was to the thriller, a form that grew out of the sensation novel anyway. In Rinehart and Burns and Ostrander we have a number of mysteries for the amateur or professional to solve, but more important than these is the excitement experienced by the hero. Here speed dominates. Another form that replaces the sensation novel was the narrative (short story or novel) which presages the Golden Age story. These stories depend on the assembly of disparate, sometimes goofy, evidence, they emphasize the detective using his brains and their prose is light, urbane and witty. This shows best in Futrelle and Adams. Ottolengui fills the same place as Freeman Wills Crofts, a humdrum writer whose attention to careful analysis marks a break from the old slipshod kind of motivation found in older detective stories. Finally, turn of the century fiction looks forward to the hard-boiled story. The hero isn't there and the prose isn't there, but the attitudes are. Loss of faith in government and authority is there with Post, Flynt and Burns, and the same three writers establish the necessity of the hero acting according to his own concept of justice, even if it means bending or breaking the law.

# Chapter 5
# Contexts
# 1917-1940

Between 1917 and 1940 America's cities developed in some new ways. Of course the population continued to grow, but the wholesale immigration of earlier periods slowed. In 1900 one third of Americans lived in cities, but by 1920, for the first time, more people lived in cities than in the country. The heady rush to the cities stopped with the depression of the thirties, only to begin again with World War II. During the period the governments of America's cities went through cycles of corruption and reform, illustrated best in New York with the swing from the laissez faire administration of James J. Walker to the house-cleaning years of LaGuardia. Some cities, though, resisted change: Chicago Mayor "Big Jim" Thompson's determination to make his an open city gave Chicago a world-wide reputation as the gangster capital.

In the twenties the notion of city planning appeared, and its first real impact was in the adoption of zoning laws which, in fact, solidified the segregation of cities into business, industrial, shopping and different kinds of residential districts that had been going on since the 1840s. The suburbs, which likewise had been around for a long time, grew rapidly during the 1920-1940 period. Cities now expanded not only in population density but in area as well, beginning the metropolises we know today. They grew up with the skyscraper and out with the suburb. Suburbia increased not only because public transportation improved but also because America went for the automobile in a big way: in 1919 there were 9 million cars in the United States but ten years later there were 26 million. All of these cars served as yet another complication for American police forces. The police now needed to enforce traffic laws on an unwilling public that saw them as an infringement on its liberty.

Automobiles also helped to create a new American phenomenon, California. In 1869 California had a population of half a million, by 1910 it ranked 25th among the states in population and by 1965 it ranked first. During the decade of the twenties Glendale grew 3,000 per cent and Beverly Hills by nearly 2,500 per cent. That's a lot of people moving from east to west. Edgar Rice Burroughs moved from Michigan to found the city of, what else, Tarzana. The Joads left the dust bowl for the land of opportunity. No matter whether you were rich or poor, it was still warm there. And then there was Hollywood; in the first quarter of the century the American film industry moved to the Los Angeles area and from there made movies

95

that dominated the world market. If Chicago of the period held the title of crime capital, Hollywood became the dream capital of the United States and the world.

As we move from period to period, crime in America became increasingly more organized and violent. There were 12,000 homicides in the United States in 1926. In the period between 1924 and 1926, Chicago became more than hog butcher to the world, experiencing ninety-two gangland murders, almost all of them unsolved. America was inventing new kinds of cities and was also inventing new kinds of crime and a new kind of criminal.

In the 1920s and 1930s the relationship between criminal gangs and politicians changed. At the turn of the century, politicians protected gangs involved in extortion, prostitution, gambling, drug distribution and for-hire violence because the gangs were the means of ensuring electoral victory. On election days gangs in New York and other American cities got out the vote by intimidating voters, stuffing ballot boxes and by voting "early and often." Because of this relationship, political bosses exerted a measure of control over the crime and violence in their cities. The most famous case in point here occurred in New York. The trouble began in 1901 with friction between the two most powerful territorial gangs in the city, the Five Pointers, led by Paul Kelly (born Paolo Viccarelli), and the Eastmans, led by Monk Eastman (Edward Osterman). On and off for three years the gangs shot at one another leading up to the August 1903 gun battle under the Second Avenue elevated railroad. At that point the politicians had had enough and Tom Foley, the Tammany district leader, held a ball for the two gangs which culminated in Kelly and Eastman shaking hands in the middle of the dance floor. The battles continued, however, until another form of mediation was arranged: Kelly and Eastman accompanied by their followers, met in a barn in the Bronx for a prizefight. Kelly and Eastman boxed for two hours until the fight was called a draw. In spite of the violence, then, gangs could be brought together and accepted that some kind of settlement, other than victory in battle, was possible. Also, at this point, politicians still had a measure of control over criminal gangs. This changed.

It changed because the access to money changed. Up until the 1920s politicians paid off their debts to crooks by providing immunity from prosecution as well as giving them a shot at making some easy money through rigged city or state contracts. But in 1920 Prohibition hit. Why make a few dishonest bucks by overcharging the city on a construction job when selling booze will make you rich almost overnight? Across the country gangs discovered that their money made them the bosses, that they could buy politicians instead of being bought. For a time in the twenties and early thirties the real power in many American cities lay in the hands of criminal bosses. In 1929 Frank Loesch, President of the Chicago Crime Commission, actually went to Al Capone and asked him to help Chicago hold an honest election. The underworld bosses of the '20s also had their own way of solving their political and economic problems: if throwing money at a problem didn't work then they threw lead. A case in point, in 1931 Vincent "Mad

Dog" Coll sought a part in Dutch Schultz's New York beer business. Schultz declined the merger. Coll responded by hijacking Schultz's beer trucks. In apparent retaliation, Coll's brother Peter was shot in Harlem. Raiding the Helmar Social Club, run by one of Schultz's friends, Coll and his gunmen accidentally shot five children playing on the street. Schultz went to the police and offered the prize of a house in Westchester to anyone who would kill Coll. In February, 1932 Schultz's gunmen, looking for Coll, killed two of Coll's assistants and a woman. On February 9 Schultz's gunmen found Coll talking on the phone in a booth in a drugstore and riddled him with a Thompson submachine gun. Unlike the Eastman-Kelly feud, a number of innocent people were killed, the level of violence was substantially higher and nobody controlled the gangs. Taking someone for "a ride," the cement overcoat and the double-decker coffin were all underworld inventions of the period. Violence was the sole arbiter.

During Prohibition the money to be made in bootlegging, rum-running and hijacking changed the organization of American crime and spawned a new level of violence in the cities. Toward the end of Prohibition there was yet another new direction. Following the example of industry, a number of powerful underworld figures perceived the virtues of limiting competition as a means of fleecing the public. They also realized that violence made bad press and gummed up the money machine. Therefore, in the late twenties and thirties, American crime became organized. "Syndicated" crime was the brain-child of former Chicago gangster Johnny Torrio who, in 1927, formed the Seven Group, a syndicate that included New York's Luciano, Lansky and Costello; Nucky Johnson from Atlantic City; Waxey Gordon, Nig Rosen and Boo-Boo Hoff from Philadelphia; and alliances with King Solomon in Boston, Moe Dalitz in Cleveland; Detroit's Purple Gang boss Abe Bernstein; and Boss Tom Pendergast from Kansas City. The east coast members met at Atlantic City in 1927 to settle spheres of influence, to discuss the possibilities for easy money when Prohibition gasped its final breath and to convince Al Capone to take the fall on a minor charge so as to get his name and associated Chicago-style violence off of the nation's front pages. Big city gangsters came to see New York gambler Arnold Rothstein, "fixer" of the World Series, as a model, dressed by the best tailors, mixing with celebrities from the worlds of sports and politics, speaking cultivated English, and yet wielding the power generated by fortunes built on other people's vices.

Even before 1933 and the actual repeal of Prohibition, organized crime settled into the cities, mining their profits from other vices: gambling, prostitution and narcotics. Just as the feuds of bootleggers disappeared from the nation's headlines and the "syndicate" sought a lower profile, up sprang another class of outlaw. Spawned by the Depression and given mobility by Henry Ford, a number of notorious, even famous, gangs popped up in the south and mid-west. During the Depression nobody much liked banks: they disappeared your savings, they sold your place at public auction, they deserved to be knocked over. And so they were, by Ma Barker and her boys, by Bonnie and Clyde, by Dillinger, by Pretty Boy Floyd, Baby Face Nelson and Alvin Karpis. Rob the bank, shoot up a few policemen and move on. Their cars loaded with pistols, shot guns and a tommy gun or two, the gangs moved up and down America's heartland bringing the wild west to the rest of the country.

Guns and cars symbolize crime in the 1920s and 1930s. A lasting image of the period is the black sedan taking a corner at full speed with machine guns blazing from its windows. Crime had never been so mobile, and cars made this possible. Dillinger, in fact, wrote a letter of appreciation to the Ford Motor Company. A famous picture of Bonnie and Clyde shows them horsing around with guns in front of one of their automobiles. Until the mid-thirties a criminal's car was not simply the means of a fast get-away, it was insurance against prosecution, because all one had to do is to cross a jurisdictional line and the cops couldn't touch you. Automobiles did the same thing as horses, they gave you mobility, but they gave their drivers and passengers more excitement and more power.

The same can be said for criminals' weapons of choice in the 20s and 30s. At the end of World War I, Colonel John M. Thompson invented the submachine gun, the "trench broom," to be used in trench warfare. Too late to be manufactured for wartime use, Thompson after the war formed the Auto Ordinance Company to market his submachine gun, with Colt manufacturing the weapon. Only no government agencies really wanted to buy submachine guns: the army didn't and neither did police departments (the Chicago police had a demonstration in 1927). The only substantial sale was to the Irish Republican Army. Kennett and Anderson in *The Gun in America* observe that

> Chicago gangsters were the first to discover the submachine gun's formidable attributes in the winter of 1925-1926. It appeared in Philadelphia in 1927 and in New York in 1928. By the early 1930s the Tommy Gun had become a household word, winning the endorsement of Mad Dog Coll, Ma Barker, and Pretty Boy Floyd.

Al Capone himself is reputed to have been the first to use the Tommy gun in Chicago in the murder of two rival gangsters and Assistant State's Attorney William McSwiggin. Anyone could get one. Capone's men bought the machine gun that killed Frankie Yale at Peter von Frantzius' sporting goods store in Chicago. Submachine guns cost $175 when ordered through the mail. In addition to the new Tommy gun, American criminals favored the sawed-off shotgun, the use of which the Germans had labeled as contrary to the laws of war. Clyde Barrow had a special quick draw holster sewn into his pants for his sawed-off and in 1935 Mendy Weiss used one in the shoot out at the Palace Chop House that left Dutch Schultz dead. As machines for making a person dead, neither the submachine gun nor the sawed-off shotgun was more effective than the rifles and pistols of the period. These weapons, however, possess the power not only to kill but to grotesquely mutilate the victim. The submachine gun and the sawed-off shotgun, moreover, were designed for indiscriminate destruction by an individual surrounded by enemies. That the sawed-off shotgun and the submachine gun, the chopper, the Tommy gun, the Chicago piano, are so closely identified with crime and criminals of the twenties and thirties tells a great deal.

Local and state police forces of the period were in no shape to deal with crime in the twenties and the thirties. The subjection of law enforcement to politics and politicians continued to hamper police forces: as late as 1933, newly elected Governor Miriam Ferguson fired all of the Texas Rangers and replaced them with her less than competent political friends. In the early '30s the Seabury Commission replayed the Lexow Commission, revealing widespread corruption in New York City's government and, ultimately, forcing the resignation of mayor Jimmy Walker. The Boston police strike of 1919 which lead to wholesale firings may have established the principle that those responsible for public safety do not have the right to strike, but it also demonstrated that the police were inextricably bound to government by politicians and had little chance to demand their rights or to keep their own house in order.

And the house was as disorderly as ever before. Graft was as popular as ever. Smedley Butler, Philadelphia's Public Safety Director, estimated in 1923 that most of the city's police received from $150 to $200 a month in payoffs. Charles Fitzsimmons held that sixty percent of Chicago's police were in the bootlegging business and that at one precinct, Maxwell Street, one hundred percent were. Lewis Valentine, Mayor LaGuardia's police chief, in his first six years in office, fired 300 policemen, officially rebuked 3,000 and fined 8,000. Even when the police had the will to enforce the laws, they seldom had the way. The Chicago police presented the bullets from the St. Valentine's Day massacre with the frank admission that they lacked the technical means to analyze and identify them—whereupon two private individuals funded the crime laboratory at Northwestern University.

And in many cases it was simply futile to make arrests. Witnesses testified at their own peril. In a celebrated case in 1912 New York police lieutenant Charles Becker commissioned the murder of Herman Rosenthal who was about to blow the whistle on Becker's underworld connections: Becker was convicted and executed for the murder. By the '30s things were different. When Frank "Jelly" Nash was going to testify about his crime connections to the F.B.I., he and several federal agents were machine gunned outside of Union Station on June 17, 1933 in the Kansas City Massacre. No one was ever arrested for it. Even when cases arrived at trial the courts or the politicians let the criminals go free with disturbing frequency. On the trivial side, of the 6902 liquor cases that went before the New York courts, 400 never went to trial and 6074 were dismissed. On the less than trivial side, juries were bought and intimidated (William Burns got in trouble for this) and if these things failed, it paid to own a politician. Governor Len Small of Illinois pardoned 1000 convicted felons during his term.

If the temptations of illicit gain and the new complications presented by the dense and mobile city population were not enough, more voices were being raised against the policeman's traditional practice of violence. The

American Bar Association in 1930 issued a report on the Third Degree estimating that hundreds, probably thousands of cases were never reported; the same year Emanuel Lavine's *The Third Degree: A Detailed and Appalling Expose of Police Brutality* appeared. Indeed, breaking some laws for what was considered the greater good was an accepted practice. Maybe the most prominent, and ironic, case of this involved the celebrated detective Ellis Parker who, in his efforts to solve the Lindbergh kidnapping, kidnapped Paul Wendel and beat a false confession from him.

At the beginning of the twentieth century, the federal government began to cast its eye on corruption and crime in American cities. The first federal glance came in a series of laws intended to curb vice. Anti-vice movements go back at least to the mid-nineteenth century, with citizens banding together against smut or strong drink or other vicious personal practices. By the turn of the century some states had taken legislative stands against gambling— without apparent success. Then the federal government stepped in. With the Pure Food and Drug Act (1906) and the Harrison Act (1914) Congress restricted the sale of narcotics. The Mann Act of 1910 made it a federal crime to transport women across state lines for immoral purposes. And then came the biggie: Congress ratified the 18th Amendment to the Constitution on January 16, 1920 and alcohol was supposed to go the way of the dinosaur. Of course it did not. The federal government did not have the means to enforce the law. Prohibition agents were grossly underpaid and frequently inept or corrupt. And the American public simply did not want to abide by the law. Whatever else Prohibition did to America, and it did many things, it gave money and energy to criminals and it cut off or seriously hampered the movements toward police reform begun at the turn of the century. It took the federal government over a decade to undo its mistake.

In 1929 The Wickersham Commission, the National Commission on Law Observance and Enforcement, began to meet. It eventually reported that American police, on the whole, were inadequate:

The general failure of the police to deter and arrest criminals guilty of many murders, spectacular bank, payroll, and other hold-ups and sensational robberies with guns, frequently resulting in the death of the robbed victim, has caused a loss of public confidence in the police of our country.

The Commission found that crime cost the citizens of the United States one billion dollars a year. Part of the problem was the linkage between police and politicians:

The chief evil, in our opinion, lies in the insecure, short term of service of the chief or executive head of the police force and in his being subject while in office to the control of politicians in the discharge of his duties.

The Commission's report recommended some specific reforms, such as putting police into the civil service system, and it went on to imply that Prohibition exacerbated the problems of crime and policing crime, suggesting the utility of repealing the 18th Amendment. And so it was, on December 5, 1933. Legislating against vice in a sprawling, democratic nation, no matter how worthy an action, had the effect of promoting the prosperity of the criminal and, across the board, diminishing the dignity of the law.

Up until the 1920s the federal government perceived crime and criminals to be the concern of the states. Except for the Secret Service's investigation of currency crime, the federal government had little to do with the active protection of American citizens. The F.B.I. of the period was a small, inept bureau and efforts to enforce federal law were at best feeble and misguided. Neither Congress nor the executive made enforcement of Prohibition a priority (President Harding had his own bootlegger) and responding to the red scare of 1920 with the Palmer Raids (which rounded up 4,000 "suspected" reds) was, in retrospect, farcical. As we approach the 1930s, however, the executive branch became more and more concerned with crime in the country's cities. President Hoover repeatedly asked Andrew Mellon, Secretary of the Treasury, "Have you got that fellow Capone yet? Remember I want that man Capone in jail." The problem, however, was that the federal government had no jurisdiction over most lurid and heinous crimes. The first solution was to nail gangsters not for murder and extortion, which were state crimes, but with the federal law against income tax evasion. In 1931 Al Capone went to federal prison for under-reporting his income. Thomas Dewey made his reputation in New York in the Federal District Attorney's office going after gangsters by way of their income tax returns. Form 1040 did more damage to the country's gangsters than whole police forces.

The second federal approach to crime came in the early 1930s. Partly as a result of the Lindbergh kidnapping, the federal government looked for ways to step into the enforcement of criminal laws. In 1934, therefore, Congress passed laws making it a federal crime: to rob a federally chartered bank, to take stolen property worth more than $5,000 across state lines and to assault or kill a federal officer. The same package of bills put some oomph into the F.B.I. In the late '20s J. Edgar Hoover gave new life to the incompetent Bureau. He insulated its agents from politics and fought to make it a modern organization. He won, for instance, the battle of fingerprints: before 1930, when Hoover won the tug-of-war in Congress, convicts at Leavenworth Penitentiary were in charge of the Country's centralized fingerprint records. In 1930 the F.B.I. also began to compile statistics on crime in the United States. Still, F.B.I. agents had no power of arrest and they were not allowed to carry firearms: when agents wanted to arrest someone they had to depend on local police to do the arresting. The 1934 crime bills gave agents full powers of arrest and allowed them to carry firearms. They were in business.

Part of F.B.I. business in the mid-thirties was gathering up the flamboyant bank robbers looting the country's banks. Dillinger, Baby Face Nelson and Pretty Boy Floyd bit the dust in 1934; Bonnie and Clyde along with Ma Barker and her boys went in 1935; Alvin Karpis was captured in 1936. From Florida to Ohio and Illinois to Louisiana "Public Enemies" were reeled in, sometimes by the F.B.I. and sometimes by local police. The other part of Hoover's business was establishing the image of himself and his bureau. The Director flew to Memphis to personally capture Alvin Karpis; Hoover delighted in the report that Machine Gun Kelly said, "Don't shoot, G. Men" when F.B.I. agents entered his room. Hoover's public relations bumpf inflated the image of his bureau, establishing the G. Man as incorruptible, tough, scientific and dogged, an image never before associated with public law enforcement. The trouble was, that to do this also meant building up the images of the Bureau's antagonists; it meant inflating mean, pathetic and sometimes petty bank bandits into premiere Public Enemies not only distorted the true picture of crime and criminals in the United States but every so often it backfired and romanticized the criminal.

In the process of romanticizing the criminal, the American cinema industry played no small part. In the first two decades of the century, silent films featured detectives with some regularity. The first Sherlock Holmes film appeared in 1903, and Raffles made his film debut in the same year. British detectives dominated the American cinema of the period, not only with numerous Holmes films but also with films about Sexton Blake (1909), Bulldog Drummond (1922), The Old Man in the Corner (1924), *The Moonstone* (1915) and Alfred Hitchcock's version of *The Lodger*. American film-makers shied away from dime novel American detective stories (there were Nick Carter films made from 1909 to 1912, but they were made in France) and concentrated on the more genteel tradition with films of *The Leavenworth Case* (1923) and *The Circular Staircase* (1915). Arthur B. Reeve was one of the few "new" detective writers to appear on the screen with *The Adventures of Elaine* of 1915 and several other Craig Kennedy films. Silent detective films were scarcely the most prominent film products of the period, and American films of American stories never received the attention or status that British detectives gained: John Barrymore played both Raffles (1917) and Holmes (1922) on the silent screen; Arnold Daly played Craig Kennedy. But then there were Mack Swain, Slim Summerville, Chester Conklin and Fatty Arbuckle: Max Sennett's Keystone Kops. Satire or assault on authority? Both are traditional purposes of comedy. It is telling that the silent era's most persistent image of American law enforcement makes the policeman the subject of farce.

The development of the cinema coincided with a move toward intellectualism in detective stories. Detective stories of the last century intertwined a detective plot with a good deal of sentiment suited silent films, but in the twenties, detective stories came to stand on their own. They became more dependent on complex dialogue (Golden Age stories, in fact, have many similarities to stage plays) and had subtlety beyond the range of silent screen. In 1928 talking pictures appeared in America, and they provided a possible new venue for stories about crime and detectives. Unlike during the silent era, the works of American authors dominate the new films about crime, criminals and detectives. In 1929 Paramount made its first S.S. Van Dine film with William Powell as Philo Vance: there would be a total of eleven of them before 1940. Ellery Queen made his debut with Republic's

*The Spanish Cape Mystery* of 1935. The most popular of the American Golden Age writers at the movies was Earl Derr Biggers: there were twenty Charley Chan films between 1931 and 1940. After *The Case of the Howling Dog* of 1934 Perry Mason appeared in five more films before 1940. Hard-boiled writers, too, made it to the movies in the thirties. Coxe's Flash Casey took to the screen in *Women are Trouble* (1936). Hammett, though, was the most filmed of the hard-boiled writers: Paramount trashed *The Red Harvest* in *Roadhouse Nights* of 1930; three films based on his short stories were released (*City Streets* (1931), *Woman in the Dark* (1934) and *Mister Dynamite* (1935)); *The Thin Man* series began in 1934; *The Glass Key* met celluloid in 1935; and Warner Brothers made *The Maltese Falcon* twice, in 1931 and 1936. What impact did these films have? The hard-boiled detective films were negligible. Hard-boiled fiction on film made no real impact until the 1940s, beginning with Bogart in John Huston's version of *The Maltese Falcon* in 1941. Golden Age pattern fiction translated into the film chiefly in terms of oddity. William Powell as the foppish Philo Vance, Warner Oland as Mister Chan with his numbered sons and Peter Lorre as Mr. Moto (starting in 1937) come across decades as the dominant cinematic detective images of the 1930s. Like the silents, American talkies did comedy very effectively, but dealt less effectively in the 1930s with America's heritage of detective fiction. They could not yet portray the detective hero. This would wait until the 1940s.

The film industry, though, did much better with criminals than it did with detectives. Film makers, in fact, looked to criminals before they took up detectives in the thirties. Criminals did appear in silent films during the twenties. Boston Blackie was a favorite, portrayed by Lionel Barrymore, among others. Bad guys, though, did not smash the box office until Mervyn LeRoy's 1930 film version of W. R. Burnett's *Little Caesar*. Edward G. Robinson's portrayal of Rico's rise and fall formed a pattern for other gangster films that followed: *The Public Enemy* in 1931, *Scarface* in 1932, *I am a Fugitive from a Chain Gang* (1932) and *Blood Money* in 1934. Robinson, James Cagney and George Raft personified the gangster for the film-going public. The gangster films of the thirties can be seen as either amoral portraits of the gangster, one of the outstanding public figures of the age, or they can be seen as Depression parables superimposing the criminal on the capitalist. Gangster films, however, did not long hold the industry's attention; responding to pressure from the Production Code Administration, the film companies replaced the gangster with the detective. By the late thirties the film industry, in fact, helped out the F.B.I.'s public relations campaign, with Warner Brothers' conversion of gangster star James Cagney into the star of *G-Men*, with Universal's 1937 film about G. Men, *You Can't Get Away With It* and with, perhaps as the reductio ad absurdum, *Dick Tracy's G-Men*.

During the thirties the American film industry participated in what can be called a brain-drain as far as writers are concerned. Burnett, Paul Cain, Hammett, Chandler, Horace McCoy, James M. Cain and a bunch of other crime writers migrated to Hollywood and wrote for the movies. Very simply, they made a great deal more money writing screen plays than they could writing fiction. Also, very simply, many produced some of their worst material working for the movies. But most of this went on in the 40s.

For a time in the 1920s people could experience pictures without talk in the cinema or stay at home and listen to talk without pictures on their radios. In 1921 KDKA in Pittsburgh opened the radio era with the first regular broadcast. From 1922 when there were only 60,000 radios in the United States the number of radios swelled until it reached 7,500,000 in 1928. By the end of the decade most Americans listened to the radio. But radio broadcasting did not spring full blown from the head of Westinghouse. Stations did not broadcast all day until 1930, the electronics companies who owned many of the early stations could not figure out how to pay for the broadcasts until they invented radio commercials in the middle of the twenties and scattered local stations sporadically filled the airwaves until NBC became the first radio network in 1926. Then, too, during the twenties no one really knew what to broadcast, what shape the new medium was going to take, or even what American accent to use on the air. There was a lot of music, especially opera, some sports (the Dempsey-Carpentier fight), eviscerated news (WJZ had to agree not to report fist fights and other disturbances at the 1924 Democratic Convention in New York) and some Vaudeville comedy. Radio did not discover the detective until the 1930s.

In the thirties radio responded to crime in ways that fiction and film could not. Microphones captured the verdict at the Lindbergh kidnapping trial, but before the verdict radio commentators gave the proceedings so much play that the American Bar Association saw a danger to American justice and adopted Canon 25, barring microphones and cameras from courtrooms. If newscasts featured true crime, semi-dramatic and dramatic radio programs did too. The most striking of these was on C.B.S.: *True Detective Mysteries* (beginning in 1929). Like other programs that began in radio's desperation to fill air-time, *True Detective* on the radio simply took material from *True Detective Magazine* and presented it on the air. The program claimed to present "a real story of a real crime, solved by real people, with a real criminal brought to justice." In 1934 *True Detective Mysteries* tacked onto the end of the program a description of a wanted criminal, beginning with "Baby Face" Nelson. Documentary or semi-documentary crime broadcasts appeared with some frequency in the thirties: Lewis E. Lawes, warden of Sing Sing, introduced dramas about his prisoners in *20,000 Years in Sing Sing* (1932); Chief James Davis, of the Los Angeles Police, introduced *Calling All Cars* (1932); Norman Schwartzkopf, formerly of the New Jersey State Police, narrated *Gangbusters* from 1936 until Lewis Valentine, LaGuardia's corruption busting chief of police, took over in 1945. In the late 30s, J. Edgar Hoover discovered the power of radio, and real and fictitious F.B.I. agents began to hit the air, culminating in the 40s with *The F.B.I. in Peace and War*. This type of documentary or pseudo documentary program presented America's war on crime in simple terms: no corrupt cops, no third degree and no criminals eluding prosecution. Gangsters were bad and police officers were good and competent. Radio self-censored itself far more stringently than did newspapers, magazines and books: if America had a problem with crime the authorities could handle it. But if the authorities could handle crime, why the super hero shows?

Radio in the thirties often emphasized the adventure or thriller potential of detectives and detective stories. The late series *I Love A Mystery* with Jack Packard and Doc Long's A-1 Detective Agency looks into bizarre cases in exotic locales and perhaps sums up many radio detective shows of the period. No matter how much derring-do these action detectives displayed, they paled in comparison to the voice that said, "Who knows what evil lurks. . ." *The Shadow* began much the same way as *True Detective Mysteries*: in 1930 Smith and Street presented dramatized versions of stories from its *Detective Story Magazine* introduced by a narrator named The Shadow. Realizing the sales potential of the narrator's name, Smith and Street hired Walter B. Gibson to create a hero named The Shadow. The new character, the Shadow, soon took over Smith and Street's *Detective Story Hour* and in 1932 the show was his own. With his corps of assistants and with his mysterious powers The Shadow brought the thriller tradition to American radio and he helped to wipe out crime that the police could not handle. This simplistic yearning for solution spun out into *The Shadow* pulp magazine, films and comic books. It also generated the other mega heroes: Green Lantern, Bat Man, Doc. Savage and Superman. All of these heroes moved from radio, film and print into comic books.

On the more elevated side, radio participated in other developments in detective fiction. Sherlock Holmes entertained listeners from 1930 onward: William Gillette added the radio to his stage and screen impersonations of Holmes, and Basil Rathbone and Nigel Bruce took their act from the screen to the radio in 1939. From very early, a number of shows aired which connected to the guessing-game feature of Golden Age detective stories. WMAQ in Chicago developed a local series in 1929 called *Unfinished Play* in which the program would stop before the end of the drama and the listener who provided the best ending would receive a $200. prize. The same thing happened on the networks with *The Eno Crime Club*, broadcast between 1931 and 1936: on Tuesday night a crime drama aired without a solution and on Wednesday the program presented the solution. Ellery Queen took the game show concept from 1939 to 1948 with *The Adventures of Ellery Queen*, only this time a panel of celebrities would discuss their solutions before Queen put his finger on the real criminal. Although these programs possessed a more up-town atmosphere and stressed the game aspects of the Golden Age detective story, they did have a garnish of realism. J. Fred MacDonald, in *Don't Touch That Dial*, for instance, says that while antagonists on *The Eno Crime Club*, such as Finney the Slug and Pretty Boy Gregory, were only fictional characters, listeners were certainly aware that their real-life counterparts were operating with impunity throughout the country.

Radio, however, did not do much with hard-boiled fiction in the thirties. Hammett did not reach the air waves until the 40s and then it was with Nick and Nora rather than his earlier down and dirty detectives. It was perhaps the language or the violence—radio being prudish about these things—that kept hard-boiled writers off of the radio; or perhaps the bleak outlook of hard-boiled fiction kept it off the air. Some of the features of hard-boiled fiction did work their way into other kinds of radio crime shows (the prevalence of private eyes in the adventure detective shows and the clipped narration of police shows), but, on the whole, people found the total hard-boiled experience only in print.

While these new mediums developed, new blood appeared in the American book publishing industry. New publishers, like Alfred Knopf, made their mark, and many of the old family-owned firms, like Scribners, showed renewed vitality. In spite of the cinema and the radio, Americans appeared to be reading more, partly because of the emphasis put on reading in the armed forces—five and a half million books were donated for soldiers' libraries during the war—and partly because illiteracy diminished (in 1910 the rate was 7.7%; in 1930 it was 4.3; and by 1940 it was 2.9, although these figures are suspect). Books were a way for the immigrants of the turn of the century to insure the success of their children. Books rose in price during the twenties, up to $2.00, but publishers did very well. Partly they did well because of marketing. Some publishers (notably Doubleday and Brentanos) owned book stores, but they also found other successful ways to peddle books. Following the Everyman series in Britain, Random House issued the Modern Library to bring classics to readers at a modest price. There were omnibus volumes, again following the pattern set abroad. The book club began in America in 1926 with both the Literary Guild and the Book of the Month Club.

Detective stories played a part in the new publishing scene. Although American publishers had recognized mystery/crime/detective stories as a separate, if not discreet, genre by the 1890s, they did not do much with them. In the '20s and '30s they did. Most major publishers had both American and British detective writers on their lists: Dodd had Christie and Anna Katherine Green; Simon and Schuster had Ronald Knox and Anthony Boucher; Dutton had H.C. Bailey and Harry Keeler; Little Brown had Oppenheim and J.P. Marquand; Harpers had Freeman Wills Crofts and John Dickson Carr. Everybody had at least one detective writer: Stokes had Ellery Queen, Morrow had Earle Stanley Gardner, Farrar had Rex Stout, Lippincott had Carolyn Wells, Scribners had Van Dine. Knopf had the best with James M. Cain, Chandler, George H. Coxe, Hammett and Raoul Whitfield. Doubleday had the most. Not only did they publish A.B. Cox and Georgette Heyer from England, they also had Sapper's Bulldog Drummond books and Edgar Wallace. On the American side of Doubleday's list they had, among others, Paul Cain, Mignon C. Eberhart, Mary Roberts Rinehart, Van Wyck Mason, Jonathan Latimer, Vincent Starrett and Rufus King.

In the twenties and thirties, American publishers applied one innovation after another to sell their detective writers. Doubleday reprinted Sayers' *Omnibus of Crime* and other omnibus volumes followed: Edgar Wallace's *Mammoth Mystery Book*, Frank King's *Big Book of Mystery Stories* and so on. To identify books by genre instead of by author, many publishers adopted special names and logos for their detective books: Simon and Schuster had its Inner Sanctum Novels, Lippincott had Main Line Mysteries, Dodd and Mead had Red Badge Novels and Knopf had Borzoi Murder Mysteries. Harpers introduced in 1929 a line called "Sealed Mysteries" in which the last pages were sealed with an onion skin-wrapper; return it with seal uncut and get your money back. Hot upon the heels of the Book of the Month Club, in 1928 The Detective Story Club and The Crime Club made their debut. Doubleday, which owned the Crime Club, began the club by publishing the first novel of Kay Strahan, *The Desert Moon Mystery*. Just as publishers ran contests for regular fiction, in the twenties publishers encouraged prospective detective writers by running detective story contests— surely the most famous of which was won by Ellery Queen.

Then, too, crossword puzzles had some impact. Through a front company, because they did not want to compromise the dignity of their list of titles, Simon and Schuster published the first crossword puzzles in 1924, and began one of the crazes of the 20s. Crosswords fuse play with the illusion of mental exercise and this corresponded to latent tendencies in the detective story, especially as it was coming to be written in Britain. Scribners' publication of Van Dine's novels in 1926 inaugurated a trend of combining ultra-cultured reference, facts of scientific criminology and a pedantic emphasis on logic—the later manifested in long lists of questions, footnotes and other supposedly thought-provoking devices. Echoing this, 1928 Doubleday introduced the puzzle book with Wren and McKay's *The Baffle Book*, which took most of the embellishments of fiction out of the detective story, emphasized readers' knowledge of scientific criminology and their ability to observe and reason, thereby reducing the detective story to a party game of 30 cases given to readers to solve. Doubleday did a second and third puzzle book by Wren and McKay and Crowell published their fourth (*The Mystery Puzzle Book*, 1933). H.A. Ripley wrote *Minute Mysteries* for Houghton in 1932 and then two more for Stokes in the 30s; the first book for Stokes, *How Good a Detective Are You* (1934), went through five printings by 1937.

In spite of some successes, like Christie's *The Murder of Roger Ackroyd*, publishers discovered that detective and mystery titles rarely became best-sellers. They did, however, have more staying power than one shot affairs, like *Mrs. Wiggs of the Cabbage Patch*. This made detective stories ideal candidates for reprinting just when publishers were in the process of creating reprint houses as subsidiaries: Doubleday had the Garden City Press and

Harcourt Brace, Harpers, Dodd Mead and Little Brown joined to form Blue Ribbon Books. Many of the reprint houses published detective stories, but they were still hard cover books and, to some, too expensive. And so American publishers moved toward the paperback, imitating what Penguin had done in Britain. Detective stories played a significant role in this. Simon and Schuster chose to experiment in paperbacks with their Inner Sanctum Novels, by publishing them in soft covers and offering to bind them for one dollar if the reader wanted to keep them. In 1937 Mercury Publications introduced another early paperback series, American Mercury Books. *The Postman Always Rings Twice* led off this series which, in 1940, changed its name to Mercury Mysteries. Paper covered Seal Books, published by Modern Age Books in the late thirties, advertised that they covered "a wide range, from detective fiction to serious political, social or economic studies," publishing Paul Cade's *Death Slams the Door* and David MacDuff's *Murder Strikes Three* and reprinting *Little Caesar, The Leavenworth Case, Peril at End House* and Sayers' *Suspicious Characters (Five Red Herrings)*. Pocket Books began the real paperback revolution in 1939, and *The Murder of Roger Ackroyd* (a book thirteen years old) was on their first list. Paperbacks, however, did not make their real impact until after World War II.

Between 1920 and 1940 American book publishers exercised little in the way of discrimination toward stories of crime and detection. Looking backward in "The Simple Art of Murder" Chandler put his finger on the crux of detective and mystery publishing of the period when he said

> It seems to me that production of detective stories on so large a scale, and by writers whose immediate reward is small and whose meed of critical praise is almost nil, would not be possible at all if the job took any talent. In that sense the raised eyebrow of the critic and the shoddy merchandising of the publisher are perfectly logical. The average detective story is probably no worse than the average novel, but you never see the average novel. It doesn't get published. The average—or only slightly above average—detective story does. Not only is it published but it is sold in small qualities to rental libraries and it is read.

Although Knopf stands out as a publisher who nurtured the best in American detective writing, most publishers saw detective books not as literature but as a commodity to be sold through the use of gimmicks. It stands to reason, then, that the publishing successes of the period, like *The Murder of Roger Ackroyd* and the Philo Vance books, lived not because of their literary power or intellectual insight, but because of their precocious artificiality and their cleverness.

In the twenties and thirties, crime and detective fiction appeared in a number of publishing strata. Going back to the 1860s, America has had papers and magazines which emphasize the grotesque in crime and which intend to titillate their readers with sensation. When Richard K. Fox bought the *National Police Gazette* in the 1870s he pepped the magazine up by adding features like "Vice's Varieties." There were other police gazettes published toward the end of the century, the crudest of which, Professor

Mott tells us, was Boston's *Illustrated Police News*: articles like the one on January 6, 1883 about a woman giving birth while buried alive give us some inkling of the paper's nature as well as its readership. In the 1920s *True Detective Mysteries*, begun in 1924, carried on the tradition of linking crime and sensation, only with a bit more dignity. Patterned on the romantic confession magazine *True Love Stories*, *True Detective Mysteries* led to a handful of other true crime magazines in the twenties: *Master Detective*, *True Detective* and, in the 30s, *Official Detective Stories*. Even though these crime magazines lean toward sensation and the "strange but true" quality of crime, they do present crime and the detective in a more real light than that provided by the detective stories of book publishers. Readership of true detective magazines however, has always been limited and they remain largely outside the loop of literary history. Pulp detective stories however, are another matter.

During and after World War I, pulp magazines took up where story papers and detective libraries of the nineteenth century left off. The line of inexpensive fiction did not quite die when the story paper bit the dust and postal regulations strangled the dime novel at the end of the last century. A number of detective "libraries" bridged the century: the *Old Sleuth Library* went on until 1905, Young and Old King Brady's *Secret Service* library continued until 1912 and Smith and Street's Nick Carter Stories moved from the *Nick Carter Library* (1891-1896) to the *Nick Carter Weekly* (1897-1912) to *Nick Carter Stories* (1912-1915). Some of the old dime novel firms, went under at the end of the nineteenth century, but others got a second wind when they discovered the pulp magazine.

Frank Munsey invented it. Munsey emigrated from Maine to New York city determined to make a dent in the publishing business. In 1882 he launched his new career with a magazine for children, *Golden Argosy, Freighted with Treasures for Boys and Girls*. Running Horatio Alger serials and doing much of the work himself, Munsey kept the magazine afloat, although it often lived on the financial edge. With a successful middle-class magazine, *Munsey's Weekly Magazine,* going, Munsey tinkered with *Golden Argosy* throughout the '80s and '90s: in 1886 he dropped the "children" from the subtitle and, in 1888, he dropped "Golden," making it, in 1896, an all-fiction magazine aimed at adults, principally male adults. Part of the cost-cutting at *Argosy* involved cutting production costs, the switch from coated stock to pulp paper, and a no-frills approach to the contents, no illustrations, no fancy stuff. The transformation of *Argosy* worked: in 1894 the circulation was nine thousand, but after it became an all fiction, pulp magazine, circulation reached 500,000 in 1907 and *Argosy* made a profit of $300,000 a year. Munsey's fiction magazines, printed on pulp paper (colored covers entered the pulp field with Munsey's *All Story*), had considerable impact on American popular fiction. First of all they demonstrated that there was money in popular fiction. Munsey's magazines contributed to the evolution of popular fiction by printing Mary Roberts Rhinehart (*The Circular Staircase* appeared as a serial in *All Story*), O. Henry, serials by Upton Sinclair,

Zane Gray, Edgar Rice Burroughs and others. Munsey's *Argosy* and *All Story* provided the bridge for the detective stories of the last generation until in 1915 Smith and Street followed Munsey's lead and changed *Nick Carter Stories* into a pulp magazine, *Detective Story*, specializing in, what else?

By the early teens the pulp magazine had become a significant force and publishers began to target specific audiences with new pulp magazines. Love pulps began (including two briefly owned by H.L. Mencken); railroad pulps, war pulps, western pulps, sports pulps and science fiction pulps appeared. Although in the '30s and '40s these magazines became synonymous with sensation, sex and the depraved taste of the young and the unsophisticated, in the twenties pulp magazines broke new ground not only in the detective story but also in other genres of literature, popular and otherwise.

By the 1930s enough detective pulps appeared to fill a news stand: *Action Detective, Clues, Greater Gangster Stories, Nickel Detective, Black Aces, Black Book Detective, Double Detective, Triple Detective, Strange Detective, Spicy Detective, Thrilling Detective, Top Notch, Scotland Yard, Detective-Dragnet, Ten Detective Aces, All-Detective, Crime Busters, Pocket Detective, Secret Agent X, The Complete Detective, Popular Detective, Detective Tales, The Shadow, Black Mask, Racketeer Stories* and more. William Nolan in *The Black Mask Boys* lists 178 detective or crime related pulps. Many of them did not last long and few of them broke new ground. In the twenties they sold for five to twenty cents, they came out weekly or bi-monthly and they ran fiction by writers forgotten by history, the likes of Arnold Duncan, Margie Harris, Riley Dillon and Hugh Kahler. *Detective Story Magazine* for November 19, 1921 can serve as an example. The cover art shows two tough-looking coppers, one holding his coat open to flash his badge, confronting a submissive crook who has his hands in the air: it is better than the contents. *Mr. Britlach Breaks the Law* by Hugh MacNair Kahler is advertised on the cover. The magazine runs 144 pages and features "one complete novel," *The Picaroon Discovers Christmas* by Herman Landon; two serials, *Whispering Tongues* by Cecil Bullivant and *Treasure for Scoundrels* by J.B. Harris Burland; and seven short stories: "Mr. Clackworthy's St. Nicholas Company," "Christmas Eve at Doctor Bentiron's," "Thubway Tham's Chrithmath," "Santa's Promise," "Greatest Gifts," "Santa Claus," and "Too Much Evidence." There are four departments, What Handwriting Reveals, Expert Legal Advice (here on the Workmen's Compensation Act), Under The Lamp (on solving ciphers) and Missing (six pages of missing persons ads sent in by subscribers). There are twelve filler items tagged Miscellaneous, including "Use Automobile Horn as Weapon in Bank Robbery" and "Ex-Chief of Secret Service Opens Detective Agency" (the William J. Flynn Detective Agency). Except for an ad for imitation diamond jewelry, the ads here are for correspondence schools, including one offering training in fingerprinting. Aimed at working-class readers the fiction drips with sentiment, especially as this is a Christmas issue, true crime raises chuckles—robbing a store with an automobile horn under your coat!—and the whole issue seems the conception of a mediocre school teacher. Pulps like this one flash us back to the story paper and the fiction of the last decade; indeed Ottolenqui wrote for *Detective Story Magazine* through 1916. Pulps were conceived to make money, not to make literary progress, but a few of them did.

If most of the early pulps were as disposable as the family story papers of the 1870s, some of them did introduce readers to new developments in detective fiction. Pulps, like *Flynn's*, brought English Golden Age writers to the American audience: in the twenties *Flynn's* published R. Austin Freeman, H.C. Bailey, and Edgar Wallace. *Adventure*, according to Robert Sampson in *Yesterday's Faces*, began in 1910 the move toward a male audience and introduced in the character of "Don Everhard" one of the first hard-boiled heroes. But insofar as the American detective story goes, the most important pulp was the *Black Mask*.

H.L. Mencken and George G. Nathan in April, 1920 founded the *Black Mask* as a money machine to supply their tottering "clever" magazine, *The Smart Set*. They had earlier done the same thing with two risque pulps, *Parisienne* and *Saucy Stories*, and now though they would try a detective pulp. In November of the same year Nathan and Mencken, having invested $500 to get the *Black Mask* off the ground, sold the pulp to E. F. Warner and Eugene Crowe for something over $10,000. Originally Ms. F. M. Osborne, the first editor of the *Black Mask*, ran it as a general fiction magazine (its advertised contents changed from "A Magazine of Mystery, Thrills and Surprise" in 1921, to "Romantic Adventure, Mystery and Detective Stories" in 1923, to "Western, Detective and Adventure Stories" in 1927, to "Gripping, Smashing Detective Stories" in 1933). The magazine's subsequent editors, George Sutton, Phillip Cody, Harry C. North and Joseph Shaw, made it a new force in American detective literature. They did this principally by publishing new writers and in shaping their submissions into what became known as the *Black Mask* style. Sutton bought the first stories of Carroll John Daly, Erle Stanley Gardner and Hammett, Cody found Raoul Whitfield and Frederick Nebel and Shaw bagged Chandler, Horace McCoy, Paul Cain, George H. Coxe, Norbert Davis, W.T. Ballard and other notable hard-boiled writers of the thirties. The *Black Mask* introduced American readers to hard-boiled detective stories. By the early thirties, hard-boiled fiction became the thing for pulp magazines. The metamorphosis of *Flynn's* shows this: in the '20s it dealt in English imports, but in 1928 the magazine changed its name to *Detective Fiction Weekly* and numbered among its contributors Chandler, Paul Cain, Carroll John Daly, Frederick Nebel and George H. Coxe. *Dime Detective, Detective Story Magazine, Crime Busters, Top Notch, Detective-Dragnet, 10 Detective Aces,* and *Phantom Detective* all dealt in hard-boiled fiction. Most of the writers of the period, however, felt that the *Black Mask* was the cynosure of hard-boiled fiction.

There are lots of ways of approaching hard-boiled fiction, as a publishing phenomenon, as a literary movement, as a social response, as a philosophical statement, as an approach to language and so on. Considering only the period before World War II, Carroll John Daly and Dashiell Hammett invented the hard-boiled detective story in the early '20s. Especially through the influence of *Black Mask* editors Phil Cody and Joseph Shaw, other writers like Nebel, Whitfield, McCoy and Ballard followed the pattern that Hammett set. At the same time that these writers continued to fill in those things often only implied by Hammett's original vision, others in the thirties developed hard-boiled detective heroes who stress he-man action and attitudes more than the somewhat restrained character of the essential hard-boiled hero and other writers created super detective heroes like the Shadow and Doc Savage who retain only a whisper of their origins. Then in the mid-thirties Chandler began to disassemble and reassemble the hard-boiled story, especially its language, and to establish a model for writers from Ross Macdonald to Robert B. Parker.

In one way, Daly and Hammett did the same thing: they introduced violence into the detective story. Whereas in earlier American detective stories readers saw almost no violence other than either extremely sanitary descriptions of the collision of good and evil or off-stage violence of the crime that drives the fiction, Hammett and Daly made violence a usual part of their experience of crime fiction. Hard-boiled fiction left behind the one-book-one-crime standard of detective fiction and heaped violence upon violence, crime upon crime. *The Red Harvest* perhaps holds the record body count, but even short fiction always contains more than one physical confrontation and frequently contains more than one death: one of Hammett's early pieces was "The Bodies Piled Up" and this gives some indication of the incidence of violence in this kind of story. Hard-boiled fiction, especially in its early days, connects to the shoot-em-up western story (Daly's Race Williams extolls his own quick draw), or, like Hammett's "The Gutting of Couffignal" or "The Big Knockover," it leans toward the war story. Whatever the context, hard-boiled stories deal in lead:

My shot drowned out the racing engine. The white face showed, splotched suddenly crimson...Not a person had heard the shot; not a living being had seen me drop to one knee. Only I knew that a big touring car turned the corner at Sixth Avenue with a dead man in the back; a dead man who still held a Tommy gun. A Tommy gun that was cold; as cold as the fingers that clutched it. (Daly, *Murder from the East*)

A squint-eyed Portuguese slashed at my neck with a knife that spoiled my necktie. I caught him over the ear with the side of my gun before he could get away, saw the ear tear loose. A grinning kid of twenty went down for my legs—football stuff. I felt his teeth in the knee I pumped up, and felt them break. A pock-marked mulatto pushed a gun barrel over the shoulder of the man in front of him. My blackjack crunched the arm of the man in front. He winced sideways as the mulatto pulled the trigger—and had the side of his face blown away. (Hammett, "The Big Knockover")

Violence brought a degree of realism to the detective story, but hyperbole often characterizes hard-boiled violence, it being too frequent and too romantic to be absolutely real. More importantly, it brought danger and excitement to American readers who had hitherto only experienced suspense, and often naive or intellectual or spinsterish suspense at that.

Hard-boiled crimes are not antiseptic crimes committed as an aberration in a community. Not only do the stories contain many crimes, they also portray crimes different from the body in the library type. *The Big Sleep* starts off with pornography and drugs. Bootlegging, confidence games, gambling, dope pushing and extortion appear regularly. Although for the sake of construction, hard-boiled stories center on one reasonably conventional crime problem like murder, during the progress of the plot the hero uncovers crime upon crime, corruption upon corruption. The rottenness of the world comes from its inhabitants. Depraved and corrupt people inhabit both the underworld and the upperworld of hard-boiled fiction. Matter of factly, hard-boiled writers describe the mindless and psychopathic reality of leg-breakers and professional killers; they describe the obscene reality of the rich in the same way. Occasionally hard-boiled fiction strips away the covers and deals with the ultimate sources of corruption: *The Red Harvest* and *The Fast One* show the linkage between crime and politics. Chandler's portrayal of Bay City sums it all up. Bay City's police and Bay City's mayor are controlled by a gangster. Corruption flows up and down the chains of command. And nothing is going to change it, just as nothing can make the gunman human or the rich humane.

Violence and corruption also create the detective hero's character. Hard-boiled writers make a point of breaking apart sentimental codes of behavior and action. Take this:

> I brought down my right hand and pounded the nose of the gun across her forehead. Blood flowed into her eyes...
>
> As for crashing her on the head! Did I have a conscience about that? Don't make me laugh. I know, according to the accepted formula for heroes I should have waved her gun aside, taken her in my arms and kissed the murder out of her eyes. But I didn't. That's why I'm alive to tell it. Any explanation for my brutal act? Sure! She had it coming to her. (Daly, *Murder from the East*)

or this:

> 'Adieu!' she said softly.
> And I put a bullet in the calf of her left leg.
> She sat down—plump! Utter surprise stretched her white face. It was too soon for pain.
> I had never shot a woman before. I felt queer about it.
> 'You ought to have known I'd do it!' my voice sounded harsh and savage and like a stranger's in my ears. 'Didn't I steal a crutch from a cripple?' (Hammett, "The Gutting of Couffignal")

Social convention and civilized behavior too often serve in this world to cover and protect individual and social rot; in his search for the truth the detective needs to follow the truth rather than convention. In a world so full of warped people and values, the hero finds truth in himself. The hard-boiled code of behavior is an unspoken one predicated on fundamental values of which a boy scout could approve: friendship, courage, protection of the weak, truthfulness, perseverance and hard work. The hero knows the extent of sickness in society—politicians, criminals and the leisure class are all the same—but he also knows, as Flynt did at the turn of the century, that reform doesn't work. Preferring isolation to collaboration, the hard-boiled hero lives a minimal life with few possessions and few friends. He is, nonetheless, neither a monk nor a cynic, but a romantic who keeps the faith and who keeps on fighting whether he's going to win or lose the battle.

Take the violence and take the hard-boiled hero away and you can still have a hard-boiled story if you have the style. In essential ways hard-boiled fiction lives on literary style. Hard-boiled style liberated crime fiction in America. First of all, it enabled writers, for the first time really, to convey action and violence to their readers. Pow, you are there with the staccato sentences, fragments of sentences and fresh verbs made out of nouns. Equally important, hard-boiled writing for the first time in American literature uses the language of the streets in a natural and realistic manner. Part of this has to do with working to have characters speak the truth without straining it through a cultivated sieve; part of it has to do with the writers' use of slang which contributes reality and immediacy to their language. Finally, hard-boiled writing adopts the wise-crack and other comic effects and these essentially contribute to the tone of the narrative as well as to the character of the hero.

But crime fiction between the wars was more than the hard-boiled detective story. Naturalistic hard-boiled novels reporting the lives of down-and-outers and criminals made an emphatic appearance. Formal, classic, Golden Age detective writers in this country made, for the first time, a real impact on British fiction. Indeed, an American, John Dickson Carr, was one of the chief voices for the Golden Age of the detective story in Britain. For the first time crime fiction achieved a considerable audience of readers, as well as film goers and radio listeners. The police novel did not prosper during the period mainly because the police of the period did not prosper. With this exception, crime fiction became a truly American form of literature in the years between the wars.

# Chapter 6
# Texts
# 1917-1940

Between the two world wars American crime and detective fiction came into its own. The twenties witnessed a number of innovations that matured in the thirties. Three strands of crime/detective literature emerged during the period.

First, there was the hard-boiled story. Hard-boiled detective fiction merged certain basics of American popular fiction (the western, the adventure story and the semi-fictional literature dealing with crime) with certain elements of detective plotting and the detective character. Often critical of the English or Golden Age school of detective fiction, as witnessed by Joseph Shaw's editorial comments and Chandler's "The Simple Art of Murder," the hard-boiled school of detective writing, nevertheless, shared some traditional detective story devices with Golden Age writing. Hard-boiled writing, however, also developed, for lack of a better term, a sociological side that omitted consideration of the romantic detective hero and in the hands of James M. Cain, Horace McCoy, Edward Anderson, and others concentrated on the realistic depiction of the lives of losers and criminals, producing some of the bleakest portraits in American literature. At the same time, the English Golden Age came to this country. American writers of the Golden Age, often less secure about their culture and intellect than European writers, split the detective story and its readers into opposing camps (hard-boiled and classical, liberal and conservative, proletarian and elitist) in spite of the best efforts of the most outstanding writers.

*Boston Blackie* by Jack Boyle, 1919.

Forward: the author tells of meeting a man caring for orphaned children in Golden Gate Park after the San Francisco earthquake. "This was my first meeting with the stranger but, to me, wonderfully human character I have tried to picture..." hidden under the made-up name of Boston Blackie. "To the police...he is a professional crook, a skilled and daring safecracker, an incorrigible criminal made doubly dangerous by intellect." But the author sees him in another light: "university graduate, scholar and gentleman, the 'Blackie' I know is a man of many inconsistencies and a strangely twisted code of morals—a code he guards from violation as a zealot guards his religion."

Boston Blackie's Little Pal: in the act of burgling the Wilmerding jewels, Blackie is interrupted by a small boy searching for his stuffed animal. Blackie comforts the boy and takes him back to his bed. The boy's mother then returns from a dance with an admirer who implores her to desert her husband for him. She finally agrees to elope and sends the family's jewels off with him. Blackie intercepts the lover, robs him of the jewels and scares him off. He then sends telegrams to both wife and absent husband that bring the family together again.

The Cushions Kid: the Cushions Kid, refusing to squeal on his accomplices, is sentenced to hang. His girl, Happy, has tried everything and at last turns to Blackie. Blackie travels to Folsom Prison and, with the help of inmates, arranges for the Kid's escape. One of the inmates, though, turns traitor and the guards thwart the escape. A gambler in town notifies the prison authorities of Blackie's presence in town, but he escapes with the aid of the gambler's former girl, Rita. Blackie appeals to a political boss to get a commutation for the Kid, but fails. He returns to Happy and Mary, his wife, with the sad news, but Rita has used her wiles on the political boss to get the Kid's commutation.

Fred the Count: Fred, the convict who squealed about the attempt to free the Cushions Kid from Folsom, leaves prison with time off for spying on his fellows. Blackie and his gang keep watch on Fred as he resumes his old trade of preying on rich women. They follow him to the Northwest where Fred prepares to bamboozle a lumber baron and his daughter. As Fred prepares to scoot with a $10,000 check, Blackie robs the local bank and leaves Fred handcuffed to a drugged guard. Fred is returned to Folsom to face the wrath of the inmates whom he had so often betrayed.

Clancy's Gold: To even the score with Clancy who had caused Mary's father to be unjustly imprisoned, Blackie and Mary determine to rob the gold that James J. Clancy is sending from Alaska to Seattle by sea. Mary flirts with the purser and takes an impression of the ship's vault's keys. Blackie enters the vault and transfers gold to Mary's trunk. Another gang makes a try to open the vault but this is foiled. Leaving the ship in Seattle, the other crooks are arrested, but Blackie, with the help of Mary and a group of girls, smuggles the booty off of the ship. Detective Rentor, although he knows that he is innocent, arrests the purser, third-degrees him and suborns perjury to frame him. Mary arranges, through a sympathetic lawyer, to return the gold if the innocent man is released.

Alibi Ann: Alibi Ann, a clever and experienced jewel thief, falls in love with the Glad-rags Kid, a worthless fop. Ann tries to make a home for the Kid, but his actions become more flamboyant and egotistical. The Kid shoots a man in a nightclub and the prosecutor determines to hang him. Blackie arranges an escape but the Kid's bragging thwarts it. Ann then makes a deal to save the Kid's life, turning herself in and accepting a twenty-year prison term. In their only meeting before she leaves for prison the Kid spurns her.

Prison: Mit-and-a-half Kelly cracks a safe but shoots a policeman in his escape. Blackie helps him get away but is falsely arrested as one of Kelly's gang. The police withhold evidence and Blackie is sentenced to fifteen years. In prison Blackie organizes an effective strike against cruel punishment and rotten food. But the Deputy Warden, Martin Sherwood, has it in for him. He cuts off Mary's visiting rights and Blackie, enraged at the guard's insinuations about his wife, attacks him. Sherwood subjects Blackie to cruel punishment. Blackie then executes a daring and original escape from prison. When Sherwood tracks him down, Blackie gets the drop on him but cannot shoot the defenseless man. He offers a duel, but Sherwood refuses. Blackie cannot take Sherwood's life and offers to return to prison. Sherwood sets him free and they part with mutual admiration: "He is a man even though he's a copper;" "He is a man even though he's a convict."

Boyle's Boston Blackie stories originally appeared in *Redbook*. He wrote a few transitions for the stories when they appeared as the book *Boston Blackie*, but this is in no sense a novel.

*Boston Blackie* depends in small part on the tradition of E.W. Hornung's gentleman crook, Raffles. American versions of Raffles, like O. Henry's Jimmy Valentine, however, are far more moral and sentimental than Hornung's aesthete burglar. The Boston Blackie pieces drip with sentiment and sentimentality. Part of this is standard Victorianism: reveries about the innocence of children, ecstasies about the loyalty and self-sacrifice of women and yearning for home and hearth. Part of this, though, comes from the sentimentalizing the underworld. Boyle portrays the honor and loyalty among thieves and convicts as well as the righteous revenge for wrongs suffered in order to evoke more sentiment than sympathy.

Boston Blackie is not much in the way of a fully developed character. Readers know very little about him. We know about his general appearance, but that is about all. He is not the central character in any but the last story. Rather, Blackie exists more in the line of a moral force. We know what we do about him because of his relations with people around him. He is, surely, an underworld leader, and this role drives several of the stories. Occasionally Boyle shows Blackie in the role of the brains behind a well-organized crime, as in the theft of Clancy's gold, but in most cases his underworld associates turn to Blackie for help: Happy comes to him to do something about the Cushions Kid, Alibi Ann seeks out Blackie for domestic advice and the whole gang turns to Blackie for leadership in the affair of Fred the Count. Rather than a person, Boyle represents Blackie as the personification of a code of behavior, a code which is only in part the criminal's code.

Boyle knew Flynt and Walton's *The Powers That Prey*; he alludes to it in *Boston Blackie*, and some of this book needs to be seen as an extension of the earlier book. Boyle pictures the subjugation of the police to political pressure:

Chief Rentor spat out the mutilated remnant of his cigar and eyed his phone speculatively and with growing gravity. Over it but a moment before he had been told by James J. Clancy, aged and irascible president of the Northwestern Steamship Company, that unless the *Humbolt's* mysteriously missing gold was recovered, the resultant police shake-up would jar loose the gold star on the breast of Rentor's uniform.

So Rentor does what he has to do: the next two chapters are "The Frame-Up," and "The Third Degree." He also speaks to the inevitable issue of graft: Rentor "is getting rich on the graft he is collecting from gambling houses and red light dens." Boyle, having been inside, renders prison brutality far more vividly than Flynt and Walton could have. Here is part of his description of the use of straight jackets on recalcitrant prisoners:

Fully tightened, the jacket shuts off circulation throughout the body almost completely. For the first five minutes, oppressed breathing is the only inconvenience felt. Then the strangulating blood commences to cause the most excruciating torture—a thousand pains as if white-hot needles are being passed through the flesh run through the body. The feet and limbs swell and turn black. Irresistible weights seem to be crushing the brain.

Yet there is not too much bitterness about policemen, even corrupt ones, and there is even some admiration in the last piece for Martin Sherwood's courage and integrity: "he is a man even though he's a copper." The upper world, by and large, has ravenous attitudes toward those in the underworld, demanding harsh sentences and allowing a brutal treatment. At the same time, the morals of the upper world leave much to be desired. Were it not for Blackie's intervention, the husband and wife in the first story would continue in loveless isolation and the Clancys of the world, who consider "the world well rid" of the harmless and innocent poor, would continue unpunished.

Boyle only gives us glimpses of the upper world: *Boston Blackie* dwells on details of life in the underworld. He gives some snatches of their speech ("jack" is money, "stiff" a letter and so on) as well as some detail on prison life, like prisoners' silent speech. For Boyle the underworld is a mixed bag. There are plenty of paragons in the underworld; other than Blackie, Boyle chiefly emphasizes women (Mary, Happy, Rita and Alibi Ann) and convicts. But there are some real rotters too: Fred the Count and the Glad-rags kid. The bad ones seek ease and flashy living and willingly use others to possess these things, which, of course, cause their downfall. The good folk in the underworld are modest and controlled and they follow the code. Chapter Two is entitled "Boston Blackie's Code." The code is fairly simple. "Do not snitch" ranks high and so do "help your pals" and "don't complain." These precepts, in fact, embody most of the code, but as Boyle sees it they are more than simply the criminal's code. They ramify in a number of directions all of which have some connection not with do-nots, but with identity, commitment and self-sacrifice.

The Boston Blackie stories point in several directions. They point back to the English gentleman crook tradition and to the sappiest kind of Victorian sentimentalism. At the same time they serve as a connection for *The Powers That Prey* to the hard-boiled, realistic portrait of criminals and police officers. Blackie also demonstrates an internalized code of behavior which transcends one's occupation as a cop or a crook. The movies got a hold of Blackie and emphasized all of the older elements that Boyle had used to make his fiction. Hard-boiled writers fastened on to something else.

*Murder from the East* by Carroll John Daly, 1935.

Race Williams receives $1000 and instructions to appear at the information booth in Grand Central Station carrying a book in each hand. Pocketing the grand, he goes, but when an assassin tries to shoot him he shoots him first, having hidden a pistol in one of the hollowed-out books. Next, Race's professional rival, Gregory Ford, tries to hire him to work on a government case; Race refuses until he is taken to see the General who unfolds for him the plot of the country of "Astran" to undermine the United States. Through its agents, Count Jedho and Mark Yarrow, this evil eastern empire has been kidnapping family members of government employees for the ransom of government secrets, torturing the victims to death when the secrets are not forthcoming. Among the kidnap victims is the General's daughter. This hooks Race into the action. With information from the "Number 7 Man," a spy in the enemy's camp, Race sets about rescuing the General's daughter only to find out that the Flame—his old acquaintance Florence Drummond—has married Count Jedho. When Race botches the rescue, an unknown person saves him and enables him to rescue Betty. Mark Yarrow, at this point, is worked up about Williams' interference and threatens him with death on a given date. Meanwhile, Race goes to the assistance of a Senator whom the evil empire is blackmailing in order to obtain secret aircraft plans. At a posh dinner party, Race prevents one attempt on the plans and two attempts on his life. The Senator's daughter, however, takes the plans and bounces off to Mark Yarrow in order to save her father's reputation. On a yacht in the Hudson, Race saves the plans, saves the Senator's daughter and saves the Flame, who has been exposed as the "Number 7 Man," from torture and death. In this outing Race kills Mark Yarrow but still has to deal with the Count and his country's evil plans. The Count kidnaps the Senator's daughter and the Flame discovers the existence of his "Yellow Book," containing the names of all of the foreign agents in the United States and Panama. Race steals the Yellow book, but Jedho has wised up and knows that the Flame is the Number 7 Man. He threatens her with torture and death but seems willing to do a swap for the return of the Yellow book. Race goes along with this, but the Count goes back on his word and is about to murder both Race and the Flame. Race then reveals that his assistant, Jerry, holds the Count's niece as surety for their release. Jedho starts to free them but one of his servants, loyal

to the homeland, kills the Count and has a go at Race and the Flame.
Race blasts him, saves the Flame and the whole darned country.
*Murder from the East* appeared in serial form in the *Black Mask* from May
to August, 1934.

Carroll John Daly is a gift to literary historians and critics: everything
that he did is so definitive and obvious that one can simply cite dates and
titles and then quote passages from the book of Race. Unless one chooses
to follow one of the -isms of literary criticism, discussing Carroll John Daly
is about as difficult as dynamite fishing.

Daly wrote the first hard-boiled story, "The False Burton Combs" which
appeared in The *Black Mask* in December 1922, and he invented the hard-
boiled detective in "It's All in the Game" (*Black Mask*, April 23, 1923) and
in "Three Gun Terry Mack" (*Black Mask*, May, 1923). His *The Snarl of
the Beast* of 1927 was the first hard-boiled detective novel. He was the first
and one of the worst of the hard-boiled writers, but if he didn't exist someone,
probably Mickey Spillane, would have to invent him.

Daly established the voice of the hard-boiled story. First came the voice
of his narrators: most of his heroes, Race Williams, Three Gun Terry, and
so on, recount their own adventures. Although later hard-boiled writers turned
first person narration to other uses, for Daly it primarily gave his characters
repeated opportunities to establish themselves, and to justify their own acts
and attitudes. Although they may technically be confessional narratives,
Daly's fictions are more in the nature of advertisements or boasts. Further,
he does not simply tell a tale for his readers' excitement or enjoyment, but
frequently turns to comment directly to the readers, repeatedly referring to
"you" the reader. Daly's heroes give a running personal and social
commentary on the specifics of the action. This is one of the reasons that
they are so quotable:

I do a little honest shooting once in a while—just in the way of business. But my
conscience is clear; I never bumped off a guy that didn't need it. "Knights of the Open
Palm" (1923)

Right and wrong are not written in the statutes for me, nor do I find my code of
morals in the essays of long-winded professors. My ethics are my own. I'm not saying
they're good and I'm not admitting that they're bad, and what's more, I'm not interested
in the opinions of others on the subject. *Snarl of the Beast*, (1927)

I must admit that I'm strong for a little loose shooting against loose thinkers. There
may be laws of the state or of the government that aren't so good, but the laws of God
and man can't be improved upon. Them that live by the gun should die by the gun,
is good sound twentieth century gospel. *Snarl of the Beast*, (1927)

In addition to the vigor Daly achieves by using first person narration, his
use of ungrammatical expressions, concrete terms and slang ("I had picked
Jerry up in the underworld and his jargon, if inelegant, was expressive"
*The Tag Murders*, 1930) made a rudimentary pattern for later hard-boiled
writers to complete and polish.

Daly's second contribution to the American detective story was in establishing a number of conventions which became part of the private eye genre:

The hero begins with a voracious attitude toward money, but this disappears once the action begins.

The hero exists between law and outlaw: Daly repeats "I'm just a halfway house between the law and crime; sort of working both ends against the middle" in a number of stories.

The hero's absorption in his profession and himself gives him not only self-confidence but also casual attitudes toward other areas of life, dress, living conditions, food, and so on.

The hero is an emphatically lower class individual, uncomfortable or hostile to upper class speech, culture and etiquette.

The hero disregards accepted decorum associated with age, rank or sex.

The hero maintains attitudes of aloofness and selfishness but is essentially committed to larger values, friendship, love, honor and patriotism.

The hero lives in the present, the past having little meaning and the future offering only despair ("Better to die now than forty years from now, with pains in the stomach" *Snarl of the Beast*).

The hero's actions are competent whereas corporate action by the police is not.

The hero's violence (Daly goes through various permutations of "You can't make ketchup without busting up a few tomatoes") is real but different in kind from that of the villains.

In creating these and other attributes for his heroes, Daly allows no gradations or subtlety: aggressiveness in self-assertion and aggression when facing a problem mark them. His heroes are men of action, and Daly consistently not only has them assert this ("When I hesitate things get mixed up. I'm a man of action—not a man of deductions and thoughts and reasonings" [*The Hidden Hand*, 1929]) but he contrasts them to flabby detectives like Gregory Ford who use what passes for their brains.

Race Williams and Three Gun Terry and all of the rest are the way they are because of opposition, because of the criminals. Daly draws almost all of his criminals as sub-human. There are constant animal or monster references: in *Murder from the East* Mark Yarrow seems to have pointed teeth that have been filed down, the Beast in *Snarl of the Beast* actually snarls, and the gangster family in *The Third Murderer* is named the gorgons, after monsters of myth. Worse still they are foreigners:

Dr. Michelle Gorgon was just a wop, just a human, physical, rotten bit of life he controlled and stood above. (*The Third Murderer*)

All three with something the same in their faces; something the same in their blood. And I knew. Eurasians, all of them. The deadly mixed blood of the European and the Asiatic. (*Murder from the East*)

The Palmer Raids and the xenophobia of the twenties formed almost all of Daly's attitudes and color both hero and villain. Separating hero and villain so graphically from one another puts Daly outside the principal traditions of detective fiction which either hides corruption or taints all characters with it. Additionally Daly catches himself up in something of a paradox: his criminals are all contemptible, rotten, sadistic, cowardly but at the same time hugely powerful, organized and awe inspiring. That's what one gets when crossing hard-boiled story, which deals in real crime and criminals, with the master criminal thriller, which deals in Napoleons of Crime.

It is difficult to speak of Daly's most conspicuous failure, but aesthetically his largest failure was fusing a new American hero with Old World plot. Daly repeated the same character, often using patches of the same dialogue, through a bundle of short stories and sixteen pieces of book length fiction. They are all the same: Race or Terry Mack or another hero shoots his way into and then out of a problem that ordinary people and organizations cannot solve. The novels are all thrillers built on the formula of the super hero versus the super villain. The hero must master situations of increasing menace and danger until he confronts the Giant of Evil who has managed to dupe or intimidate or beat everyone else. Daly uses Buchan and Sapper and Edgar Wallace as his models for action and atmosphere—the gothic accoutrements of hooded criminals, secret passages, torture appliances and so forth.

Daly, therefore, combined the variety of fantasy developing in England, in the form of the thriller, with a new kind of fantasy, that of the hard-boiled detective. Real crime, real criminals, real action and real people have no place in his fiction. Tapping the fantasy of power is not unusual in popular fiction; most genres do it in one way or another. Daly wrote at one of the times that Americans felt particularly helpless when faced with the problems of both criminals and police, and he wrote after America had flexed its military muscle in the international ring of World War I. Considering this, it is no surprise that he brought his own particular fantasies of power to the detective story. As I said above, if there were no Daly it would be necessary for Mickey Spillane to invent him and it would also be necessary for Hammett and Chandler to invent him to be reinvented.

### *The Red Harvest* by Dashiell Hammett, 1929

The plot is well-known, so let's be brief. Donald Willsson, a reform-minded journalist, summons the Continental Op to Personville, but is murdered before they can meet. The Op discovers that Personville is the totally corrupt city. Willsson's father, Elihu, called in gangsters to break a strike at his mining company and the gangsters not only broke the strike but took the town over. Peter the Finn, a bootlegger, Lew Yard, a loan shark and receiver of stolen goods, Whisper Thayler, a gambler, and Noonan, the chief of police, run the town. The Op puts pressure on Elihu until the old man unwillingly hires the Continental Detective Agency to clean up the town. While cleaning up Personville, the Op solves several discrete crimes: he pins the murder of Donald Willsson on Albury, he unravels Tim Noonan's last words to prove MacShane guilty of his death, and he cops Reno for ice picking Dinah Brand. In each case the Op points out an unsuspected culprit. Woven in and around these murder cases is the purging of Personville. The Op achieves this by setting the gangsters against one another. Through false information and several varieties of dirty tricks, the Op stirs up trouble. He sets Noonan against Thayler, Noonan against Pete the Finn, Reno against Lew Yard and so on. They shoot at one another's persons and property until they are all gone. Speeding cars, machine guns, riot guns, automatics, knives, ice picks, bootleg liquor, laudanum and fast women: *The Red Harvest* is the detective novel of the twenties. Andre Gide, in 1943 wrote in his *Journals*:

> Read with very keen interest (and why not dare to say admiration) *The Maltese Falcon*, by Dashiell Hammett, by whom I had already read last summer, but in translation, the amazing *Red Harvest*, far superior to the *Falcon*, to *The Thin Man*, and to a fourth novel, obviously written on order, the title of which escapes me. In English, or at least in American, many subtleties of the dialogue escape me, but in *The Red Harvest* the dialogues, written in a masterful way, are such as to give pointers to Hemingway or even to Faulkner, and the entire narrative is ordered with skill and implacable cynicism. In that very special type of thing it is, I believe, it is the most remarkable I have read.

Gide here is off about many of the particulars, but he is right in feeling that nothing quite like *The Red Harvest* had ever been written.

*The Red Harvest* appeared first in the *Black Mask* beginning in November, 1927. It was Hammett's first novel and it illustrates in many ways Hammett's accomplishments as one of the founders of the hard-boiled school of detective fiction.

Hammett began writing at almost the same time as Carroll John Daly: his first *Black Mask* piece was "The Road Home" (December, 1922), and his first Continental Op story was "Arson Plus" (October, 1923). Indeed, *Black Mask* editors Cody and Shaw did their best to Hammettize their pulp magazine. In some ways Hammett did the same things as Daly. He wrote about a tough private detective, his stories emphasize violence and movement and he introduces dialogue appropriate to his characters—American English peppered with slang, police and criminal jargon and wisecracks. Hammett, however, is a very different kind of writer from Daly. His experiences as a Pinkerton detective made him different, made his fiction more authentic. More importantly, though, Hammett developed. Throughout the twenties he worked on the style and substance of his fiction, making it increasingly better. Additionally, Hammett matured in the twenties not only as a writer but also as a thinker. As Gide read Hammett he matured until *The Maltese Falcon*, and this may be correct.

Although Hammett's detective character, the Continental Op, participates in some of the same conventions as Daly's Race Williams, he is also a substantially different kind of character. For one thing the Op is not a lone wolf private eye: he is an employee of the Continental Detective Agency. This means several things. It means, first of all, that the Op perceives detecting as work deserving devotion and dignity: he, therefore, tells Elihu "If you've got a fairly honest piece of work to be done in my line, and you want to pay a decent price, maybe I'll take it on." By and large, in the short stories leading up to *The Red Harvest*, the Op is a competent and loyal employee. His work and his employer mean something to him. The Op may complain about The Old Man, the agency executive, but he is not overly insubordinate. The same thing holds true for *The Red Harvest*: here the Op insists on a contract with Elihu Willsson, he is parsimonious with the agency's expense money and even at the end of the novel, after having broken many of the agency's rules, the Op returns to catch "merry hell" from the old man rather than quitting or just walking away. Further, in the short stories the Op, much in the manner of contemporary Pinkertons, works with the police, who are often competent and effective individuals. Not so with Race Williams. The Op also is no matinee idol—he's short, fat and forty. He is a veteran detective, wise in ways of crime and the world. At the same time he can be as tough and violent as the younger Race Williams. The Op is ready and able to use his gun, sap, fists, feet and teeth if necessary. Hammett presents the hard-boiled detective in a more realistic context and as a more realistic person.

Hammett's realism, though, goes deeper than simply making his hero fat and forty. We know that he built many of his subordinate characters on details he observed in people during his Pinkerton days. But this is the kind of realism that we expect of any writer. The singular aspect of Hammett's realism lies in his description of the milieu in *The Red Harvest*. Here he describes Personville/Poisonville/the generalized American city as no earlier detective or crime writer had:

> The first policeman I saw needed a shave. The second had a couple of buttons off his shabby uniform. The third stood in the center of the city's main intersection—Broadway and Union Street—with a cigar in one corner of his mouth. After that I stopped checking them up.

In *The Red Harvest* Hammett mixes an action plot (the Op cleaning out the bad guys) with several classically plotted mysteries (who killed Donald Willsson) and sets them in a place that verifies the details revealed in the Lexow and Andrews Reports. The police are for sale to the highest bidder (policemen help Whisper escape from Chief Noonan's raid and whisk him away in an official car), they are violent (Chief Noonan sends MacSwain downstairs in the station to the "wrecking crew") and they are incompetent. The gangsters, bootleggers and gamblers, run the town using the police or their own private armies of gunmen. This state of affairs has evolved after Old Elihu, the capitalist, lost control of the town. Nowhere in *The Red Harvest* does Hammett mention such a thing as a mayor or a city council; Dinah Brand keeps trying to sell the Op information about how much money Elihu and the gangsters made on the construction of City Hall, but the Op again and again refuses her. Politicians and politics are an irrelevance in a town run by money and guns. *The Red Harvest* in some ways is *The Shame of the Cities* brought to the detective story, and after Hammett's novel the decayed city became a given for all hard-boiled writers who set their aim above the belt.

In addition to making the city a vital part of hard-boiled fiction, Hammett contributed to elevating the hard-boiled school by altering the sensibility of the detective hero. Race Williams tirelessly talks to the readers and to the inhabitants of Daly's fictional world about himself, his values and his abilities. He is not reticent about anything. Hammett's detectives are reticent: they don't talk to strangers and they hardly talk to friends. In *The Red Harvest* when Mrs. Willsson tries a bit of conversation on the Op he hardly replies to her, telling us at one point "I let her get whatever she could out of a grin." Near the end of the novel, Mickey Linehan sarcastically tells the Op that "You're going to ruin yourself sometime telling people too much." As a matter of course, Hammett's heroes don't talk much, and they only talk about their values in intense rhetorical outbursts, usually near the end of the narrative. Part of this comes from the laconic speech of the cowboy in the background of the hard-boiled fiction. Part of it, if you are inclined that way, can be blamed on ingrained American attitudes about how and when men talk: real men don't brag, don't whine and don't chatter about things that can't be or don't need embellishment. This is the hard-boiled part. But the detective part is just as important; keeping one's opinions to oneself is the bed-rock of the detective's trade.

Their restrained speech is only one difference between the sensibilities of Hammett's heroes and Daly's. Attitudes toward violence also set them apart. Throughout the twenties Hammett showed different phases of the Op's attitude toward violence. There are places in which the Op approaches violence with a certain relish:

'Hurry!' he panted again as he left me to run upstairs, while I went back to my hiding place and hefted the lead pipe, wondering if Flora had shot me and I was now enjoying the rewards of my virtue—in a heaven where I could enjoy myself forever and ever socking folks who had been rough with me down below. ("The Big Knockover," 1927)

In other places Hammett emphasizes the Op's experience with violence as a routine part of the detective profession:

Anyway, a row was coming. Ordinarily I am inclined to peace. The day is past when I'll fight for the fun of it. But I've been in too many rumpuses to mind them much. ("The Whosis Kid," 1925)

Most significantly, however, Hammett in *The Red Harvest* develops in his hero a consciousness of what obsessive violence can do to people:

'To show you how my mind's running. A couple of days ago, if I thought about it at all, it [the ice pick] was as a good tool to pry off chunks of ice.' I ran a finger down its half-foot of round steel blade to the needle point. 'Not a bad thing to pin a man to his clothes with. That's the way I'm getting, on the level. I can't even see a mechanical cigar lighter without thinking of filling one with nitroglycerine for somebody you don't like. There's a piece of copper wire lying in the gutter in front of your house—thin, soft, and just long enough to go around a neck with two ends to hold on. I had one hell of a time to keep from picking it up and stuffing it in my pocket, just in case—

'You're crazy.'
'I know it. That's what I've been telling you. I'm going blood-simple.'

Here the Op gains a degree of, shall we say, maturity; he realizes the effects of violence on others and on himself, but he does not lay down his gun and walk away—and he does not go blood simple.

He does not go blood simple because he sees people, even criminals, as more than targets. As central to *The Red Harvest* as the Flitcraft parable is to *The Maltese Falcon* is the Op's visit to Myrtle Jennison in the hospital:

'What do I care what anybody does now? I'm done. Hell with them all!' She sniggered and suddenly threw the bedclothes down to her knees, showing me a horrible swollen body in a coarse white nightgown. 'How do you like me? See, I'm done.'

This experience, along with his watching Reno die, gives the Op knowledge that a finder of facts or a gunman can never possess. The Op certainly does his job as a detective, finding information, making arrests, shooting people, but it does not diminish his compassion. When he arrests Albury for Donald Willsson's murder,

On the way down to the City Hall with the boy and the gun I apologized for the village cut-up stuff I had put in the early part of the shake down...

Likewise, when he takes MacShane back to jail the Op does not tell Noonan that MacShane killed his brother, thereby saving MacShane's life. As the events in Personville drain the police chief, the Op expresses some compassion for Noonan—someone whom he had formerly seen only as a corrupt slob. Most significantly, when Dinah Brand slugs Dan Rolf, the Op knocks Rolf to the ground to give the man back a shred of dignity:

So I poked him to give him back some of his self-respect. You know, treated him as I would a man instead of a down-and-outer who could be slapped around by girls.

When the Op needs to be a detective he is, but this does not extinguish his humanity. It does not, to use Hammett's metaphor, completely form a shell around the Op's soul. Nor does the Op's humanity rob him of the capacity for decisive action, make him a wimp. Here Hammett creates humane insights, instincts and impulses for the Op rather than conscious ideals, romantic or otherwise. Honesty, respect for others' dignity and doing one's job rank high on the Op's list of values. In *The Red Harvest* the Op experiences betrayal (Elihu's attempts to cancel his contract) and separation from his Continental colleagues in Personville: these presage the betrayal and isolation in later hard-boiled works. Here, however, the hero accepts these things as part of his world and survives not with cynicism, as Gide would have it, but with balance, flexibility and maturity. Hammett, nevertheless, makes the Op know that neither he nor his values can survive without conniving and violence.

*The Red Harvest* does things that no detective tale had ever done. It reflects with some accuracy its culture, and it presents a character whose nature is made not only interesting but complex and significant because of his profession as a detective.

*The "Canary" Murder Case* by S.S. Van Dine, 1928.

Philo Vance and John Markham, New York District Attorney, meet at the Stuyvesant Club and discuss detection, with Vance maintaining that the legal mind and material evidence hinder crime solving and that what Markham condescendingly calls "psychological theories and aesthetic hypotheses" can do the trick. Markham vows to put Vance to the test of a real crime. Hot upon this, news hits of the murder of Margaret Odell, an ex-showgirl known as "the Canary." Vance, Van Dine (the narrator) and Markham go to the scene of the crime and meet Sergeant Heath. The Canary's apartment yields all the signs of a burglary or murder. Gradually Markham and Heath unearth four of the The Canary's suitors, one of whom was, admittedly, her escort for the evening. All four of the middle-aged swains have alibis, but all of them have a motive for doing away with Margaret Odell, who was blackmailing them. Sergeant Heath, convinced from the beginning that a burglar committed the murder, arrests Tony Skeel, a gentleman of that profession who left fingerprints in Odell's apartment; Markham, however, has insufficient evidence to hold him and lets him go. Meanwhile, the alibis of the four suspects begin to unravel; not only do they unravel but it turns out that all four of the men were in the vicinity of the apartment on the night of the murder. Sergeant Heath then discovers that one of the apartment building's telephone operators is an ex-convict and arrests him for the murder. But at this point Skeel, the burglar, calls Markham and tells him that he will name the murderer the next day, but this is too bad since he's strangled before Markham, Vance and company get a chance to see him. Vance then demonstrates how, by fiddling the outside door, it would be possible for almost anybody to enter Odell's apartment unobserved. Now the investigators have two murders, but one of the four suspects gets off the hook by being in the hospital the night of the second murder. With no real inkling of which of the three to tag, Vance arranges a poker game with the suspects. He introduces a card-sharp into the game to fix a couple of hands so that he can observe the suspects' play. From this Vance determines that one of them is the culprit and tells Markham, who is not convinced. Vance and Markham return to Odell's apartment for another look and Vance discovers that the record on the record player is a fake, that it is a specifically made record of a man's falsetto voice intended to give the illusion that The Canary was speaking through the door of the apartment when she, in fact, was dead. Markham and Vance go to the criminal's club, he confesses and then Vance arranges it so that he can commit suicide.

*The "Canary" Murder Case* was the second detective novel (the first was *The "Benson" Murder Case* of 1926) by W. H. Wright who reputedly adopted the pseudonym, S.S. Van Dine, so as to avoid the obloquy of being known as a detective novelist. Van Dine was America's first real Golden Age detective writer. The British had been doing the same thing for a few years: Christie's first book was in 1920 and Sayers' was in 1923. Indeed, Sayers' Lord Peter Wimsey and Christie's *The Murder of Roger Ackroyd* (1926 U.S.) have much to do with *The "Canary" Murder Case*, the one providing some of Vance's character and the other suggesting the record player as a means of providing an alibi.

In its structure this, and all of Van Dine's other books, follows what was the typical Golden Age pattern: the scene of the crime, the initial line-up of suspects, the peeling away of alibi and motive, the complication, the collection of final proof for the surprise solution, the confrontation and finally the explanation. In Van Dine there is the expected pattern from one stage to the next, but as this is one of his early novels there is not yet the kind of tired and predictable bump between sections that caused even mystery writers to comment on the predictability of his plotting. *The "Canary" Murder Case* includes, at the beginning, a list of "Characters of the Book," as well as two architectural plans of Odell's apartment and a drawing of the trick used to bolt the door. In spite of having some of the apparatus of the logic-oriented puzzle story, Van Dine does not yet single out reason and logic as the principal theme of the hero and the main justification for the reader. Indeed, although Van Dine uses the metaphor of the puzzle to describe the crime-solvers' dilemma, Philo Vance here alludes a number of times to coming upon bits of the solution by inspiration. " 'That's the terrible thing about logic,' said Vance. 'It so often leads one irresistibly to a false conclusion.' " Van Dine had not yet moved into the sort of emphasis on reason that makes him include a list of 97 points for readers to wrestle with in *The Greene Murder Case*.

On one hand *The "Canary" Murder Case* attempts to be criminologically real. Van Dine intends the introduction and includes footnotes simply to add verisimilitude. Here is the note on page 7:

> The Loeb-Leopold crime, the Dorothy King case, and the Hall-Mills murder came later; but the Canary murder proved fully as conspicuous a case as the Nan Patterson-"Caesar" Young affair, Durant's murder of Blanche Lamont and Minnie Williams in San Francisco, the Molineux arsenic-poisoning case, and the Carlyle Harris morphine murder. To find a parallel in point of public interest one must recall the Borden double murder in Fall River, the Thaw case, the shooting of Elwell, and the Rosenthal murder.

As a detective Philo Vance shows a second stage of the impact of modern criminology on fiction. Writers like Arthur B. Reeve popularized scientific discoveries that helped read a criminal's actions from the scene of the crime. Van Dine assumes not only that his readers know about things like fingerprints, but that criminals do as well. He concentrates, therefore, on modern analysis of the criminal's nature. Vance cites Lombroso's work (with its Italian title, of course) and he alludes to Freud a couple of times. Throughout the novel Markham twits Vance on his dedication to psychology, but in the end Van Dine uses the poker game to demonstrate the efficacy of the science: he even provides a footnote reference to an article by Dr. George Dorsey which says "I have studied humanity all my life from the anthropomorphic and psychological point of view. And I have yet to find a better laboratory [than a poker game]..." Sporadically throughout the novel Vance cavalierly tosses off bits of what Van Dine naively thought were scientific psychological observations. Take this groaner:

'Really, y' know, Markham, old thing,' he added, 'you should study the cranial indications of your fellow man more carefully—*vultus est index animi*. Did you, by any chance, note the gentleman's wide rectangular forehead, his irregular eyebrows, and pale luminous eyes, and his outstanding ears with their thin upper rims, their pointed tragi and split lobes?...[sic] A clever devil this Ambrose—but a moral imbecile. Beware of these pseudo-pyriform faces, Markham...'

In charity to Van Dine, in *The "Canary" Murder Case* he chose material that in 1928 he could not treat: the crux of the matter here is that Margaret Odell is a society tart and the four suspects are her sex-besotted middle-aged victims. In 1928 this was a subject that could not be dealt with with candor.

Partly because he couldn't really use psychology and partly because Van Dine wants more semi-relevant talk, Vance also uses the techniques of the art critic to help him solve the case. In analyzing the scene of the crime, Vance gives Markham a lecture on the difference between an original painting and a copy, scattering references to Botticelli and Rubens: the original shows elan while the copy shows mechanical perfection. There is this, and there is also the fact that the final solution to the case does, in fact, turn on the discovery of material evidence—the phonograph record which provided the illusion that Odell was alive when she wasn't. But it doesn't matter so much here, for in *The "Canary" Murder Case* Van Dine had not yet taken up the cause of detective fiction as reason and he still wanted to provide other kinds of literary fulfillment.

It is difficult to say for sure whether Van Dine intended Philo Vance as a joke or not. I suspect that he did and he didn't. Vance pretty clearly draws on Sayers' Wimsey: he's a sort of American aristocrat with lots of money and leisure; he has cultivated taste, especially when it comes to art, and flawless manners; he has an extensive education; he seems indolent but is capable of great energy; and he talks funny. Van Dine constructed Vance's speech out of Britishisms, dropping letters from words, flinging in foreign words and phrases, as well as literary quotations and, most especially, filling his diction with excruciatingly erudite and obscure words. In the early books, like this one, I suspect that Van Dine did this for the fun of it, but this is hard to say since he does not display much instinct for comic writing.

If Philo Vance was amusing in the beginning, as the books rolled on this became merely pedantic and Ogden Nash echoed informed opinion when he wrote that "Philo Vance needs a kick in the pance." Van Dine also intended Vance's bantering relationships with Sergeant Heath and Markham to lighten the tone of the book, and it does, somewhat.

The problem is that Van Dine, in addition to making Vance an amusing character and a solver of problems, also made him a spokesman for attitudes toward crime and criminals. Near the beginning of *The "Canary" Murder Case* Vance looks down his nose at the notion of organized crime:

> Personally, I don't much stock in the theory that a malevolent gang of cutthroats have organized an American cammora, and made the silly night clubs their headquarters. The idea is too melodramatic. It smacks too much of the gaudy journalistic imagination: it's too Eugene Sue-ish. Crime isn't a mass instinct except during war-time, and then it's merely an obscene sport. Crime, d' ye see, is a personal and individual business.

This at about the time that Mad Dog Coll and Dutch Schultz were splitting lead all over Philo Vance's home town. But never mind that: Golden Age fiction frequently denies the real world to achieve its particular effects for its readers. Vance becomes involved in the investigation because he has gotten into an argument with Markham about material, circumstantial evidence, a theme going back to the crime fiction of the last century. He enters into the whole business as an aloof participant who claims to have no purpose other than an objective, scientific one. As things progress, however, Vance changes. First he says that he's determined to free those who have been falsely accused by the bumbling Heath, and then, at the end, he advocates a romantic view of criminals:

> 'Don't be so confoundedly moral, old thing. Every one's a murderer at heart. The person who has never felt a passionate hankering to kill some one is without emotions. And do you think it's ethics or theology that stays the average person from homicide? Dear no! It's lack of courage—the fear of being found out, or haunted, or cursed with remorse.'

Not only do Vance's pronouncements clash with the image of the insouciant aristocrat, they are also inconsistent as all get out. Indeed Van Dine's books do not really compare to those being written in England. English writers did some of the same things that Van Dine attempted and did them better in part because they were, very simply, better writers. But this didn't bother Van Dine, and it didn't bother lots of readers and cinema-goers. He was the most popular and prosperous American detective writer of the era. And he made a good target for hard-boiled writers.

### *The Roman Hat Mystery* by Ellery Queen, 1929

During the second act of *Gunplay*, William Pusak leaves his seat and excuses himself down the aisle until he bumps into the body of Monty Field. The play stops, the audience is held and Inspector Queen, his son Ellery and miscellaneous policemen descend on the Roman Theater to investigate the murder. In their initial investigation the Queens discover that the dead man's top hat is missing, and they collect some members of the audience who seem suspicious: Morgan the lawyer, Field's former partner; Parson Johnny, a professional crook with connections to Field; and Frances Ives-Pope, a society celeb whose purse was found in Field's pocket. The police thoroughly search the theater, but find nothing useful. At Field's apartment the Queens discover Mrs. Russo, Field's mistress, and Charles Michaels, Field's ex-con valet. They take a look around but find nothing. Then things slowly unravel. Monty Field, it seems, had important underworld connections and practiced blackmail on the side. The Queens discover that Benjamin Morgan was one of his victims, being blackmailed for having an illegitimate child. Inspector Queen interviews Frances Ives-Pope with the deference due the rich, permitting her whole family to be present along with a handful of others including Stephen Barry, the lead in *Gunplay*. Field picked up Frances' purse that she dropped in terror of Field's advances to her during intermission. Doc. Prouty, the Assistant Medical Examiner, with a toxicologist in tow, tells the Queens that a poison extracted from gasoline killed Field.

The police reinterview selected members of the audience and recomb the Roman Theater and then let it reopen. Ellery and his father witness a performance of *Gunplay*. Finally the Queens return to Field's apartment and give it a thorough search. Here they find Field's hiding-place and filing system, papers hidden in the lining of hats. They also figure out that Field sold forged documents to his victims and kept the originals himself. We do not learn precisely what they found in the hats, though. Ellery departs on a fishing holiday leaving his dad in a funk. Then Inspector Queen stirs himself. He has an unidentified apartment burgled, and then intimidates Michaels into writing a blackmail note to an unmentioned addressee. At night in the park the murderer stalks the policeman posing as the blackmailer, but is captured holding a hypodermic full of poison. It is Stephen Barry, the leading man and fiancé of Frances Ives-Pope. At his apartment Inspector Queen explains the case to the District Attorney and one of his assistants: Field had discovered that Barry had mixed blood in his background and was blackmailing him. Barry slipped out of his dressing room and murdered Field and took along his topper, which contained incriminating evidence.

Frederic Dannay and Manfred Lee joined forces to write a mystery for a contest run by *McClure's* offering a $7,500. prize. Their Ellery Queen book *The Roman Hat Mystery* won, but *McClure's* went bankrupt and they never got the prize. They did, however, get their book published by Stokes.

*The Roman Hat Mystery* makes a significant contribution to the development of the detective story, but, at the same time, it exhibits flaws endemic to its type. Even though the authors give some hints about the attractiveness of their characters, they are merely hints which do not develop much. The narrator or editor, J.J. McC., introduces Ellery Queen as an author of detective stories but presents us not with one of Ellery's fictions but with a narrative of one of Ellery's files of actual cases he worked on with his father, Inspector Queen. There's some needless confusion here that the writers ironed out later by getting rid of J.J. McC. What the writers want to do here is give us the Sherlockian notion that they are providing an actual criminal investigation not only because of its interest for "the dilettante of criminology" but also because it serves as an example of and exercise in reason. The Queens specifically encourage the readers to see the fiction as a challenge to their reasoning powers.

Yet *The Roman Hat Mystery* cheats and messes up. If the police give the Roman Theater such a thorough examination, even bringing in an architectural expert, why do they neglect to give the victim's apartment the same treatment? When Inspector Queen's tame burglar searches Barry's rooms and reports that he found neither papers nor poison, how can Barry have poison in the park? Even though *The Roman Hat Mystery* is more precise than many of its type, if you live by minutiae you die by it. Furthermore, why is it that the Queens have concocted a case here in which neither means (anyone can make the poison), nor motive (Field is a nasty piece of work with many enemies), nor opportunity (almost anyone in the theater could have done it) has any relevance? Why near the end of the novel do the authors start leaving things out, things like the details of the documents in Field's hats? Why do they pay little attention to the cast of the play or the layout of the dressing rooms? They do these things because if they did not their book wouldn't work—if they tell the readers what they find in Field's hats it doesn't take much wit to figure out that Barry committed the murder. They can justify tagging a minor character as the murderer because they say that "seemingly unimportant characters...[may] prove of primary significance in the solution of the crime." In reality, nevertheless, the authors mainly want to trick the readers and want them to leave the book impressed by its cleverness.

But this is the sort of carping to which most Golden Age pattern books leave themselves open. It really doesn't get to the significance of *The Roman Hat Mystery*. One of the things that the novel demonstrates is the popularity of S.S. Van Dine. Part of Ellery Queen's character, the part that is the cultivated lounger, comes from Van Dine. So does edging a deductive problem with a filigree of reality, which at the same time pooh poohs that reality. *The Roman Hat Mystery* alludes several times to gangsters. The drama at the Roman Theater is, after all, *Gunplay*, which uses

the noises customarily associated with the underworld. Automatics, machine-guns, raids on night-clubs, the lethal sounds of gang vendettas—the entire stock-in-trade of the romanticized crime society was jammed into three swift acts.

District Attorney Sampson, when he fills the Queens in on Field's background speaks of a golden age for crime, but one that is past:

You'll remember that in that period some highly shady things were happening in New York. We got faint inklings of a gigantic criminal ring, composed of 'fences,' crooks, lawyers, and in some cases politicians.

Just as this attitude which skims over massive crime to concentrate on a bizarre case comes from Van Dine, so does the emphasis on logic, reason and deduction. Ellery Queen could have become another Philo Vance but for several significant things.

First of all, the authors didn't make their detective prigs like Philo Vance. Ellery is far less presumptuous, less dilettantish and more likable than Vance. He may occasionally talk funny, but the authors never intended his diction to be the sort of thesaurusical speech that Vance uses; indeed, as an allusion in the novel indicates, Ellery's speech is modeled, albeit badly, on P.G. Wodehouse. The authors want to present kinder, gentler characters. Their policemen, Velie, Piggott and the rest, are both more competent and more human than the stereotyped flatfeet in Van Dine. The authors also reveal that Inspector Queen, manhunter, has a heart of gold. He is not only a friend to his son Ellery, but to Djuna their house boy, and to his officers as well. The authors portray in the Queens, father and son, an intimacy that may for modern tastes be almost cloying, but which is far different from the sterile relationships in Van Dine. While Van Dine makes Vance an aesthete who stoops to solve problems in a world far beneath him, the Queens attempt to provide what is almost an Enlightenment atmosphere for *The Roman Hat Mystery*. Inspector Queen has his snuff box, Ellery has his antiquarian book hobby and some of the narration has a particularly eighteenth century sound. All of the chapters begin with "In Which..." and sound like chapter titles in Fielding. The narrator, and Ellery, occasionally break into aphorisms: chapter four begins with "Some natures, through peculiar weakness, cannot endure the sight of a whining man," an eighteenth centuryish echo of Shakespeare. Ellery Queen, I suspect, wants the books to have something of Chesterfield in them, along with the wit and lightness of touch associated with Enlightenment authors. And here the authors grew something out of Van Dine that isn't planted in the original.

This is not quite the case with the Queens' other innovation. One of the most important things about *The Roman Hat Mystery* and about the subsequent achievement of the Queens is that they realized that their book was part of a tradition of detective fiction and that detective fiction was, in many ways, a self-conscious medium. And so they played this up. They make Ellery a detective story writer, they refer in the text of their novel to Poe and Doyle, and they talk about conventions of the detective story, like that of the incompetent policeman. What they are doing here is establishing the fellowship of readers, as well as creating the special artificial world necessary for the formal detective to work. In addition to this, the Queens realized that in many ways all formal detective stories are alike: there is the scene of the crime, the identification of suspects, the peeling away of lies and alibis and so on. It's what readers expected, and it's what writers interested in the building of an "intellectual" detective story had to do. This kind of detective story had, over the years, collected a number of appurtenances: maps, room drawings, footnotes, lists and so on. Since tradition demanded that these things had to be there, why not make a feature of them instead of trying to fit them in smoothly as a part of the narrative? Why not emphasize the artificiality instead of trying to cover it up? And that is what the Queens did in *The Roman Hat Mystery*, they invented editorial apparatus that speaks directly to the reader, not as someone experiencing fiction but as someone solving a puzzle or playing a game. Thus they begin the novel not simply with a list of dramatis personae, but with a list of characters with enigmatic clues attached to them—"Stephen Barry. One can understand the perturbation of the juvenile lead." And they end the list with the most relevant question "Who Killed Monty Field?" Then comes a plan of the Roman Theater. The Queens divide the novel proper into four parts, and preface them all with fictional epigraphs about detection. These divisons correspond to the inevitable parts of the formal story. The fourth section is Queens' famous Challenge to the Reader where the editor says "the alert student of mystery tales, now being in possession of all the pertinent facts, should at this stage of the story have reached definite conclusions on the questions propounded." And with this question they added a new slant on something that had been going on for a long time.

   *The Roman Hat Mystery* began moving the detective story out of literature and away from reality and into the realm of games. Lee and Dannay also contributed mightily to the preservation and continuation of the detective story as literature with their editorial and scholarly work appearing in *Ellery Queen's Mystery Magazine* (which began in 1941) and in their anthologies. They began, in short, to look at sensational fiction in a new way, in a number of new ways, and this began in *The Roman Hat Mystery*.

### *Little Caesar* by W.R. Burnett, 1929

   Cesare Bandello, Rico, a small-time hood from Youngstown arrives in Chicago, by way of Toledo, with his Mexican pal, Otero. In Chicago they become members of Sam Vittori's gang. The book opens with the gang robbing the Casa Alvarado night club on New Year's Eve. During the robbery Rico shoots Courtney, a policeman. The gang's wheel man, Tony, shows signs of losing his nerve and Rico kills him. In spite of the heat from shooting a policeman, provided by Officer Flaherty who dogs him, Rico begins a meteoric rise in the underworld. He takes over the gang from Sam Vittori, and its members acknowledge him as their new leader. As the new boss Rico comes under the protection of the Big Boy, a politician who, along with the more powerful Old Man, provides protection for Chicago's underworld. Discovering that Little Arnie, the owner of a gambling joint, has been welching on his pay-offs, Rico drives him out of town. Pete Montana, the town's most powerful gangster, makes overtures of alliance to Rico; indeed, the Big Boy tells Rico that Montana is on the way out and that he is the presumptive heir. When Rico is at the height of his power, a witness identifies Joe Sansone as the inside man in the original night club robbery. The police arrest Joe and, in spite of his best attempts to keep quiet, he spills the details to the police and to the new Crime Commissioner.

The police arrest Sam Vittori but Otero gets word to Rico. On their way to a hideout Otero dies in a police shoot-out but Rico reaches safety. Rico leaves Chicago and stays for a while in Hammond, Illinois but Scabby, one of his underworld enemies, sees him and so he goes to Toledo to look up the bootlegger who gave him his original stake. Old Chiggi has been put away by the feds, but Rico goes to his son where he finds a safe hideout. Rico then becomes a partner in the booze business with young Chiggi and Chicago Red. On a bender Red lets Rico's real identity slip, the police find him and shoot him down in an alley as he tries to escape.

*Little Caesar* is a short novel that contains far more dialogue than description. The dialogue records uncomplicated, often terse speech of the characters and the description gives a minimal amount of scene setting, brief comments on the internal state of some characters and some distanced analysis of the characters and their actions. It is earlier than Horace McCoy's *They Shoot Horses, Don't They?* (1935) but has the same mood and much of the same impact. It is, for want of a better term, a naturalistic or a sociological hard-boiled novel. *Little Caesar* is one of those books that gives the illusion of letting the readers form their own conclusions but that, in reality, stacks the deck so as to force readers to conclude certain things. Burnett, moreover, is the first American writer to present criminals in a new way. As much as they tried, there is a distance between the criminal and the writer in Flynt and Walton and in Jack Boyle. Here the writer recedes into the background, and largely attempts to let the actions and words of criminals portray Chicago's underworld in the late twenties. In all, *Little Caesar* was a revolutionary book.

In some ways Burnett works on pace, on speed: Paul Cain, doing much the same thing, entitled his novel *Fast One. Little Caesar* contains sparse scene-setting. Readers don't know that they are in Chicago until they are well into the book. But they do know that they are in a crime-ridden place. Pete, the hash-house operator says "I wish to God that I was back in Sicily. The Mafia, what is that? That is kindergarten." Burnette mentions meals of spaghetti and wine and a few other details of Little Italy, but not often. The only two places he dwells on to any extent are Sam Vittori's Club Palermo and the Big Boy's apartment. The former stands out because its sign is reproduced several times in the book. The latter is somewhat different: it is Rico's first real exposure to what money can buy: imitation Old Masters, $1,000 dinnerware and a library full of real but unread books. More than places, Burnett concentrates on snap shots of people. There is Sam Vittori, fat, complacent, timid and middle-aged. Otero, "The Greek," isn't a Greek at all but a Mexican, weak around money and women, who idolizes Rico. Joe Sansone is a professional dancer who has some sense of fashion and the ability to succeed in the night club world, but who follows Rico in part because of the intimidation and in part because of the money. Burnett characterizes a number of gunmen—Killer Pepi, Ottavio Vittori, Blackie Avezzano and Bat Carillo—by merely giving their names. And there are a few underworld women as well: Blondy, Arnie's girl who attaches herself to Rico, and Seal Skin, Otero's girl. All of these people are limited—limited in intelligence, and aspirations. Burnett describes some of them as "stupid," but he does not condescend in portraying them. Their needs are recognizable and insofar as they have strengths, they have strengths. Tony Passalacqua stands out a bit more than the other gang members. Tony's mother nags him about his associates and Father McConagha counsels him about the straight and narrow when they meet on the street. After the night club murder Tony suffers not so much remorse or conscience as fear of capture. He instinctively knows that he needs the relief of confession and goes to seek out the priest when Rico shoots him. In addition to Tony, Otero and Sam Vittori, Burnett pays some attention to the Big Boy. Without specifying his particular office, Burnett makes clear that the Big Boy is some variety of Chicago ward-healer and power-broker. The Big Boy is wily enough to profit from and manipulate gangsters without being identified with them— he gets suddenly shy when the newspaper photographers enter Rico's party. The Old Man, whoever he is, holds more political power than the Big Boy, but he never appears in the novel—presumably because he is too important to have direct dealings with gangsters. Burnett, in describing the Big Boy's apartment, points out his misdirected attempts to live like the elite, but at the same time opens to question whether the elite themselves have any but wallet aesthetics.

All of the people and all of the places in *Little Caesar* really serve as background for Rico. Indeed Rico is complicated enough to change under Burnett's hand. Burnett begins describing Rico as a simple gunman: "Rico was a simple man. He loved but three things: himself, his hair and his gun. He took excellent care of all three." But by the end of the book Little Caesar assumes far more sophistication and complexity than that of a vain gunman. Rico becomes, if not a hero then a person. Burnett gives him foibles shared by many people: he constantly combs his hair, he is proud of having his name or picture in the papers, he likes fashionable clothes and jewelry and he rejects most associations with Italy insisting that he is an American. Unlike those around him, Rico is something of a puritan. He does not drink and does not especially like music. Although he needs women, he does not like them:

> Rico had very little to do with women. He regarded them with a sort of contempt; they seemed so silly, reckless and purposeless, also mendacious and extremely undependable.

Rico, indeed, cannot enjoy much either sensual or intellectual, and he especially cannot relax. Part of this has to do with notions of independence: "He fought shy of any kind of ties. A slight relaxing of this principle and you are tangled up before you know it. The strong travel light!" Burnett, perhaps with some awe, pictures Rico as a type A personality:

Rico lived at a tension. His nervous system was geared up to such a pitch that he was never sleepy, never felt the desire to relax, was always keenly alive. He did not average over five hours sleep a night and as soon as he opened his eyes he was awake. When he sat in a chair he never thrust his feet and lolled, but sat rigid and alert. He walked, ate, took his pleasures in the same manner.

All of this works out in Rico as a need for order and control. Sam Vittori's sloppiness as a person and as a leader bothers him. The drunkenness and womanizing and general asinine behavior of his men irks him. "Rico's great strength lay in his single-mindedness, his energy and his self-discipline." And herein is one of the roots of what happens to Rico: he brings order and control to a world that is by its nature both disorderly and uncontrollable. All of this, however, does not mean that Rico is an inflexible or unrealistic person. Burnett tells us that one of the things that "distinguished him from his associates was his ability to live in the present." Superficially we can see Rico's adaptability with his clothes. He begins wearing flashy and vulgar suits—black with red pin stripes—but when Joe insists that he wear evening dress to go to Big Boy's, Rico quickly sees the appropriateness of it. More essentially, Rico demonstrates a quick and essential grasp of reality when he falls. At one moment he is heir presumptive to the Chicago underworld and at the next he is a fugitive,

Rico stood in the middle of the room staring. By an effort of the will, he rid himself of an attitude of mind which had been growing on him since his interviews with Montana and the Big Boy. He was nobody, nobody.

In some ways Rico is Burnett's study of people existing and working in an organization. Rico replaces Vittori because Sam had become complacent and timid. The men give Rico their respect because of his capacity for definitive action. He is a new kind of leader who "did not swagger, he seldom raised his voice, he never bragged." Rico is an executive. In *Little Caesar* murder is an act of policy, not emotion: Rico shoots Courtney because he threatens to ruin the Casa Alvarado heist and, likewise, he shoots Tony because it has to be done. Far from being blood-thirsty, Rico survives Arnie's attempt to kill him and then simply runs him out of town. Burnett abandons his early description of Rico the gunman as the novel progresses. Vittori, Montana and the Big Boy all see in Rico executive material. The problem is that in this world, defining executive material, defining one's place in the organization, depends on whether one is hard or soft. The world of *Little Caesar* defines not only conscience or cowardice but also the desire for peace or domesticity or pleasure as softness. Hardness means scrupulously following the implications of the first premise, that the gang makes its living by breaking the law. And it is this premise that brings all of those in the book to grief.

Burnett has, in reality, written a tragedy: Rico's strengths are his weaknesses ("The very virtues that had been responsible for his rise were liabilities in the present situation") and the acts that propel him to greatness—

the night club robbery and murder—contain the seeds of his destruction. We see very little of Rico at the top, but then we don't see much of Macbeth at the top either. It all happens very quickly: one day Rico is simply Vittori's gunman, the next he's the boss and the next he's dead in a Toledo alley. Rico is a force unto himself and he fulfills the ideal of his world, but it's the underworld. Rico's name, Cesare, stretches back to antique greatness; nevertheless, he's not Big but Little Caesar, and the world doesn't tremble and readers' lives don't change after experiencing his life and death. *Little Caesar* isn't a tragedy because that's the way things are in the twentieth century.

*How Good A Detective Are You? The New National Game*
*"Minute Mysteries" by H.A. Ripley, 1934.*
The work begins with a brief introduction entitled "The Author":

H.A. Ripley, a police enforcing officer of the most crime-ridden city in America, working with Professor Fordney and the police in almost all countries of the world, has obtained from the professor's case book his most interesting and dangerous experiences and reduced them to THE WORLD'S SHORTEST DETECTIVE PROBLEMS.

. . .

Here's *your* chance to match *your* wits with *both* the criminal and Professor Fordney. Also you will find some humorous and baffling problems which do not deal with crime.

Here's a *real game!* Two minutes should be sufficient for you to solve these WORLD'S SHORTEST DETECTIVE AND CHALLENGING PROBLEMS!

Then there is an introduction by Calvin Goddard, Professor of Police Science and Managing Director of the Scientific Crime Detection Laboratory of Northwestern University. Goddard reminisces about how people used to gain satisfaction from reading about Old King Brady and other dime novel heroes, but notes how this was considered a "puerile pastime." But now, he notes, "times have changed. The detective thriller has been elevated to high estate. Great men are known by the crime magazines they read. To eschew these is to confess oneself—just not bright." Goddard comments on fast-paced modern life and applauds Ripley for reducing crime fiction to tabloid or digest proportions.

Sixty single page problems compose the body of *How Good A Detective*. Each has a narrative followed by a bold face, upper case question like: "WHAT TOLD THE PROFESSOR THE INVALID HAD BEEN MURDERED?" On the following page there is small graphic (most often a stylized owl or detective), a quotation from classical world literature (Shakespeare has 4 but there's also Virgil, Cervantes, Rousseau and Emerson along with a heap of other greats) and, printed upside down, the solution to the problem. To bulk the book up, a full-page line drawing often faces the page containing the narrative. Half of the problems in the book involve murder. In 19 cases there is no crime at all—some of these are labeled "Class Day" and feature Fordney challenging his class to solve posers. The remainder feature problems of theft, blackmail, kidnapping, arson, desertion from the army and counterfeiting.

Ripley's game book clearly follows the fashion of Wren and McKay's *Baffle Book* (1928). Here the problems are not only much shorter but they are also far less technical: Wren and McKay provide, for instance, facsimiles of tire tracks, handwriting, room plans, maps and fingerprints. The earlier writers also provide much more in the way of editorial apparatus with a score sheet and instructions about how to play the game—including "How To Give A Baffle Party." *The Baffle Book* includes "Hints for Solving," "The Importance of the Small Clue," and insists that "The Baffle Book Keeps the Faith." By 1934 the notion of "fair play," I suspect, had become so engrained that Ripley didn't see the need to talk about it. Also Ripley skates lightly over the notion of the game, maybe because of fear of copyright infringement (Doubleday plasters "Inventors of the Detective Problem Form" under the authors' names in *The Baffle Book*) but also because Goddard, at least, saw the book as presenting the essence of the detective story for people too busy to read. Finally, Ripley—in spite of his invocation of the Northwestern Crime laboratory, and giving us a criminology professor as the solver—avoids the kind of technical details which Wren and McKay feature because, as he says twice in his introduction, "crime is simple." The whole implication here is that the sort of wide cultural knowledge supplied by the classical authors of all of the wise quotations, a smattering of medical knowledge plus some plain common sense is enough to solve most crimes. All of the 60 problems in *How Good A Detective* turn on some kind of inconsistency, which a supple mind can detect.

First let's take a look at the non-criminal "Class Day" problems in the book:

—*Problem 12:* a French peasant prays at a shrine and asks to have his money doubled and promises to leave $20 at the shrine in thanks. His prayer is answered. He does the same thing at two more shrines but ends up broke. How much money did he have at the first shrine?

—*Problem 18:* surgeons enable a child blind since birth to see. Her father holds up a red card and is overjoyed when she identifies the color. What was the discrepancy in the story?

—*Problem 24:* On what day of the week was Christ born?

—*Problem 30:* fleeing robbers cut down the sign post at a place that the road forks in four directions. How did the pursuers, unfamiliar with the countryside ahead, know the correct road to take?

—*Problem 36:* officials at the British Museum receive notice that the body of a pharaoh who reigned from "1410 to 1426 B.C." had been found. How did they know the note was authentic?

—*Problem 42:* one race car drove around a mile track at ten miles an hour, another drove at fifty miles an hour. What was the average rate of speed for two laps of the course?

—*Problem 59:* a hunter shot two migrating geese when the leader dropped down and flew backward to join the rear of the formation. Why wasn't this story true?

Three of these problems (12, 18 and 42) require the kind of word problem math that school teachers say develops mental agility and shows math at work in the real world. Most of them turn, though, on having some general knowledge and using it to catch impossibilities or discrepancies: no one knows the date of Christ's birth (24), B.C. dates are written descending and not ascending (36), geese can't fly backwards (59) and a child blind since birth cannot know colors to identify them (18). Problem 30, about the sawed-down sign post, has the only half-way ingenious solution: put the post up so as to correctly point to where you've been and you'll be able to identify the roads properly.

Most of the non-criminal problems in *How Good A Detective*, however, are not specifically academic, "Class Day" problems. They, nevertheless, involve the same kind of solving. "Tough Tim's New Year's Eve Party" requires the mathematical formula for discovering the day of the week for any date after 1752; in "Threat" we need to know that you can't handle hot light bulbs; "The Missing Millionaire" turns on the fact that ship-to-shore radio wasn't around in 1908; and we need to know that a President cannot sign legislation until after inauguration in "A Fisherman's Tale." Some of the problems do require a bit more observation: in "Madame Klunk," Fordney notices that the cheap alarm clock is still ticking and this indicates that the room was recently occupied. "An Old Spanish Custom" calls for knowledge of human nature: the suitor who must choose the paper marked "win" understands that the king has rigged the contest and bets on the king's dignity to win.

Just as the "Class Day" and other non-criminal problems turn on the same sort of solution, so do the criminal problems in *How Good A Detective*. Although none of them requires mathematical solution, "The Death Warrant" demands an elimination graph of the if A was X but not Y and B was Y but not X variety. Ripley usually stays away from this in the crime puzzles. The solutions in most of the crime problems depend either on elementary knowledge of physics or medicine. He usually depends on physics. In "At The Cross Roads" and "An Illustrative Case" we need to know that bodies in moving vehicles will roll about; "The Clown Dies" and "Detective Tom Manahan" focus on what can and cannot fit through a gun's trigger guard; and several pieces turn on what one can and cannot see in the dark. Far fewer problems pivot on medical facts, either because Ripley was uncomfortable with them or because much forensic medicine and toxicology is not quite common knowledge. He tends to rely on facts about blood: it doesn't circulate after death, bodies immersed in water aren't bloody, and so on. What the detective needs to solve the crime problem, then, is some common-sense knowledge of science plus close, not minute, observation and the ability to discover contradictions.

Indeed, Ripley is largely up front with most of the crime problems. Some of them turn on precise definition of words ("Professor Fordney in Edinburgh" is solved with the difference in meaning of "place" and "address"), but this is hardly etymologically abstruse. Many depend on detecting inconsistent statements (the man who asks "who shot her?" when he couldn't know his ex-wife was shot) or inconsistent facts (one cannot write precisely on a rolling ship). Most depend on applying common knowledge. None of the problems is particularly hard to solve once you assume that almost everyone who speaks to Professor Fordney lies and that there is something wrong with the circumstances the book presents to us.

Ripley, though, hardly gives us problems from the real world of crime. He does bring gangsters into some of them. One piece, "Rubbed Out" is about "Poker Face" Hamlin being machine gunned in a Bleaker Street phone booth, but when Ripley brings in gangsters, which he does not do much, they are pussy cats like those in "Tough Tim's New Year's Eve Party," yeggs sitting around trying to figure out how to reckon days of the week of past years. "A Grisley Threat" brings up martial law and a Red scare. But, truthfully, Ripley isn't attempting social comment or even literature. He is not quite giving his readers a game, but an evening's entertainment. He has framed *How Good A Detective* so that the reader can say "I'm a pretty good detective." By keeping away from minutiae, by building his problems so as to be simple without being quite transparent, by giving his readers the illusion, through his academic bits, that they are engaged in the basic American pastime of self-improvement and by counterpointing crime problems (which themselves sanitize crime) with non-crime problems Ripley concocted what a lot of readers thought detective stories ought to be—entertaining.

*Thieves Like Us* by Edward Anderson, 1937.

Bowie Bowers, Elmo (Chicamaw) Mobley and T.W. (T-Dub) Masefeld escape from the Alcatona Prison in Oklahoma. They hi-jack two cars and make it to the Keota, where they find refuge with one of Mobley's relatives. They then set off to rob banks in Texas. Carefully setting up safe houses and escape routes, they successfully rob several Texas banks. Bowers and Mobley return to Oklahoma, but Bowers' car becomes involved in an accident in Texaco City: Bowers is hurt and Mobley kills two policemen. Recuperating in the original hide-out in Keota, Bowers falls in love with Keechie Mobley and they leave together. Keechie and Bowers return to Texas and, disguised as T.B. patients, set up housekeeping in a cabin at a disused sanitarium. They live together peacefully until Bowers determines that he must meet his old colleagues for a planned bank robbery in Gusherton. T-Dub, Chicamaw and Bowie rob the bank and Bowers sets off to return to Keechie. On his return he learns that his friends have been trapped by the police, the T-Dub is dead and Chicamaw in jail facing the death penalty. Bowers and Keechie settle down until a plumber recognizes Bowie and the two set off on the run. They stop and give a lawyer enough money to ensure that

Chicamaw will have a competent defense and escape the electric chair. Bowie and Keechie then go to New Orleans and there set up housekeeping. They live peacefully there until Bowie learns that Chicamaw has been sent to one of Texas' infamous prison farms. He convinces Keechie that they are going to head for Mexico, but on the way they stop at McMasters, Texas. Keechie is now pregnant and ill from travelling. Bowie obtains a sheriff's badge and a fake warrant and rescues Chicamaw from the prison farm. Chicamaw insults Bowie and Bowie makes him leave the car. When Bowie returns to the tourist cabin where Keechie is staying, the police, acting on a tip from T-Dub's sister-in-law, close in and shoot them both to death.

What *Little Caesar* does for gangland Chicago, *Thieves Like Us* does for midwestern outlaws, only more so. Anderson presents echoes of Dillinger, Machine Gun Kelly and Bonnie and Clyde. In T-Dub, Anderson gives us the reality of Kelly's flamboyant but unrealistic nickname: responding to a newspaper labeling him Tommy Gun Masefeld he says "It tickles me... about this tommy gun they're putting on me. I never did have but one machine gun in my life and I never did even try it out." Bowie and Keechie, on the other hand, although they may have Bonnie and Clyde in their background, have little similarity to the real criminals. In addition to bouncing off of the biography of contemporary criminals and presenting realistic pictures of bank robberies and prison farms, in *Thieves Like Us* Anderson extends his demythologizing to the Laws, specifically to the F.B.I.:

> 'I don't see where these fellows they call G-men, them big shots, get that stuff about thieves not having no guts. I don't see how they get that.'
> 'Me neither,' Bowie said, 'They don't do anything unless they got ten carloads and when they jump anybody they use about fourteen hundred rounds of ammunition.'

Perhaps just as important as Anderson's allusions to actual persons and events are his attempts to come to grips with the public attitudes toward criminals. The first time that this issue hits is when Bowie and Chicamaw head north after their set of successful bank robberies. A service station attendant recognizes Chicamaw:

> 'Boy, it ain't none of my business, but I know you.' I says to him, 'Brother, you just think you know men.' He says, 'You're Elmo Mobley as sure as hell, but after you leave here, I never seen nobody that looked like you.'
> 'He really knew you, did he?'
> 'Sure he did. But I never did let on, see. He says to me: 'Boy, I just wish you had got this bank here 'fore it went busted and took my wad. I'd rather for a poor boy like you to have it than them goddamned bankers. Both of them bankers are out of prison now and still living swell on what they stole from me and about four or five hundred more folks here.'

It's an honest rendering of Depression thinking. Much later in the novel Keechie and Bowie visit lawyer J. Archibald Hawkins. Hawkins treats them to doses of socialist commentary and then goes on to point out the peculiarity of a fourteen dollar a week wage slave who works "for a millionaire" being whipped up by newspaper publicity to think "that red-hot spikes are too mild for bank robbers." Indeed, throughout the novel readers gradually see that newspapers are almost always wrong. This builds up to the news clip that closes the book. The clip not only badly distorts the characters of Keechie and Bowie ("the escaped convict, bank-robber and quick triggered killer, and his woman aide"), but it also inflates the prescription that the doctor had just given Keechie into "a quantity of what officers declared was narcotics." At the same time that Anderson documents the mendacity of the press he also documents its romantic pull. Some criminals actually want their names in the papers: they want to be described as daring and quick-triggered and dangerous. At the end of the novel Bowie and Chicamaw fall out because of Chicamaw's jealousy over his reputation:

'You'r no more a criminal than that damned radiator cap there. And yet you do it. It rips my guts out. You're just a big sunday-school chump and yet you can pull a thing like that back yonder and run these roads and make me look like thirty cents.'

Anderson's novel gets its title from the gang's repeated comparisons of themselves to other professions: politicians, bankers, policemen, druggists, lawyers, and so on, "are thieves like us." Bowie, T-Dub and Chicamaw see it that everybody is on the take and no one can be trusted—"I wouldn't trust Jesus Christ." Lawyer Hawkins gives Bowie and Keechie a socialistic answer for their society's malaise:

There are more millionaires in this country than in any other...and at the same time more robbers and killers...Extremes in riches make extremes in crime. As long as the social system permitted the acquisition of extreme riches, there would be equalizing crime and the government and all law enforcement organizations might as well fold their hands and accept it.

*Thieves Like Us,* on the one hand, presents a predatory world in which money and the media distort humanity. On the other hand it presents a bunch of dumb Okies who do what they do because they do it.

T-Dub is 44 years old, Chicamaw is 35 and Bowie is 27. The older men are veteran bank robbers—T-Dub has robbed 27 banks at the beginning of the book. Insofar as the readers know, neither of these men has ever worked, ever farmed, labored, clerked or anything else. "I never was cut out to work for any two or three dollars a day and have to kiss somebody's behind to get that," says T-Dub. All they have been is bank robbers and they like being bank robbers. Their conversation is limited to prison anecdotes and superstitions, reminiscences of past crimes, plans for future robberies, statements about their own successes and occasional simplistic social observations. They talk about hunting, but never hunt, and they romanticize life in Mexico. But from past to future, being thieves makes their identities. They are efficient but not particularly smart thieves. Although they carefully plan their bank robberies and preach about how women and whiskey will undo any criminal, Chicamaw is a habitual souse and T-Dub takes up with a silly woman who is ultimately the cause of his death. They have generous impulses, sending money to impoverished relatives, and they stick together. When others display honesty or principle they call them "real people." They are not wantonly violent or vicious, insisting that they do not shoot up banks, just rob them. The money that they rob means very little to them: they spend it on frippery. Chicamaw loses most of his $20,000 share gambling. A number of times in the novel when the bank robbers are asked their occupation they identify themselves as baseball players, and in some ways they are like double A ball players shagging from one town to the next, mindlessly gossiping to pass the time, not even dreaming of the big leagues any more, mechanically doing the only thing that they know how to do.

Anderson sets Bowie apart from the other two. He is younger and in jail for a first offense—killing a man during a robbery that he was roped into as a teenager. Bowie begins the novel with plans; he intends to continue robbing banks until he has a stake and then quit the trade. We witness some of his dreams and see him scratching at feelings of unreality, that he died in the electric chair and is living out other lives. He has not the vices of the other two; he neither drinks nor gambles. Chicamaw and T-Dub call him Country Boy and Sunday School Boy. Bowie's relationship with Keechie is sensitive, tender and protective and their stays at the sanitarium and in New Orleans are domestic idylls. Keechie is an anomaly in the criminals' world. Little affected by material things, she wants to live in a safe world with Bowie. She cannot, however, articulate what it should be or lay plans for attaining it. Additionally, at first she does not have the strength to overcome his bond with his friends, and then passively goes along with Bowie because she loves him. Bowie's love for Keechie makes him suspicious and aggressive to those they meet, the caretaker at the sanitarium and the drunk in New Orleans. Bowie can neither reconcile his love for Keechie with his allegiance to this friends nor can he give up either one. In spite of Keechie's objections, Bowie goes off for the final bank robbery in Gusherton, goes to see lawyer Hawkins about Chicamaw and finally breaks Chicamaw out of prison. Anderson makes Bowie the main character of *Thieves Like Us* and he presents him as having slightly higher horizons than his pals. In spite of coincidence and irony of the Texaco City car crash that brands him as a murderer just as he could have left the life of crime and the irony of his death after rescuing Chicamaw, Bowie is no hero. Unlike Rico in *Little Caesar*, Bowie would never have amounted to much: he could have, maybe, risen to the status of Average Joe. *Thieves Like Us* isn't tragedy. It's hard-boiled social observation.

Anderson gives his readers a taste of West Texas and Oklahoma: arid, flat, broken down by the Depression. *Thieves Like Us* is the most authentic social document (not social commentary) about criminals of its time. It does contain bits of socialistic commentary but they come either from the thieves or from lawyer Hawkins, people from whom we expect them. *Thieves Like Us* nevers shows the other side of the tracks, never portrays either wealthy or middle-class individuals. Sure, readers can make inferences, but even though Anderson may agree, he doesn't make them. Readers can also make observations about the losers Anderson concentrates on, T-Dub, Chicamaw, Bowie and Keechie. This is what I've been doing. But Anderson doesn't. He presents them without superimposing generalizations on them. The gang members talk, motor around the country, rob banks, get killed. That's all; readers supply the rest from the selection of material that Anderson supplies. *Thieves Like Us*, like most hard-boiled writing, detective or non-detective, stays away from pathos and other varieties of sentiment, but it cannot, does not wish to, avoid irony. This is the contrast of the world as it is and as it should be, and irony is the accepted burden of being hard-boiled.

### The Big Sleep by Raymond Chandler, 1939

The aged General Sternwood calls Marlowe to his estate where he tells Marlowe about the disappearance of his elder daughter's husband, Rusty Regan, and hires the detective to find out who has attempted to blackmail him over his younger daughter, Carmen's, indiscretions. Marlowe watches the pornography shop of Geiger, the blackmailer, and follows him to his home. At Geiger's house Marlowe finds Carmen Sternwood drugged and posed for pornographic pictures and Geiger dead. After depositing Carmen at her home, Marlowe discovers that Brody has carted off Geiger's stock of books and photos. Meanwhile the Sternwoods' chauffeur, and Geiger's murderer, bobs up dead, apparently a suicide. At Brody's apartment Marlowe finds the stolen photographs of Carmen as well as Carmen herself who bursts in and tries to shoot Brody. She doesn't, but minutes later Carol Lundgrin, Geiger's homosexual lover, bursts in and shoots Brody, thinking that he killed Geiger. This wraps up the blackmail angle, but Marlowe begins to pick away at the disappearance of Rusty Regan. He begins with Eddie Mars, the owner of a gambling club who bumped into Marlowe while he was looking into the Geiger mess. Regan, word has it, ran off with Mars' wife; additionally Vivian Sternwood has some sort of connection to Mars. While all of this is going on both Sternwood sisters make passes at Marlowe but he declines both of them. Harry Jones, a small grifter, tells Marlowe that he and his girl, Agnes, know the whereabouts of Eddie Mars' wife. Mars' hired gun, Lash Canino, poisons Jones, but Marlowe finds Agnes and gets directions to Mrs. Mars' hideaway. When Marlowe arrives, Canino saps him and leaves him bound, with Mrs. Mars; she releases Marlowe and he shoots Canino when the killer returns. Marlowe then drags out to the Sternwood estate and the General asks him to find Rusty Regan. As he leaves, Marlowe sets up a test for Carmen Sternwood which proves that she killed Regan. Vivian then tells Marlowe that she had Mars and Canino dump Regan's body into the sump of a disused oil well. Marlowe forces Vivian to put her sister into a mental hospital and, although it makes him seem unclean, he withholds the information from the General.

"The Killer in the Rain" (1935) and "The Curtain" (1936), both published in the *Black Mask* contain material that Chandler reworked for *The Big Sleep*. In a sense, all of Chandler's early fiction featuring Mallory, who appears in his first story, "Blackmailers Don't Shoot" (1933), and Carmady, who appears first in "The Man Who Liked Dogs" (1936), leads up to the voice that became Marlowe. As a novel, *The Big Sleep* is hardly a seamless work. It tends to break in half when Marlowe wraps up the Geiger killing, Canino seems very much to be a late addition and Chandler is tentative in the appearances of Eddie Mars early in the book and his wife at the end. It is not, however, construction that holds *The Big Sleep* together, it is Chandler's drawing of Marlowe and, more importantly, Chandler's writing that make the book.

When *The Big Sleep* appeared the hard-boiled story had been around for seventeen-odd years. Everybody knew the conventions and readers expected them. Chandler gave them full value with Philip Marlowe. Marlowe is a big man unperturbed by violence. He has some official connections but Chandler colors these by firing him from the D.A.'s office for insubordination. He lives an austere life, with a minimal apartment and office. Marlowe's Los Angeles is the city gone to seed, where money means more than justice and where the corrupt are beyond the reach of the law. His private life he keeps private. Although it can't be called a passion, being a detective holds some significance for Marlowe. Neither the rich nor the powerful on either side of the law intimidate him. Marlowe's investigations literally cover a great deal of ground and although he thinks, his solutions to crimes come in surprising bursts. In these and in other things Chandler learned much from Hammett.

But Marlowe is not Race Williams or the Op or the Sam Spade or Nick Charles. For one thing, by the late '30s law enforcement in American had become if not efficient, then more professional. In *The Big Sleep* Marlowe tells General Sternwood that:

'I'm not Sherlock Holmes or Philo Vance. I don't expect to go over ground the police have covered and pick up a broken pen point and build a case from it. If you think there is anybody in the detective business making a living doing that sort of thing, you don't know much about cops. It's not things like that they overlook, if they overlook anything. I'm not saying they often overlook anything when they're really allowed to work.'

And it's not just Philo Vance and Sherlock Holmes that Marlowe can cite, he is more intellectual than any of his hard-boiled predecessors. He actually admits to General Sternwood that he has gone to college. He plays solitaire chess and knows, though he pretends not to, Marcel Proust. Marlowe, in fact, is literary enough to apply the image of the knight to himself early in *The Big Sleep* and, although he rejects it in the middle ("Knights had no meaning in this game"), maintains the image at the end. Although Marlowe embodies some hard-boiled notions about violence—he bashes Agnes at Brody's apartment—Chandler precipitates less physical violence than other hard-boiled writers. Marlowe does not, in fact, carry a gun in *The Big Sleep* and Chandler uses the shoot out with Canino as something like an action cap for the novel.

Far more than any of the previous hard-boiled detectives, Marlowe is not alienated from, but aloof from, the world in which he participates. Before the final summation, every conversation that Marlowe enters has an edge, is a contest. He holds things back not only because he is a detective but also because he inclines that way as a person. Marlowe's aloofness is the case partly because Chandler peoples *The Big Sleep* with numerous bent people: Carmen Sternwood, the childish nymphomaniac killer; Geiger, the epicoene pornographer; Lundgrin, the homosexual lover with "a face as hard and cold as mutton fat;" Detective Cronjager, "as hard as the manager of a loan office;" and Lash Canino, the hired killer. Not the kind of people who can share intimacy with the hero. And then there are pathetic losers: Brody, Agnes, Vivian Sternwood, Eddie Mars and his wife. These people are so wrapped in their losing struggles to master their own predicaments that they do not acknowledge others. While Marlowe is not exactly contemptuous of these people, he has little sympathy for them and when they clear off they lay no claim upon him or his actions. Because he is no longer a public servant, Marlowe cuts himself off from the company of Bernie Ohls and other honest law officers. Harry Jones, Rusty Regan and General Sternwood have the most pull on Marlowe. He does not know any of them well, has never met Regan at all, but something about them, their courage or honesty or generosity, or authenticity, makes Marlowe sympathize with them. This sympathy, a motif essential to Chandler, is something that Marlowe cannot share with them, for two of them are dead and Marlowe wishes to protect the General from grief.

Marlowe is the most alone of all of the hard-boiled heroes. Although he is able to master his world, Marlowe despises modern garishness (evident when he reflects on the decoration and furnishings at Eddie Mars' club) and in *Little Sister* he confesses a nostalgia for his own small town background. The next novel, *Farewell, My Lovely*, partly focuses on Marlowe's sympathy for Moose Molloy who, upon his return from prison, is sandbagged by the present. Marlowe is also isolated because he has extremely high standards for institutions (his being fired for insubordination no doubt shows this) and for intimacy (he refuses the sexual advances of both Carmen and Vivian Sternwood). Maintaining his values in a world that largely flouts them and finding part of his identity in being a detective does not make for a comfortable existence. As he says after exposing the grotesqueness in *The Big Sleep*, "I was part of the nastiness now." Nevertheless, Marlowe perseveres in holding together both the ideal world where people care about people worth caring about, and the real world where they don't. And Chandler was the first to fully articulate this theme latent in earlier hard-boiled fiction.

Although Chandler emphasized different aspects of the hard-boiled hero's sensibility, there was little that was revolutionary about this aspect of his fiction. The really revolutionary part of Chandler is in the writing. Chandler took a form which had developed a specific style of dialogue (terse expression mixed with slang and wisecracks) and narration (active and sometimes startling descriptions of events) and made it different. He made it different, first of all, by adding detail. Earlier writers, like Hammett, add detail only occasionally and for specific purposes—like the description of the contents of Joel Cairo's wastebasket in *The Maltese Falcon*, which is important for the articulation of the plot. Chandler uses much more detail and uses it for different purposes. Take the description of the Fulwider Building in *The Big Sleep*:

> An old man dozed in the elevator, on a ramshackle stool, with a burst out cushion under him. His mouth was open, his veined temples glistened in the weak light. He wore a blue uniform coat that fitted him the way a stall fits a horse. Under the grey trousers with frayed cuffs, white cotton socks and black kid shoes, one of which was slit across a bunion. On the stool he slept miserably, waiting for a customer. I went past him softly, the clandestine air of the building prompting me, found the fire door and pulled it open. The fire stairs hadn't been swept in a month. Bums had slept on them, eaten on them, left crusts and fragments of greasy newspaper, matches, a gutted imitation leather pocketbook. In a shadowy angle against the scribbled wall a pouched ring of pale rubber had fallen and had not been disturbed. A very nice building.

By adding up concrete things leading up to the discarded condom Chandler conveys the feel of the desolation of the Fulwider Building in a way that earlier hard-boiled writers could not.

Chandler also made the simile a standard part of hard-boiled style. While earlier writers like Daly and Hammett used similes, they used them as simply a routine element of common speech. Chandler changed that. His similes in *The Big Sleep* are numerous and unusual:

—The plants filled the place, a forest of them, with nasty meaty leaves and stalks like newly washed fingers of dead men.
—The General spoke again, slowly, using his strength as carefully as an out-of-work showgirl uses her last pair of stockings.
—...her whole body shivered and her face fell apart like a bride's pie crust.
—Her eyes became narrow and almost as black and shallow as enamel on a cafeteria tray.
...his pale eyebrows bristling and stiff and round like the little vegetable brushes the Fuller Brush man gives away.
—A case of false teeth hung on the mustard-colored wall like a fuse box in a screen porch.

Chandler used similes not simply as an element of common, slang-ridden speech, he used them to elaborate the meaning of the hard-boiled story. He used them because they were graphic and shocking—"like newly washed fingers of dead men," but he also used them to portray the hard-boiled hero's consciousness. The Fuller Brush man, cafeteria tray, pie crust, stockings with runs: all of these are items from the mundane experience of the average person. Chandler takes them and makes them signify not only the observer's points of reference but his ability to use his experience in different contexts, detective contexts, surely, but also poetic contexts as well. Indeed, Chandler made hard-boiled writing edge into poetry not just with his use of similies, but with his whole use of language. Here is a writer who deals with crime, social ills, psychiatric problems, the growth of the city, the sinking of modern life into crassness and bad taste. Chandler has nothing new to say about crime or detection. What makes Chandler powerful, however, is his ability to describe "moments of crouched intensity" and people who exude "stealthy nastiness." What makes Chandler powerful is the fact that he made prose into poetry and made detective fiction into literature—almost.

The end of the 1920s was the watershed of American crime fiction. In 1928 Hammett synthesized many of his earlier accomplishments into *The Red Harvest*. The next year Ellery Queen domesticated the Golden Age pattern developed by the English and dabbled in by S.S. Van Dine. Burnett came as close as anyone had yet come to depicting real criminal life in *Little Caesar*. The timing is convenient and significant because it means that modern American crime fiction began in books, and not in the movies or on the radio. After the late twenties this would not always be the case: in *The Big Sleep* Chandler talks of "the elaborately casual voice of the tough guy in pictures." Watershed, though, may not be the right metaphor, for in some ways the same materials (conventions, characters, style and so on) continue from the early twenties up through 1940 and beyond. Also in some ways, crime fiction got better, much better, in the thirties: in style, plot and significance it got better. At times it had the potential to rise out of the genre ghetto that the publishing world had made. But crime fiction, because there was so much more of it, also appealed to more diverse tastes than it had ever before. The main split, of course, was between hard-boiled and Golden Age detective fiction, but each of these major divisions broke down into sub-groups aimed at different kinds of readers from the high to the low brow and all the gradations in between. Hard-boiled fiction developed the Hammett school and the he-man school and the naturalistic criminal biography school and more. Golden Age fictions were either more esoteric or less esoteric, more psychological or more material, more like non-literary games or more like standard literature. It became a lot harder to make generalizations about a form read by the President of the United States (F.D.R. suggested the plot for *The President's Mystery Story* composed by 7 crime writers in 1936) and by those who wanted stuff like:

I ripped her brassiere, baring her left breast. I shoved my hand against that blood-stained, swelling mound of still-warm flesh. (Robert Leslie Bellem, from *Spicy Detective*, November 1935)

We can say that basing fictional detectives on real detectives had gone by the boards. The twenties and thirties have no Chief Byrnes or detective Burns; the principal detective heroes of the age are made up. Surely Philo Vance can only be a fictional character, and the same is true for the hard-boiled paragon. J. Edgar Hoover managed to get G. Men into some of the lesser pulps as well as on the radio and the screen, but he failed to convince any of the major writers. Indeed, writers like Anderson started the process of debunking Hoover almost at the same time that he began the F.B.I.'s publicity campaign. Elliot Ness had to wait until the fifties for television and for the eighties and Max Allan Collins to make him a hero. Although some writers do feature police heroes, the majority of detective and crime writers make their policemen corrupt, or lazy, or stupid, or intimidated and incapacitated by being part of an organization which itself is corrupt or lazy or stupid or intimidated. When writers of detective stories tried to break away from what was fast-becoming the stereotype of the private eye, they looked to professions like journalism (Nebel's Kennedy and Coxe's Flashgun Casey) that did some good rather than to the police officer.

One of the clearest trends of the period was the coming of realism to the detective and crime story. In the fiction of the twenties and thirties crime was no longer an aberration or an isolated phenomena. Van Dine and Queen speak about the prevalence of "common" crime that serves as a backdrop for their focus on bizarre cases. And even the outre cases showcased in Golden Age novels depend on strange (but nonetheless rigorous and often material) proof. Hard-boiled writers presented crime as almost omnipresent, from the grifter and gun punk up to the politician or millionaire with connections to big shot gangsters. In *The Red Harvest* Hammett portrays with some ardor the completely crime-ridden city. By Chandler's time the cities were just as infested with crime but now the fictional criminal, much in the manner of real criminals, had bought respectability and the hero realizes that there is not a great deal that he can do about the pervasiveness of crime.

Just as writers present an America in which crime is a daily fact, they also present crimes more frankly. Obviously Burnett and Anderson treated criminals and crime with a degree of realism and objectivity never witnessed before. Detective writers describe murders more graphically, they bring in other crimes—the pornography of *The Big Sleep*—and although later writers, particularly in the 1980s, stress more awful crimes, they could not have done this unless the writers of the 20s and 30s made the first step. They gave their characters blackjacks, revolvers, automatics, sawed-off shot guns, Tommy guns and even hand grenades and their characters used them sometimes almost casually. Unlike the polite combats of bygone days, the fiction of the twenties and thirties dumped the convention of the polite, quasi-violent clip on the jaw and made its characters hit and kick and bite their opponents. Excepting the crime games, American writers, far more than their British peers, stressed the impact of heinous crime on the detective. Crime and criminals clearly disgust Inspector Queen and Ellery, and dealing with them makes heavy inroads on the psyches of hard-boiled heroes, the Op's self-disgust at going blood simple, and Marlowe's feeling that he was "part of the nastiness now." Indeed, hard-boiled fiction invented a convention of the hero's dream to help demonstrate and expunge the effects of crime and violence.

The fiction of the twenties and thirties became less Victorian and more romantic. Superficially it moved away from the idea of the hero who could cleanse the corruption of society. Literature about criminals shows this most graphically. At the beginning of the period Boyle presents Boston Blackie as a moral exemplar. Burnett's Rico is no moral exemplar but he, at least, has connections to the tragic hero. Finally, Anderson's characters are just criminals. A parallel movement occurred in the detective story. Hard-boiled detective fiction moves emphatically away from the hero sanctioned by society whose acts reestablish society's values. In the place of the police officer or other legitimate representative of the law it puts the private eye, who has shady connections and who fights to establish his own values. Further, hard-boiled literature moves from the hero who always wins, as in the case of Race Williams and the Continental Op, to the hero like Marlowe whose victory is also defeat. Even with characters like Ellery Queen and Philo Vance crime fiction of the period shows the hero isolated or alienated from much around him.

With almost all crime fiction of the period the social circle has shrunk; few people deserve one's love or trust. The characters in *Thieves Like Us* talk about those few as "real people," and the same principle works in much of the other fiction—the characters just use different measures for what makes another have value. In this sense, Van Dine and Anderson show the same sort of exclusivity in their characters. And the value one character puts on another doesn't always have much to do with his status with the law: Boston Blackie comes to see the Deputy Warden as a real man, and Marlowe understands Rusty Regan's vitality. The crime fiction of the period leaves behind with some nostalgia the idea of community, and runs counter to democratic ideals: every person is not of equal worth and there are a lot of corrupt or weak or vicious people out there. The community cannot save itself. It returns to the Byronic notion of the hero who perseveres in spite of his alienation from a corrupt society. If, therefore, the society in the crime story holds little for the hero, the writers put a great deal of stress on the heroes' satisfaction (grim in the case of the hard-boiled character and smug in the case of characters like Philo Vance) gained from having a code of their own.

The crime fiction of the era also had something to say about women. Most earlier crime fiction contains female characters, but they by-and-large act out conventional roles, and it never occurs to the writers to say anything special about them. Not so in the twenties and thirties. American crime fiction has little good to say about women. The women in *The "Canary" Murder Case* are high class whores, so is Angela Russo in *The Roman Hat Mystery*, and the detectives in these books live an asexual existence. Dinah Brand in *The Red Harvest* lives by sex and Carmen Sternwood in *The Big Sleep* is a nymphomaniac. Outlaws like Rico and the convicts in *Thieves Like Us* know better than to become involved with women and, with the exception of Keechie, their women are the same frivolous sort found in detective books. Women in all of these books are dangerous: they are not only tarts, but also frequently blackmailers and they are not competent to do things right. Furthermore, women frequently both lure men but then betray them: this was a standard theme in hard-boiled fiction before Hammett enshrined it in *The Maltese Falcon*. Here the writers followed a current in early twentieth century culture reflected in Bernard Shaw's coinage of the term femme fatale and in the cinema's purposeful creation of Theda Bara as the Vamp. There are all sorts of sociological observations to be made about this phenomenon, along with all sorts of name calling. The best that can be said of the use of women in the crime fiction of the period is that hard-boiled writers simply added the paradox of women's attraction and repulson to the list of contradictory pulls on their heroes.

The city is nearly universal in the crime fiction of the period. Most of the books take place in cities and even in *Thieves Like Us* T-Dub and Chicamaw label Bowie "Country Boy" for his optimism, temperance and naivete. During the thirties the growth of the cities either slowed or stopped; they were, in fact, no longer the centers of jobs and opportunity. They were, as they had always been, the centers of corruption and violence. And the crime fiction of the period reflects this. Hammett signifies the corruption of the city by having his fictional city in *The Red Harvest*, Personville, universally known as Poisonville, and by making the disease of the city one of the themes of the novel. In some ways hard-boiled detective heroes are like Anderson's Bowie Bowers, country boys placed in environments of corruption and temptation—they are just more ascetic and, in a word, Calvinistic. Even sophisticated detectives like Philo Vance and Ellery Queen, who thrive on the accumulation of culture available only in cities, have become exiles. The editorial apparatus of both *The "Canary" Murder Case* and *The Roman Hat Mystery* tells us that the heroes are now living abroad, in exile with Philo "declaring he would never return to America." Just as crime fiction shows that there are not many people with whom one can feel safe, it also shows the same thing about places—hence Marlowe's rage at Carmen Sternwood's violation of his apartment, "it was all I had in the way of a home."

And finally there is language. It was one of the principal reasons for the renaissance of the detective story in America in the 1920s and 1930s. Finally, writers had the words to use to write crime stories. Up until the 1920s, notions of literary style limited what the crime story or the detective story could do. Accepted notions of style made detective stories verbose or elephantine or breathlessly purple or ironic in a condescending way. A number of things came together in the twenties and thirties. Internationally, detective writers rebelled at the style of nineteenth century detective fiction, and aimed at clearing up their own prose, making it more efficient: thus A.A. Milne in his preface to *The Red House Mystery* writes about the detective writer's obligation to write efficient rather than ponderous prose. Classical detective writers here and Britain paid close attention to describing their worlds, as they had to if they were going to trick readers with a turn of phrase or two and claim that they were being fair. At the same time American journalism underwent a change; it got leaner and more efficient. Writers like Sherwood Anderson and Hemingway and, some would add, Hammett, transformed journalistic style into a terse but evocative literary style. In the twenties American radio networks, after sweating over the problem, decided to adopt unaccented American English as the medium for the air waves. And there is more: Vaudeville, telegrams, radio commercials, Groucho and Chico, P.G. Wodehouse, jazz songs. America in the twenties was new and fertile ground for creating new literary styles and perhaps the most American of them all was the one that evolved in the hard-boiled detective story.

# Conclusion

Generalizations about American crime fiction come easily, too easily. They tend to speak about a country accustomed to violence with a heritage of vigilante justice that enshrines both the avenger and the lawless hero. They also speak of the standard of the hyper-masculine hero, and they split our crime fiction into two antithetical types—the classical and the hard-boiled story. I list these notions here not merely as straw men to be knocked down by cunning and sophisticated argument, but because they do embody some truth about America's crime fiction. But there are other generalizations, equally true, which can be, maybe need to be, made about the first one hundred years of crime fiction in the United States.

But first, let's tally up some of the material developed in the preceding chapters. Crime fiction in this country has resulted partly from the efforts of publishers. In the 1840s story papers discovered that they had a good thing in Miseries and Mysteries and they used Miseries and Mysteries as a bait to sell their publications: they found that advertising fiction as a Miseries and Mysteries story made people read and, more significantly, buy their product. Publishers did the same thing with the detective: Munro spent a small fortune promoting the character of Sleuth, and other story paper and dime novel publishers found that the term detective made them money. As early as the 1890s legitimate publishers began to group novels together as mystery or detective books, in part because they were, but also in part to promote their wares by linking a new author with a favorite or well-known writer. The process hit full gallop in the twenties and thirties. Publishers focused a barrage of marketing devices and strategies on the detective story. It paid off for them, and sometimes paid off for readers.

Readers, to belabor the obvious, read books because they were there. But a couple of things moved Americans to read crime fiction. They read it because foreigners wrote it and read it. Until the hard-boiled story, most American detective fiction looked to European patterns. Eugene Sue inspired the Miseries and Mysteries stories of the mid-nineteenth century just as Dickens, Collins and the British sensation writers had their impact. Gaboriau influenced both high and low-brow writers. Doyle and Hornung and R. Austin Freeman inspired turn of the century writers, and Christie, Sayers and other British Golden Age writers served as models in the 1920s. While American crime writers indisputably used foreign models, they also responded to the continuing crisis in law enforcement in their own country in a number of ways, some subtle and some not so subtle.

154

From the 1840s up through 1940 Americans have more or less continually worried about their police. The purpose and practice of American police forces has been open to question throughout our history: the questions of what should the police do and how can we get them to do it effectively rise repeatedly to the surface of the American consciousness. Although the foreign literary models take first place in authors' and readers' attention, American writers do include home-grown police themes in their fiction. During the early period, writers made images of the hobbled and over-burdened police into an American theme. Our police, the authors suggest, need all of the help that they can get. In specific ways Green focuses on the way that social prejudice hinders police work, and Hawthorne shows how the public gets in the way of serious professionals. Other early writers imply similar motifs. The police officers in *The Dead Letter* and *Old Sleuth* welcome the assistance of private individuals in dealing with crime in the upper world where money or position has put criminals above the law and both the police and the courts are all too ready to help Pinkerton do the things that they, apparently, cannot. Another early American police theme was police corruption. European writers had taken up the convention of the brilliant detective versus the bumbling policeman, but writers like Pinkerton gave it a contemporary American connection by contrasting the effective detective to the corrupt one. Later, crime fiction took these American concerns of the 1870s (they need all the help they can get and the corruption of police officers) and expanded them until they became significant themes.

If these early tribulations of American law enforcement had something to do with the development of a uniquely American crime fiction, what about crime? No matter what the objective truth, Americans from the 1840s to the 1940s perceived that with each decade crime, and especially violent crime, was growing and becoming more threatening. The detective story as a genre responds to public concern about crime in several ways. Sometimes it sanitizes it (makes it into the body in the library skewered with the curious oriental dagger) in order to reassure its readers. Sometimes it exaggerates (makes it the Napoleon of Crime who wants to take over the world or a significant part of it) it in order to reassure its readers. Thus we have the twin traditions of the formal detective story, which reassembles the reasonable world after a slight dysfunction, and the thriller, which saves the reasonable world after a titanic threat. American fiction uses both patterns, but it develops them in some uniquely American ways. It makes, for instance, the thriller more realistic, even more domestic: the aristocratic megalomaniac Master Criminal from British thrillers becomes in America the underworld king-pin. This limits some of the scope of the thriller but it also makes it more recognizable.

There is a comparable change in detective story plots. As the detective story evolved in Britain, it centered on the domestic scene, the crime or problem that concerns a family or other small group of individuals. This was a natural development given the detective story's background in romantic fiction with its lost relations and the sensation novel's emphasis on emotional travail. British crime fiction rarely engages with current fashions or fears about crime. Although American detective fiction cannot be said to courageously grapple with contemporary issues, it does move out of the domestic circle and treat other kinds of crime. Superimposed on their romantic plots, detective library stories frequently deal with American society's current fears. The New York Detective Library's #439 is *The New Orleans Mafia; or, Chief Hennessy Revenged* and other "dime novels" bounce off of the Mafia or the Black Hand. Stories about anarchists, like *Mr. Lazarus of Ludlow Street; or, Old King Brady Among the Anarchists of New York*, appear in most of the detective libraries. There is a Cap Collier number entitled *Who Destroyed the Maine?*, another in the same series that uses New York's notorious gang the Whyos, and another bringing readers *The Double Mystery; or, Tracking the Nitro-Glycerine League.* Although higher-class detective fiction does involve domestic situations, even here there is significant concern with non-domestic crime. Robbery appears with some frequency: *The Expressman and the Detective* and *The Great Bank Robbery* obviously treat this subject. At the turn of the century writers used robbery again and again: Futrelle, Reeve and Rinehart all have robberies in their fiction. And the next period follows up with bank robbery works like Hammett's *The Big Knockover* and *Thieves Like Us*. With Post's stories, robbers switch to robber barons and writers like Adams focus on corporate crime and politicians, the shame of America's cities. The point of all of this is that in the United States the crime story was about more than one family's trauma; it frequently used dangers to everyone's lives and property as either the ground or, more commonly, the background of the detective plot. This while writers in Britain stuck to the family tragedy.

In nineteenth-century Britain detectives never got the press that they received in America. Dickens and Collins may have modeled their detectives on real men, but they submerge them in fictional identities. Indeed, in Britain police forces ran on the principles of organization and duty, as well as the idea of civil service. Cults of personality do not fit any of these concepts. Not so in this country. Pinkerton, Byrnes and Burns actively sought public recognition and they got it. American police officials courted the press, and this wasn't just Chief Byrnes. As Police Commissioner, Teddy Roosevelt treated reporters Jacob Riis and Lincoln Steffens almost as colleagues. Additionally, the most prominent police officers of the late nineteenth century moved from the world of journalism into the world of fiction. In its quest for realistic touches, the Cap Collier Library (in item 602) features a real detective, Inspector Byrnes. Byrnes, as we know, along with Pinkerton and William Burns became characters in fiction. Here readers had real people dealing with real or realistic crime. They had heroes to fight crime when their crime-fighting organizations broke down, and many believed that they broke down often.

One of the realities of the American police has always been money. America's civil servants did not receive anything in the way of princely wages. While police officers were poorly paid, they were put in the way of many temptations, temptations of vice and money and power. Police history resounds with money troubles. At the beginning of the history of our police there was the business of rewards and reward-splitting, of officers of law serving as the middlemen between robber and robbed—for a price. This practice enflames the various founders of American police departments, and it also enflamed Pinkerton who talks about it in his fiction. After reward-splitting came graft, the use of the police officer's position to extort money. Official and unofficial investigations across the country at the turn of the century found graft to be the police officer's occupational disease. Owners of businesses had to pay the police to ensure proper protection at the same time that felons paid the same police for the right to ply their trade. The linkage between official police and dirty money, however, only impacted on detective fiction by inference. It inspired writers to create altruistic amateur detectives, like Victor's Mr. Burton, as well as making the business practices of the private detective unique. An inevitable motif in private eye fiction is the hero's concern for money at the beginning of a case: the workman is worth his hire, and only a sap starts to work without knowing what his pay is going to be, even though the pay is inevitably modest. As things proceed, however, the claims of justice and honor and truth and just plain excitement take over and the private detective, business man that he is, forgets about money and often does the job whether he gets paid or not. Rather than condemning those police officers in the real world who were on the take, fiction largely emphasized detectives who were motivated by the higher elements of their vocation as opposed to greed or even fiscal prudence. This is, no doubt, another instance of the wishful thinking of detective fiction, but it is specifically American wishful thinking.

American crime fiction reflects other basic facts of American police reality in a more down-to-earth manner. No doubt during their first century American police forces achieved some successes, and police officers did solve many crimes with subtlety and intelligence. Their most typical techniques, however, displayed other, less intellectual, qualities. One of the earliest and strongest traditions of American police work was recognizing criminals. The published rogues galleries of the last half of the nineteenth century point to this, but they tell only part of the story: they contain portraits only of criminals who had been arrested. The other part of the story is the policeman's or the detective's personal familiarity with members of the underworld—knowing their names and relationships and being familiar with and sometimes a familiar in their haunts. Knowing who the criminals are is the first sine qua non of traditional American police work. Finding them comes next, and here the abilities of the Indian or the tracker are simply transferred from the frontier to the city. The effective police officer knows his city and can follow a trail using sophisticated knowledge of the material and human environment.

Force is the third part of the American formula for effective police work in the nineteenth century. Many of the period believed that the most effective means, perhaps the only effective means, of making the police a truly preventive force was when the policeman was tougher than anyone on his beat. The best example of this was Inspector Alexander "Clubber" Williams. During his early years he would challenge criminals, singly or in groups, and defeat them in battle with his nightstick. This reputation allowed Williams to leave his gold watch hanging on a lamp post, walk journalists around the block and find the watch where he left it. Whether it was individuals like Williams or groups like the "strong arm squads," the police of American cities felt that it was necessary to show real and potential criminals who was boss by using force. Hard upon the founding of American police departments, the notion of the preventive police underwent significant changes, not the least of which was the official arming of police officers. As early as the mid-nineteenth century, American police officers perceived that they were engaged in a battle not with abstract social ills like vice or poverty but with something specific, criminals. Look at the titles of early works about crime and police work: *The Dangerous Classes of New York, Thirty Years Battle with Crime, Our Rival the Rascal*. They suggest that the job of police officers involved strife, and that strife would naturally lead to violence. American police by the end of the nineteenth century, then, had developed the formula of know 'em, find 'em and thwack 'em as the most effective way of winning with criminals.

These police techniques influence the shapes that crime fiction in this country has taken. Although English crime fiction in the nineteenth century, in Dickens and Collins and the like, depends upon the idea of the hidden criminal, American crime fiction frequently does not: story paper and dime novel fiction, Pinkerton and Hawthorne, make little pretense of hiding the villain. The protagonists in crime stories often know who is causing the trouble; the problem is finding and getting the goods on him. Turn of the century stories, affected by the English tradition, make the unmasking of villainy one of their surprises, but hard-boiled fiction returned to the native procedure of identifying the bad guys early on, but with the added fillip that there are so many bad guys that it is hard to know which one was responsible for the crime under consideration.

Just as knowing the identity of the criminal has certain ramifications for the making of detective story plots, it has, perhaps, an even more profound impact on the character of the policeman or detective. To truly know the particulars of the underworld, the detective cannot remain aloof from it. He has to be familiar with it. In older stories, depending on the French tradition of Vidocq and Lecoq, detectives like Sleuth or Nick Carter use disguise as a means of penetrating the world of criminals while retaining their middle-class respectability. At the turn of the century, as writers slowly, even wistfully, abandoned the use of disguise, one of their choices was to create an ambiguity in their heroes occasioned by their participation in both the worlds of the law-breaker and the law-enforcer. Those who chose this route depicted heroes seen by their society as shady or irresponsible individuals, but who reveal themselves to the readers as bastions of moral rectitude: Race Williams, Sam Spade and the like. The other choice for writers, elaborated by Flynt and Walton, posits opposing sides, police and criminals, each familiar with the others' personnel and methods, much like participants in a war. This tends to be the stance of the more formal writers like Ellery Queen as well as that of those who chose criminals as their protagonists—Boyle, Burnett and Anderson—who trace back to Flynt and Walton.

Insofar as violence goes, as we have seen, tracing American detective novels shows an increasing amount of violence. But it is very easy to go overboard here. With the exception of *Old Sleuth* and some of Pinkerton's later books, nineteenth century writers show that criminals are subdued with moral or intellectual force instead of physical violence. American crime fiction does not begin as a particularly violent medium. Although Flynt and Walton write of the inclination to violence of American police officers, they temper this by acknowledging that American society cares little about law enforcement and the policeman is very often on his own in his confrontations with criminals. Real police violence does not, by and large, appear in fiction until the twenties and thirties. It is difficult to tell whether the relative absence of violence in earlier fiction reflects social prejudice that ignores violence toward lower class individuals, or the writers' extremely limited experience with real police work, or publishing taboos, or reality or some combination of these.

Nevertheless, even in hard-boiled fiction of the twenties and thirties, where violence appears without let or hindrance, police officers are more frequently portrayed as corrupt or ineffectual than they are portrayed as violent. Usually our detective stories take the point of view that it is the criminal who inaugurates violence and the police who are powerless to stop it. American crime writers tend to show arrogant police power through police officers' bearing, attitudes and speech rather than through the end of the nightstick or the third degree—which writers frequently portray as being more psychologically abusive than physically cruel. Police arrogance, however, has little effect on criminals who are just as arrogant if not more so. Thus part of the motive for writers like Daily is in making the point that the police are, for one reason or another, not violent enough in their treatment of criminals and that private individuals, not hamstrung by a bunch of rules, must supply what the police can't or won't do.

It is a given in both the detective story and the criminal biography that the police are inept. Classical or Golden Age stories often need to use official stupidity or ineptness as a foil for the amateur detective. But the amateur detective was a concept principally fostered by British fiction: America has always slightly disapproved of leisured intellectuals who have nothing better to do than poke around in other people's business. This fact, along with the historical development in this country of the working professional private detective, modifies the traditional detective story theme of the inept police, and makes the laziness of official police officers a relatively important aspect of dealing with the police in our fiction. And certain aspects of the dark side of police history reinforce it: the facts of police graft and extortion insured that many of those people called police officers viewed their jobs only as sinecures, bought with real money, or as political pay-offs. One of Teddy Roosevelt's first acts as Police Commissioner was to wander New York's streets at night looking for patrolmen who were not at their posts: he found three in a liquor store, one asleep in a butter-tub and one, er, "partly concealed by petticoats." American crime fiction reflects on the laziness documented by this history. Flynt and Walton's Detective Minick works at law enforcement only when his shrewish wife makes him. Boyle's Detective Rentor bestirs himself only when a millionaire calls and threatens his cushy job. Noonan in *The Red Harvest* does nothing all day. It is Chandler, however, who drills hardest on the motif of the slothful cop, culminating in his portrait of the inert Detective Nulty in *Farewell, My Lovely*. These guys are no help with the war going on out in the streets.

In addition to the many things that police officers mean in fact and fiction, they have come to represent the law: police officers have been called Laws and John Laws from the nineteenth century through the present. On one hand, American crime fiction shows instances of detectives observing the outward forms of the law: thus Pinkerton's scrupulous practices and Chief Byrnes' arrest and rearrest game in *The Great Bank Robbery*. Theory says that our police enforce our laws, but in fiction as well as in fact the term "law" for police officer means that they make the law—they make the rules on the streets and at the station house. The most outstanding case of this in fact was Chief Byrnes' Dead Line: Byrnes drew an imaginary line around New York's Wall Street and spread the news that any known felon who entered the district without a pass from the police would be arrested. Flynt and Walton and Boyle all testify about police making de facto law. Additionally, through coercion and manipulation, police officers have the ability to turn the innocent into the guilty. What they say matters, as opposed to what underprivileged individuals or facts say. In our crime fiction the police occasionally do suppress or manufacture evidence (the coat that proves Blackie innocent happens to disappear and the policeman withholds the confession of a murderer in *The Powers That Prey*) and by the use of the third degree and plea bargaining in the cells they can and do coerce confessions from innocent people. They are, in some ways, the law. This aspect of the law in crime stories, however, is largely an off-shoot of the theme of the inept or lazy police: in fiction when police officers twist the spirit or the letter of the law they often do so because they are frustrated but more often because they are too lazy to do things right.

But the idea of the law is far more important to American crime fiction than this small edge that touches the abuse of the law by the police. One significant fact is that, in one way or another, characters in crime fiction think and talk about the law not simply as a fact but as an idea. This shows particularly in hard-boiled stories and it turns up in one of two ways. First, writers like Daly make their heroes preach about redefining the law ("Right and wrong are not written in the statute books for me") to make it fit their own sense of morality. This, I suppose we can call the utopian approach. Other writers, like Hammett and Chandler, do not talk about remaking the law. Rather they make their heroes conscious of the fact that they must break any number of lesser laws in order to serve more important laws. This relativistic approach serves far more detective heroes. These thoughts about the law mean something and they touch, in fact, a larger body of thought about the law that goes almost all the way to the beginning of the American detective story.

Some take it that only twentieth century private eyes are in the pick and choose or make your own law business. This isn't quite so. In *The Dead Letter* Burton does not take the murderer to jail, but he lets the family decide his fate. Sleuth irons things out himself, and Inspector Byrnes lets Mrs. Nelson go free. Now, granted, that Pinkerton and Green bring their captives to the bar, but they had specific reasons for this: Pinkerton wanted to establish the legitimacy of his business and Green is telling "A Lawyer's Story." Much nineteenth century crime fiction in this country and in Britain (witness *Martin Chuzzlewit*), reflects a wistfulness for the standards of the small community rather than respect for equally applied statute law. The community solves its own problems, frequently in the most compassionate way, rather than submitting them to judge, jury, prison, hangman. Although it does not apply to criminal cases, our Supreme Court has, in fact, handed down at least one decision that establishes "community standards" as an arbiter. Part of the point here, I think, is that nineteenth century writers never even thought about the propriety of solving the crime and then personally meting out the punishment. Likewise, they never thought about how their actions fit in with the law. Some of this comes from the fact that most nineteenth century fiction deals with aberrant middle class individuals rather than members of the criminal class. At the turn of the century, however, American crime fiction became much more conscious of the implications of law than it had been before.

In the late nineteenth century crime writers often display an acute awareness of some of the implications of circumstantial evidence. Material evidence, especially, became a touchy subject because it was open to more than one interpretation; it could, they feared, prove an innocent person guilty. Ottolengui deals with this and so do other writers both at and after the turn of the century. The answer lay in science. One of the functions of scientific detective tales like Reeve's was to show that modern science does not make stupid mistakes and, in fact, can remedy the defects inherent in circumstantial evidence. It can really and absolutely prove who did it. By the time we reach the twenties, however, things become more complicated. Not only did the dangers of misinterpreting material evidence again make things difficult when looking at a crime, real or imaginary (due to a slight backlash against scientific stories), but there was also psychology, and psychology said that one should not necessarily take any person's statement at its face values. Coming out of this we get a situation in which you cannot quite trust material evidence (locked rooms are not locked rooms) and you definitely can't trust what people say. So anyone can be guilty. This is the

Golden Age formula. One answer to the dilemma that writers found was in Philo and Ellery, the genius detective who can penetrate to both the real material clues and the real human evidence. Another answer was to consider that if everybody can be guilty and material evidence is, well, protean, then it spreads out the blame, dilutes the moral consequences and the whole thing can be made into a game.

Crime writers in the American mainstream, however, resisted making either the crime story or the detective story into a game. Most of their thinking about the law goes back to certain issues articulated by Post. Post essentially says two things about the law. He says that it's for sale. You get yourself enough money or enough influence and you can buy yourself a legislature. Flynt and Walton and Boyle at the turn of the century take this view as well. Post's second point is the arch attorney's one. Randolph Mason demonstrates that the law provides enough loop-holes for everyone, you simply need to find them. This means that America's system of laws is so byzantine and so contradictory that you can use it to defend or protect anything that you do. The big boys do it all of the time, Post says: they break some laws and escape because of another set of laws, or, put another way, they break some laws in order to uphold a more important law. This sort of thinking gives you robber barons; it also gives you Thoreau. Herein lies an essential American paradox.

Is the detective, then, simply the criminal turned inside out? What is it that validates heroes, detective and criminal alike, in American crime fiction? Part of the answer is that the hero becomes part of a situation not of his own making: he responds to and consciously endangers himself by responding to circumstances made by others. Most varieties of detective fiction, American or not, begin with part of this assumption: Bucket, Holmes, Poirot, Burton, Sleuth and the Op are all outsiders. To some extent writers put criminal heroes in the same position. Boston Blackie is an outsider to both law-abiding and law-breaking society, Rico's situation and abilities are unique in *Little Caesar,* and Anderson's Bowie Bowers differs in character and situation from his criminal buddies. If the hero is an outsider who takes part in a situation not of his own making, then the corollary is true: villainous criminals and derogatory characters most emphatically initiate actions that will benefit them directly and personally. Cops on the take and criminals in their acts initiate things and manipulate events solely for themselves.

British fiction up to the nineteen twenties worked at evolving the disinterested hero, most tellingly in the figures of the consulting specialist, like Holmes and Thorndyke, and the leisured amateur. American crime fiction, however, emphasizes commitment and passion. This passion may spring from personal involvement with others, such as Blackie's acts in behalf of the Cushions Kid or the fact that Race Williams only will participate in the business of *Murder from the East* when he realizes that a small child has been kidnapped and is threatened with torture and death. Often, however, it connects with passion for an abstraction, most often one's profession but sometimes justice: Burton, Gryce, Pinkerton, Byrnes and the Op possess determination as well as enthusiasm for doing their jobs as best as they can, and many of them work not only for pay but also to achieve justice. The same thing holds true for criminals. Blackie and Rico are clearly experts— they don't want to do anything but what they are doing—and the idea of justice motivates Blackie quite as much as the prospect of gain. Most importantly, for heroes in American Fiction, contact with crime alters their personalities. This goes all the way back to Mr. Burton's conversion from businessman to crime fighter, and it extends through Average Jones' step into the Great Adventure of Life, and Craig Kennedy's life in the crime lab, and the Op's concern about going blood-simple. After their contact with crime, characters in American crime fiction cannot simply resume their prelapsarian lives. Some writers take the romantic, even Byronic route: Burton is poisoned by his enemies, Randolph Mason goes mad and both Philo Vance and Ellery Queen become exiles in Europe. Most writers, though, do not permit their heroes these luxuries. Their characters cannot opt out of their worlds, and they survive by making crime into either a crusade or job that they must do because someone must, and they are good at it.

No matter its themes or characters, though, one of the fundamental ingredients of American crime fiction has been literary style. The evolution of American English, especially spoken American English, enabled the American crime novel to come into its own. It did not start out that way. In the 1860s and 1870s prose in even the most popular literature about crime was basically indistinguishable from most other semi-literary prose in this country and Britain. Here's a passage from "A Female Detective" printed in *The New York Ledger* in 1868:

> Harvey regarded me incredulously, but I saw that the name I had used impressed him sufficiently to rivet his attention; and, in as few words as possible I told him my story. When I had concluded, and delivered the razor into his keeping, he clasped me impulsively and kissed me several times.

By the turn of the century crime writers had moved crime fiction slightly away from the somewhat stilted and artificial workhorse prose of Victorian writers when they learned how to employ ironic tone. Here is a piece from *The Powers That Prey*:

> Detective Ackeray was not given to what the young lady novelists would call assorted sentiment. He had heard members of the officially gentler sex cry out insults to which nothing but a good drubbing is the answer, and that an insufficient one; and had seen women tantalize a man to deal the blow which would dishonor him, until from the point of view of a member of the force he thought the blow had been earned and ought to be delivered.

In spite of the irony, the sentences string clause, upon clause and even though writers of this period recognized that there was another kind of language connected to crime (Flynt and Walton admit that MeKlowd uses "a language unique for its abbreviations and directness"), they could not bring themselves to use it for anything except local color effects. Later writers, the hard-boiled writers, could. Daly, Hammett, Chandler, Anderson, Burnett, the list could go on and on. Writers in the 1920s and 1930s created a new style for crime fiction. It took relatively simple and direct syntax and combined it with diction drawn from the burgeoning languages that had developed in this country: street talk, convict slang, hobo terms, western and southern dialect terms and more. They folded in wisecracks, overstatement, understatement, similes and other kinds of literary devices, not as they appear in books but as they come to appear in the language that real people use. This enabled them to depict crime and criminals, cops and private eyes with a degree of realism never before achieved. In some cases this realism was simply the impetus to fantasy, but in others it led to the creation of a significant branch of American literature, the American crime story.

# Index